Preface

This fourth volume of our *World labour report* – one of a series dealing with labour problems – takes as its theme: government and its employees. Part 1 contains an analysis of recent trends in key labour areas, such as employment, labour incomes and industrial relations. It also constitutes the socio-economic background to Part 2 which provides a comprehensive survey of employment conditions of public service employees.

In some respects, the world labour situation – as described in Part 1 – has improved since the last *World labour report*, published in 1987. There has been strong economic growth in many parts of Asia, while economic recovery and employment expansion have been sustained in most industrialised countries. However, Africa, Latin America and the Middle East have generally been outsiders to this process of resumed growth, with the result that labour incomes have fallen and poverty and underemployment have increased. Even though labour incomes rose or remained constant in Asia and the industrialised countries, unemployment hardly declined in most of them and the benefits of economic growth did not – or not sufficiently – trickle down to the vulnerable groups in society. Around the world there has been a move from the formal sector and stable wage employment to the informal sector, casual work and self-employment. Moreover, with the globalisation of capital markets and with real interest rates at historically high levels, capital incomes during the 1980s have grown much faster than labour incomes which have often failed to keep pace with inflation.

The main broad conclusions emerging from Part 2 of the Report are:

1. Pay and social security benefits of public service employees have deteriorated in many countries during the 1980s and, in almost all countries, they have deteriorated in comparison with those prevailing in the private sector.
2. Organisations of public service employees and employees as individuals have obtained a greater say in the determination of their employment conditions.
3. There are various ways in which efficiency and effectiveness can be improved in the public service. Some such measures are:
   - open recruitment and promotion procedures;
   - wage policies that provide incentives for better performance;
   - better management practices;
   - more training for management and staff.

The deteriorating employment conditions of public service employees have resulted from structural adjustment programmes pursued by many governments in the wake of lower economic growth and high real interest rates. The performance of these programmes is usually measured exclusively in financial and economic terms (such as low inflation, the reduction of government budget and balance-of-payments deficits, and economic growth). However, though good economic and financial performance is essential for social development, it is not sufficient. While it would be possible to compensate for the worst effects of structural adjustment programmes by short-term social programmes for the most vulnerable groups, long-term social development can only be achieved if social as well as economic objectives and policies are integrated in structural adjustment programmes, and if social and economic aspects of development reinforce each other. Thus, the participation of independent and representative social organisations in structural adjustment programmes is an important prerequisite for their success.

There is little systematic thinking about the optimum size of government and the activities it should be involved in. In most structural adjustment programmes it is almost automatically assumed that government is over-staffed and that public enterprises are inefficiently managed. While this may be true in some cases, there is still a shortage of personnel in several areas of public service, such as rural development, education, health and other social services, particularly in the developing countries. The proper use and redeployment of public sector employees emerges as a crucial issue. The question of privatisation is also often more complicated than many adjustment programmes assume. For instance, in some developing countries there is insufficient entrepreneurial and management experience in the private sector.

Finally, an important requirement for a well-functioning government is the efficient and equitable determination of the employment conditions of its employees. Public service employees can only be expected to perform well if their employment conditions are comparable to those in other sectors of the economy and if they have a say in how these conditions are determined. Naturally, like any other economic agent, governments have to face up to the reality of their limited resources. They often have to take a tough stance in negotiations with organisations of public service employees. But even though unilateral determination of employment conditions by the government may be expedient in the short run, only their joint determination will create a favourable climate for effectiveness and efficiency in the long run. Thus, the ILO will continue and strengthen its efforts in this vital area of labour relations.

Michel Hansenne

World labour report 1989

Volume 4

Employment and labour incomes
Government and its employees
Statistical appendix

International Labour Office Geneva

ISBN 92-2-106444-1

ISSN 0255-5514

First published 1989

ILO publications can be obtained through major booksellers or ILO local offices in many countries, or direct from ILO Publications, International Labour Office, CH-1211 Geneva 22, Switzerland. A catalogue or list of new publications will be sent free of charge from the above address.

Printed in Switzerland ROT

Contents

Chapter 3 Personnel management 63

Chapter 4 The remuneration package 83

Chapter 5 Collective labour relations 105

Chapter 6 Improving public service productivity 127

Text tables

Text figures

Text boxes

Text box figure

Text box tables

Introduction

This Report reviews the employment conditions of public service employees, that is, all those who work in public administration and government-provided social services, such as education, health and social welfare. In most countries the provision of these services is considered to be the main responsibility of the government, so that useful comparisons of employment and employment conditions of public service employees can be made between countries. The employment conditions of employees in public enterprises have not been included in the analysis because there is much less uniformity in the role of governments in the production of goods and services. However, some general trends of employment in public enterprises are reviewed against the background of the structural adjustment process and public sector deficits.

The employment conditions of public service employees cover a wide range of issues, such as employment security, recruitment and career development, pay, social security and other benefits, working time and other working conditions. Over the years the ILO has collected a wealth of information on these issues, which are discussed within the Organisation in various meetings and committees. Apart from the meetings on education and health workers, there are regular meetings of the Joint Committee on the Public Service, on which both governments and workers' organisations are represented. The last meeting of the Committee was held in 1988.

This Report is in two parts. Part 1 documents recent trends in employment, labour incomes and labour relations. Part 2 – on the government and its employees – examines the resource constraints that many governments have faced during the 1980s and then analysing how this has affected employment in the public service (public administration and government-provided social services) and public enterprises. Chapter 3 then documents how governments manage their personnel; it concentrates on the issues of recruitment, career development and the organisation of working time. Chapter 4 – the core of Part 2 – studies the development over time of public service employees' pay and social security benefits and compares them with those received in the private sector. Chapter 5 reviews the extent to which public service employees have a say in determining their employment conditions. The Report closes, in Chapter 6, with an overview of measures to improve public service productivity, including more effective management and management training.

The intention of Part 2 of the Report is to review individual country experiences of determining employment conditions of public service employees and to highlight common trends. Where feasible, some pointers are given on how certain aspects can be improved. But policies on public service employment conditions must be seen within an individual country context, including overall government policy and the extent to which public service employees' organisations and employees as individuals have a say. There are many examples cited in this Report of how governments and public service employees' organisations have found constructive solutions to the problems that arise.

Part ***1***

The current labour scene

Chapter 1

Employment and labour incomes

Since the publication of the last *World labour report* in 1987, the economic situation has improved (see table 1.1). While world GDP per head grew by a meagre 0.6 per cent a year between 1979 and 1985, it is expected to increase by 1.5 per cent a year between 1985 and 1990. This is still much lower than annual growth rates of between 3 and 4 per cent achieved during the 1960s and 1970s.

The stronger performance has been brought about mainly by the economies of South-East and East Asia, followed by South Asia and the industrialised countries. (The growth rates in some, mainly centrally planned, economies may have been overestimated due to under-reporting of inflation.) Fuelled by a stronger yen, trade between Japan and the economies of South-East Asia is booming. Moreover, the economies of the OECD, mostly rich industrialised market economies, are reaping the benefits of closer integration.

Table 1.1. Estimated growth rates of GDP per head: Major regions, 1979-90 (annual percentages)

	1979-85	1986	1987	1988	1989	1990
Sub-Saharan Africa	–2.8	–3.2	–2.8	–0.9	–0.9	–0.6
Latin America	–1.0	1.5	0.2	–0.3	0.1	1.4
North Africa and West Asia	–1.2	–0.6	–2.7	–0.3	0.9	1.5
China	6.5	6.3	6.4	6.4	8.8	7.7
South Asia	3.4	2.9	0.4	2.9	3.9	3.8
South-East Asia	3.1	4.5	6.5	4.5	4.1	3.9
Industrialised centrally planned economies	2.5	3.5	2.3	3.7	2.1	2.3
Industrialised market economies	1.7	2.1	2.1	2.4	2.1	2.0
World	0.6	1.5	1.2	1.7	1.6	1.6

Calculated from: UNCTAD projections.

There are two main outsiders in this process of resumed growth: sub-Saharan Africa and Latin America. Many countries in these regions have been faced with severe debt and balance-of-payments problems, with the result that their per capita incomes will be lower at the end than at the beginning of the 1980s. The same is true for North Africa and West Asia, mainly because of falling oil revenues. This disparity in growth rates has also led to a greater inequality of income per head on a world scale (see figure 1.1). While in 1980 per capita income in sub-Saharan Africa was about 20 per cent of the world average, it is expected to decline to less than 15 per cent in 1990. On the other hand, South Asia and in particular China, whose economies are not sufficiently open to be greatly affected by international trade, price and capital movements, are expected to boost their ranking. At the top of the scale, the industrialised market economies have considerably improved their position, from just under to over four times the world average income per head.

The distribution of income within countries has probably also deteriorated as a result of greater inequality between capital and labour incomes. During the 1970s the labour share in national income increased in many countries, partly because wages were indexed; during the 1980s the share of capital in national income appears to have grown. Capital incomes have in practice been indexed from 1981 onwards by real interest rates of around 5 per cent. As documented in the previous *World labour report* and in this chapter, labour incomes have fallen in most parts of the world. With the increasing integration of global capital markets, owners of capital incomes all over the world have benefited from historically high interest rates.

At the same time, unemployment has grown and the employment structure has moved from stable wage employment towards casual work and self-employment, with the result that poverty has increased in many developing and also some developed countries. The speed and intensity of this move away from formal sector and wage employment to informal sector and self-employment, as well as the trend towards falling labour incomes, varies significantly between major regions, which will therefore be reviewed separately for the industrialised market economy countries (IMECs), the industrialised centrally planned economy countries (IPECs) and the three developing continents: Asia, Latin America and Africa.

1. Industrialised market economies

Since the previous *World labour report* the employment situation has improved a little in the industrialised market economy countries (IMECs). While the OECD unemployment rate was 8.2 per cent in 1986, it dropped to 7.2 per cent in 1988. This reflects the sustained economic growth which the industrialised market economies have enjoyed since 1983, and to some extent their more flexible labour markets. However, the numbers of unemployed may edge up again in the next two years, particularly in Western Europe.

Employment: Levels and structure

Since the recession of the early 1980s all regions in the OECD area have significantly improved their employment creation performance. Annual employment growth was more than 1.3 per cent between 1983 and 1987, compared with only 0.2 per cent between 1979 and 1983 (see table 1.2). There is, however, a considerable difference between various subregions. North America and Oceania (Australia and New Zealand) achieved annual growth rates of more than 2.5 per cent, Central and Western Europe less than 0.6 per cent, and Southern Europe less than 0.8 per cent. Japan and the Nordic countries notched up employment growth of well over 1 per cent a year. A large part of the net employment creation in Europe since 1983 has been in part-time jobs, concentrated on women in the private service sector.

OECD employment growth is expected to decelerate between 1988 and 1990. Thus, 1988 may go into history as the peak employment growth year of the 1980s, with a 1.8 per cent increase compared with a forecast 1 per cent for 1990. The deceleration is expected to be greatest in the United States and Japan

Figure 1.1. Estimated GDP per head: Major regions, 1980 and 1990 (world average = 100)

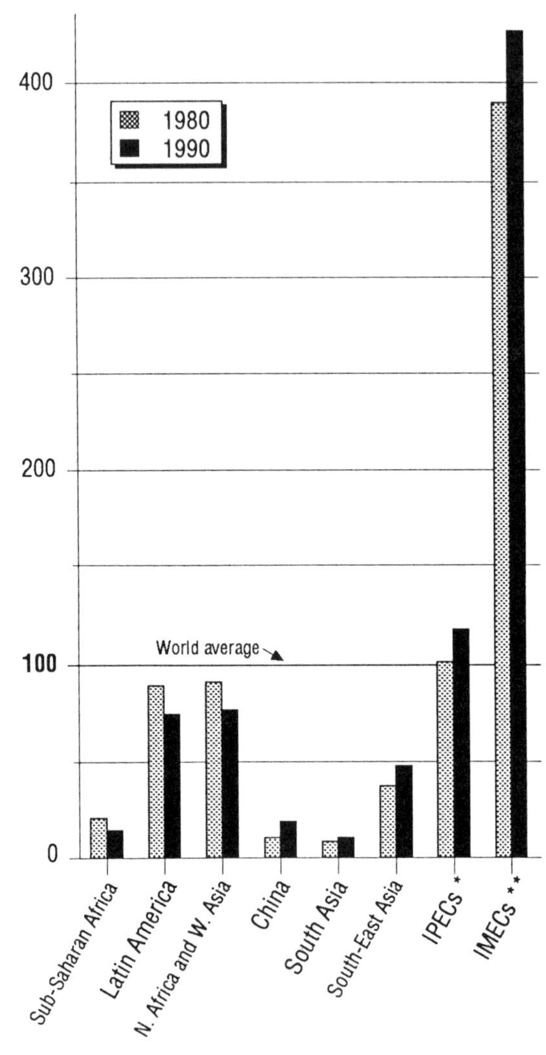

Calculated from: UNCTAD projections.

where employment growth rates may decline a full percentage point against half a percentage point for Europe. However, given labour force developments, unemployment in 1989 and 1990 is likely to remain stable in North America and Japan, but to increase in Western Europe.

These regional differences in medium-term employment trends can be explained more by differ-

Table 1.2. Annual growth rates of employment: OECD countries, 1979-90 (in percentages)

	1979-83	1984	1985	1986	1987	1988	1989[1]	1990[1]
North America	0.5	4.0	2.1	2.3	2.6	2.4	1.8	1.3
Japan	1.1	0.6	0.7	0.8	1.0	1.7	1.0	0.8
Central and Western Europe	–0.8	0.2	0.6	0.7	1.2	1.4	1.0	0.5
Southern Europe	0.2	–0.1	0.5	1.4	1.6	1.5	1.0	1.0
Nordic countries	0.5	1.2	1.5	1.0	0.8	0.4	0.3	0.3
Oceania	0.7	2.9	2.7	3.2	1.9	2.5	2.5	1.3
Total OECD	0.2	1.6	1.2	1.5	1.7	1.8	1.3	1.0

[1] Forecast.
Sources: *OECD employment outlook* (Paris, 1988 and 1989).

ences in labour absorption than by differences in average growth rates of output. These are not significant, say, between the IMECs of North America (2.4 per cent), Southern Europe (2.6 per cent) and the Nordic countries (2.6 per cent) or even Central and Western Europe (1.8 per cent) for the period 1979-88.

There has been a major shift in employment structure in the 1980s towards services and smaller establishments at the expense of industry and to a lesser extent of agriculture (table 1.3). In 1987 almost two-thirds of all workers in IMECs were employed in services; that share was only about 60 per cent in 1979. Much of the net employment creation has taken place in financial services, business services and social and community services. Overall employment growth has continued to be faster for women than for men, not only in the services sector but also in industry. As shown in box 1.1, this trend has been observed all over the world. The increasing importance of the services sector and rising female participation in the labour market has also led to more part-time employment which is concentrated in services such as commerce and social services.

The employment share of agriculture has continued to decline in line with a well-established long-term pattern. In some IMECs, such as Belgium, the United Kingdom and the United States, this share is now well below 5 per cent, though in others, such as Greece, Portugal and Spain, it still represents more than 15 per cent. The share of industrial employment dropped steeply during the slump in trade and output between 1979 and 1983. The process of "de-industrialisation" was especially marked in countries such as the Netherlands and the United Kingdom where the share of industrial employment dropped by more than 5 percentage points between 1979 and 1983. In most IMECs this share continued to decline after 1983 because of increasingly successful competition from exports from Japan and South-East Asian industrialising countries.

Over recent decades, wage employment has consistently increased its share in total employment, but since 1979 there has been a move towards more non-agricultural self-employment in some IMECs (see table 1.4). In five countries – Ireland, Italy, Portugal, Spain and the United Kingdom – the non-wage employment share increased over the whole period between 1979 and 1987, while in others it increased only between 1979 and 1983 (Belgium, Canada and Norway) or 1983 and 1987 (Australia). In the cases of Belgium, Canada and the United States this may be considered a short-term adjustment to a recession, but for the other countries it may be the start of greater employment creation in small-scale enterprises and self-employment.

Typically, around 70 per cent of the self-employed are working in services, especially in wholesale and retail trade, restaurants and hotels, real estate and business services, and personal and household services.

Self-employment has grown particularly in newer services, such as real estate and business services and recreational and cultural services, and has also been stimulated by special government measures. The most rapid growth in occupations among the self-employed has been among professional, technical and related workers and service workers. The vast majority of the self-employed in most countries are male and they tend to be older than their counterparts in paid employment. However, the proportion of women among the self-employed, and to a lesser extent that of young people, are on the increase.

There is evidence that all kinds of more precarious work, including temporary work, part-time work and home work as well as self-employment, have been growing in most IMECs over the past ten years. The most obvious explanation for growing job insecurity is the deterioration in labour market conditions, reflected most clearly in persistent high unemployment. In addition, many of these more precarious jobs are being taken by secondary workers such as

Table 1.3. Share of the three main sectors in total employment: IMECs, 1979-87 (in percentages)

	Agriculture			Industry			Services		
	1979	1983	1987	1979	1983	1987	1979	1983	1987
Large countries									
Canada	5.7	5.5	4.9	28.9	25.5	25.3	65.4	69.0	69.8
France	8.8	7.8	7.0	35.7	33.3	30.4	55.4	58.9	62.6
Germany, Fed. Rep. of	5.8	5.6	5.2	44.2	41.8	40.5	50.0	52.6	54.2
Italy	14.6	12.2	10.3	37.2	35.5	32.0	48.2	52.3	57.7
Japan	11.2	9.3	8.3	35.0	34.9	33.9	53.8	55.9	57.8
United Kingdom	2.7	2.7	2.4	38.6	33.4	30.2	58.7	64.0	67.0
United States	3.6	3.5	3.0	31.5	28.2	27.3	64.9	68.2	69.6
Other countries									
Australia	6.6	6.6	5.7	31.2	28.0	26.2	62.2	65.4	68.0
Belgium	3.1	2.9	2.7	34.4	30.4	28.0	62.5	66.6	69.3
Finland	13.6	12.5	10.2	34.2	32.7	30.7	52.3	54.8	59.0
Greece	...	30.0	27.0	...	28.6	28.0	...	41.4	45.0
Ireland	19.7	16.9	15.1	32.7	29.5	27.6	47.7	53.6	57.2
Netherlands	5.8	5.4	5.0	33.6	28.5	26.5	60.6	66.0	68.5
Spain	19.8	18.6	15.1	36.6	33.5	32.5	43.6	47.9	52.5
Switzerland	7.2	6.7	6.5 [1]	39.6	37.8	37.7 [1]	53.2	55.4	55.8 [1]

... = not available.
[1] 1986.
Source: ILO: *Year book of labour statistics.*

spouses or school-leavers in households where there is already a regular worker. The trend has been fostered by the increasingly widespread tendency of firms to employ a secure group of core workers augmented by a peripheral group of temporary and casual wage workers, or outworkers or subcontractors. And, as noted earlier, the public service and many other services have started to employ more part-timers. Non-standard employment is also a response to labour market regulation, whether through legislation or collective agreements, which limits the enterprise's control over hiring, firing and working arrangements. There are several compelling explanations why such a response has been more forthcoming today than in the past. One is that competitive pressures on firms have intensified. A second is that a growing body of regulation has increasingly limited the adaptability of firms that use only regular wage labour. A third is simply that while the desire to avoid labour regulations is not new, doing so is easier now because of higher unemployment and weaker trade unions.

Other notable changes in the structure of employment are the declining shares of young and older workers. The number of young people entering the labour force in the IMECs has dropped in the 1980s, as compared with the 1970s, reflecting the long-term trend of a falling birth rate. The share of young people (15-24) in total employment has been rising in recent years in a few European IMECs (e.g. the Federal Republic of Germany, Italy, Norway, Spain and the United Kingdom) in response to increased investment in work-oriented youth education and training schemes. However, in the United States, Canada, Japan, Australia and certain European IMECs (e.g. Finland, France, Portugal and Sweden) the share of youth in total employment has fallen in the 1980s due to a combination of a declining teenage population and falling youth labour force participation rates; a significant increase in the participation of adult women as substitutes for young people in the labour market; and, to some extent, the absence of effective labour market policies to facilitate the transition from school to work, especially against the background of structural and technological changes in industry.

The employment share of older workers (60 and over) has declined in the 1980s in most IMECs, with

1.1 Higher female labour-market participation during the 1980s

Traditionally, many women in industrialised market economies (IMECs) stopped working when they married and had children and rejoined the labour force when their children were older. But recently it has become far more difficult – in industrialised centrally planned economies (IPECs) almost impossible – to detect major differences in age-specific female participation rates as women pass through the different stages of family building. In addition, there has been a secular trend over time towards increased participation rates among women in both IMECs and IPECs. Thus, there is both a fall in the proportion of women responsible for the care of young children due to low fertility rates and a rise in the number of women carrying the "double burden" of professional and child-rearing responsibilities (many of whom work part time). As a consequence, relatively more women are building up longer periods of continuous labour market experience.

There are various world-wide factors that explain the steadily increasing participation of women in employment: the expansion of services and industrial export sectors where women have traditionally been active, the increasing access of women to education and training, various measures aimed at reducing pre-entry job discrimination, changing family values and structures and decreasing fertility rates. But the main reason may be the growing need for income, particularly in many developing countries where – as will be noted later – labour incomes have fallen.

In most developing countries the majority of the labour force works in agriculture and it often depends on cultural and social perceptions whether women's agricultural work is considered an economic activity. Thus, table 1.1.1 is restricted to women's participation in wage employment, so that the data are more comparable between countries. In almost all countries shown, women's share in wage employment increased significantly during the 1980s, usually by 2 or 3 percentage points. However, there is a great variation in the level of participation, particularly in the developing countries. In some countries in Africa (such as the Niger and the United Republic of Tanzania) and in Asia (such as India and Turkey), women account for no more than 15 per cent of wage employment. But in other Asian and most Latin American countries, women's share in wage employment is well above 30 per cent and reaches 40 per cent in some.

Table 1.1.1. Share of women in wage employment: 1980 and 1987 (in percentages)

	1980	1987
Sub-Saharan Africa		
Botswana	23.2	30.0 [1]
Kenya	17.6	25.2
Mauritius	27.2	35.2
Niger	3.3	6.2 [1]
Swaziland	25.3	28.0 [1]
Tanzania, United Rep. of	12.3	16.1 [2]
Zimbabwe	17.8	21.8 [3]
Latin America		
Costa Rica	28.5 [4]	31.2
Cuba	31.5	37.5
Panama	38.7 [5]	38.5 [1]
Puerto Rico	37.2	41.5
Trinidad and Tobago	31.6	33.0 [1]
Venezuela	31.7 [6]	32.2
Asia		
Hong Kong	36.5	38.0
India	12.1	13.0
Israel	38.7	41.6
Korea, Republic of	31.8	36.1
Philippines	36.0 [6]	36.6
Singapore	37.3	40.4
Sri Lanka	33.7	38.2
Turkey	8.9	8.8
Industrialised market economies		
Australia	36.3 [5]	41.3
Austria	37.5	39.1
Belgium	34.8	38.6
Canada	40.6	44.0
Germany, Fed. Rep. of	37.4	39.4
Greece	28.6 [6]	32.6
Ireland	33.2 [5]	37.1
Italy	31.6	35.1
Japan	34.1	36.5
Netherlands	31.0 [6]	35.3
Norway	42.0	45.9
Portugal	35.7	39.1
Spain	25.7	29.7
Sweden	46.5	50.1
United Kingdom	41.8	44.9
United States	42.9	45.2
Industrialised centrally planned economies		
Czechoslovakia	45.5	46.3
German Democratic Rep.	50.4	49.8
Hungary	44.2	46.3

[1] 1986. [2] 1984. [3] 1985. [4] 1983. [5] 1979. [6] 1981.
Source: ILO: *Year book of labour statistics*.

Table 1.4. Non-wage employment outside agriculture: IMECs, 1979-87 (percentages of total employment)

	1979	1983	1987
Large countries			
Canada	7.3	7.6	7.2
France	10.8	10.8	10.4 [1]
Germany, Fed. Rep. of	9.2	8.3	8.4
Italy	22.0	24.1	25.3
Japan	21.1	19.8	10.9
United States	7.1	7.5	7.3
Other countries			
Australia	...	11.8	12.9
Austria	8.8	7.8	7.8
Belgium	14.1	15.1	13.6
Denmark	10.4	9.5	8.0 [1]
Greece	...	32.7	31.9
Ireland	11.0	10.6	11.9
Norway	7.3	7.5	6.8
Portugal	13.7	...	16.8
Spain	10.5	10.6	20.6

... = not available.
[1] 1986.
Source: ILO: *Year book of labour statistics.*

the notable exception of Japan where older workers tend to remain longer in the labour force because pension and retirement benefits are generally low. This pattern is also related to the process of "de-industrialisation" in several IMECs, which has precipitated structural shifts in labour demand away from traditional manufacturing industries employing relatively older workers. At the same time, the employment share of female workers in the 55-59 age group has increased in countries such as France, the Federal Republic of Germany, Japan, Portugal and Spain, partly in response to the expansion of the service economy.

The anatomy of unemployment

The OECD unemployment rate reached a peak of 8.9 per cent in 1983 (see figure 1.2), with more than 32 million people out of work. It dropped to 7.3 per cent or 28 million in 1988, and is expected to remain at this level until 1990. The decline has been greatest in North America, where unemployment in 1988 was lower than in 1979. But in Europe, particularly in the Central and Western part, the unemployment rate in 1987 was still twice that in 1979. Thus, in spite of an economic recovery lasting five years, unemployment persists at high levels in most members of the European Community as well as in Turkey.

There are significant differences in the distribution of the burden of unemployment among age groups. While young people are generally more likely to be unemployed than older people, there has been a shift in their shares in total unemployment between the periods 1973-79 and 1979-87. The entry of the "baby-boom" cohort into the labour market during the 1970s resulted in an increasing share of young people in total unemployment. But since the 1980s the burden of unemployment has shifted towards older and prime age workers. Thus, the youth share of total unemployment in nine large and three Nordic OECD countries declined from 42.4 per cent in 1982 to 37 per cent in 1988.

The increasing unemployment share of older workers is directly related to the problem of long-term unemployment (i.e. those out of work and looking for a job for one year or more). This has been a persistent problem in many European countries during the 1980s and shows no immediate sign of improving. The long-term unemployed are much less likely than other unemployed people to obtain jobs. Many of them simply leave the labour force, but it is not clear whether this is voluntary or whether they should be considered as "discouraged" workers. When they do find a job, it is usually part-time or temporary work. Such jobs may be stepping stones to more permanent employment, but they are also likely to terminate in further (recurrent) unemployment. As suggested in the 1988 *OECD employment outlook*, it may well be that unemployment has now become concentrated among a minority of the labour force that is either long-term unemployed or repeatedly unemployed, interspersed with spells of employment.

Wage levels

Real wage increases have remained moderate in most IMECs, despite the pick-up in economic activity over the past five years (figure 1.3). In a few of the smaller IMECs real earnings have declined significantly. For example, in New Zealand the purchasing power of average wages in the manufacturing sector was 18 per cent lower in 1987 than in 1983, due principally to the combined effect of a devaluation and a wage freeze in 1985. In Greece real earnings increased rapidly between 1983 and 1985 but in the

Figure 1.2. Unemployment rates in the OECD area, 1979-90 (in percentages)

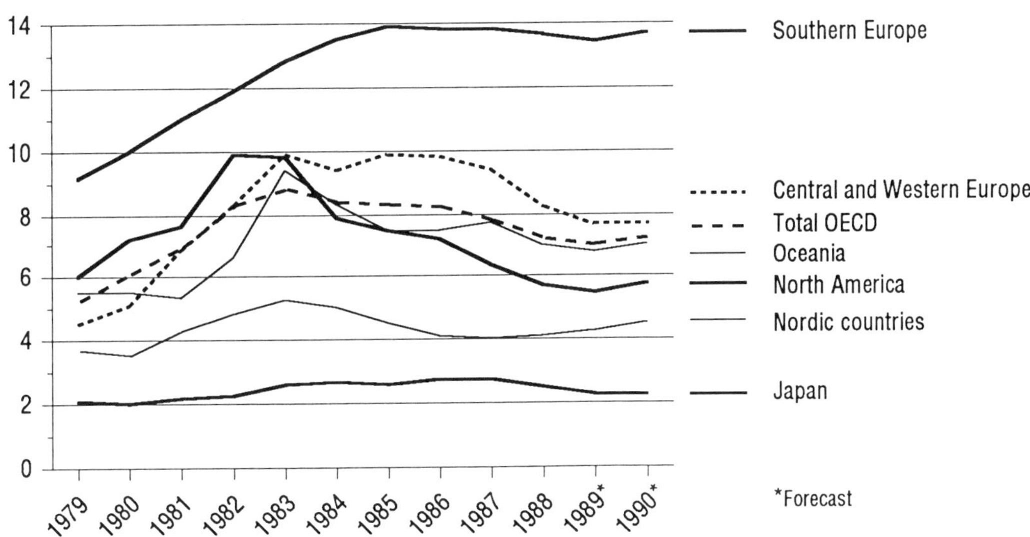

Note: North America (United States and Canada); Central and Western Europe (Austria, Benelux, France, Federal Republic of Germany, Ireland, Switzerland, United Kingdom); Southern Europe (Greece, Italy, Portugal, Spain, Turkey); Nordic countries (Denmark, Iceland, Finland, Norway, Sweden); Oceania (Australia, New Zealand).

Sources: *OECD employment outlook* (Paris, 1988 and 1989).

next two years fell by a massive 14 per cent, while in Australia real earnings declined by 8 per cent in the same period. In three of the largest seven OECD countries (Canada, France and the United States) plus Belgium, real earnings remained fairly stable; in each of these countries real earnings in 1987 or 1988 were within plus or minus 3 per cent of their 1983 level, and in no case was there any abrupt fluctuation within the period. For a further five countries in the figure (Austria, Denmark, Japan, the Netherlands and Sweden), real earnings increased by between about 5 per cent and 10 per cent over this five-year period, which corresponds to annual average real wage increases of 1-2 per cent. In only six countries (Finland, the Federal Republic of Germany, Ireland, Norway, Spain and the United Kingdom) did the total increase over this period reach double-digits, and in most cases the increase only marginally exceeded 10 per cent. However, for each of these six European countries, together with Austria and Denmark, real earnings jumped by about 3 per cent a year between 1986 and 1988 and in three cases (Denmark, the Federal Republic of Germany and Norway) by significantly more.

In the light of the wage restraint exercised generally over the past few years, a key wage policy issue is whether even more restraint is required to absorb the unacceptably high levels of unemployment persisting in some countries or, by contrast, whether it may have gone too far, thus unnecessarily aggravating income inequalities and jeopardising employment expansion because of insufficient aggregate demand. Those urging continued restraint argue that there may well be long lags before lower real wages and the concomitant improvement in profitability are translated into job-creating output expansion and investment, particularly in an economic environment clouded with uncertainties and historically high real interest rates. Another key issue is whether or not government attempts to promote a faster recovery in the labour market through expansionary monetary and fiscal policies might reignite wage and price inflation rather than produce increases in real output and employment.

Although opinions on these questions remain sharply divided, at the international level at least, there has been a growing consensus (as expressed by, for example, the Kreisky Commission (1989)) on the desirability of maintaining real wage increases, albeit at moderate levels, combined with more expansionary macro-economic policies and continuing efforts to ensure that nominal wage increases do not escalate.

While the general picture in Western Europe would suggest that employed wage and salary earners achieved moderate real wage increases, the distri-

Figure 1.3. Real hourly earnings in manufacturing – IMECs, 1983-88 (1980 = 100)

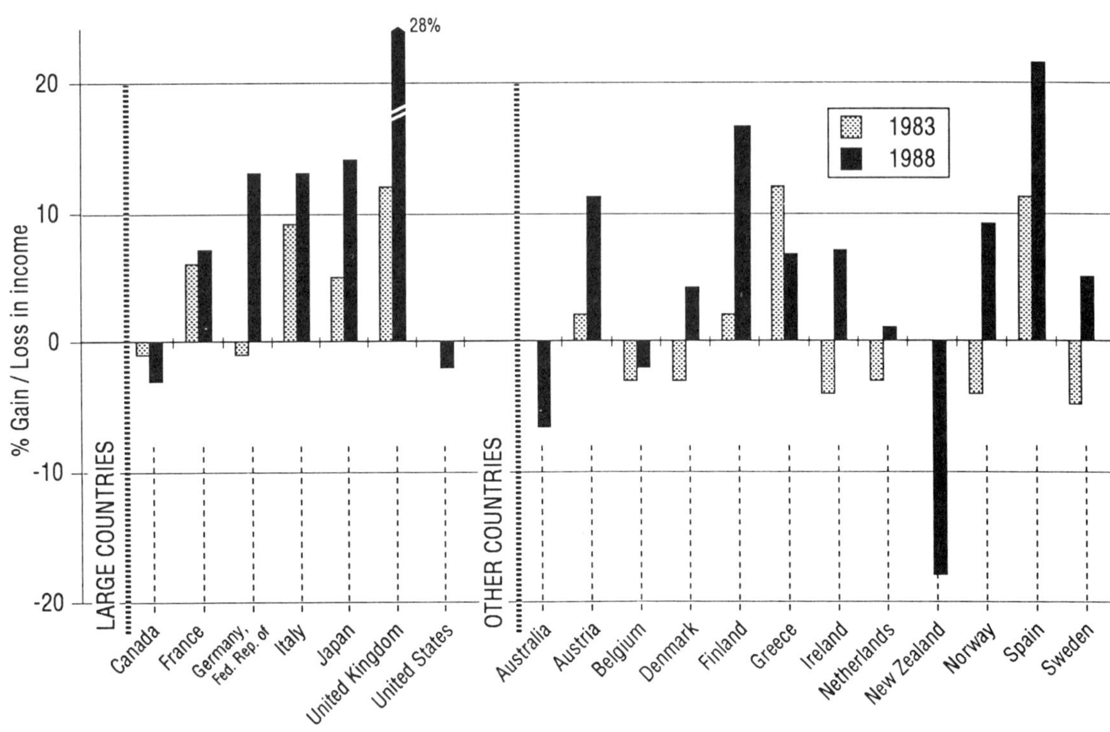

Source: OECD: *Main economic indicators*, various issues.

bution of real gains has been uneven. For example, the United Kingdom experienced rapid expansion during 1987: economic growth of 4.5 per cent, a 1.4 percentage point decline in recorded unemployment, relatively moderate inflation rates and an increase in average real earnings of about 3 per cent. However, the highest earning sections of the workforce have enjoyed large increases in pay, while real earnings among the lowest paid may have declined. The European Trade Union Institute has pointed out that the groups making the least advance have been government industrial workers and health service staff whose pay has been particularly subject to central government influence. The evidence of a geographical divide is also significant. London and surrounding regions (the south-east) have experienced stronger and more even growth of economic activity than other parts of the country, leading to a widening divergence of earnings. Average earnings in London increased by nearly 10 per cent between May 1986 and April 1987 compared to an increase of under 8 per cent for Great Britain as a whole. Moreover, the level of average male earnings is some 25 per cent higher in London than the average for the entire country.

Government's role in wage determination

One discernible general tendency in IMECs has been a move away from unilateral government intervention in wage determination, which is more difficult to justify in a context of disinflation and falling nominal wage increases. Government restrictions on wage bargaining imposed in the early 1980s were removed later in Belgium, Denmark, Greece, the Netherlands, New Zealand and Portugal, the IMECs where such interventions had become the most extensive. There would appear to be a growing belief that interventions should be reserved for short-term situations generally perceived as national emergencies and that they lose their effectiveness the longer or more frequently they are applied. They may even turn out to be counter-productive in their legacy of suppressed inflation, relative wage and price distortions and intensified industrial relations conflict.

Where difficult national economic circumstances in the mid-1980s have prompted government action, it has frequently been through formal or informal agreements reached with one or both of the social partners after consultations or negotiations at the national level. Thus, in Norway, against the backdrop of deteriorating economic conditions, the main trade union (LO) indicated its willingness to accept a legislated 5 per cent limit on pay increases, provided pay negotiations could be reopened if inflation exceeded this level and the Government undertook to control dividends and make certain changes in pensions and housing finance for young home-buyers. The minority Labour Government secured parliamentary support for a statutory incomes policy applicable throughout most of the public and private sectors based on these principles in early 1988. In Ireland the trade union sought a "social pact" with the Government covering taxation and social and economic policy as well as wages. The negotiated Programme for National Recovery comprises three agreements, covering the period 1988-90, and deals with a broad range of issues while limiting wage increases to specified levels that favour the low paid. This appears to represent a return to the practice of comprehensive national agreements followed in the 1970s but abandoned for most of the 1980s. In 1984 in Portugal the Government established a permanent tripartite negotiating body at the national level. Recently, tripartite agreements were reached setting out general criteria for pay increases linked to the expected inflation rate and anticipated improvements in productivity in the company or the national economy. Finally, it should be mentioned that the Prices and Incomes Accord, originally established as an agreement between the Australian Labour Party and the trade union movement in 1983, has evolved over the years into a flexible mechanism for national tripartite consultations or negotiations that has been used to address a wide range of economic and social issues, apart from wages. This has facilitated the elaboration of policy responses to cope with balance-of-payments pressures necessitating major structural adjustments in the economy.

However, formal or informal national tripartite agreements have not always been easy to introduce or maintain. Thus attempts in Denmark to achieve wage restraint through a tripartite agreement in 1988-89 involving pension and other reforms have encountered difficulties. After the national tripartite agreements on labour costs reached in Italy in 1983 and 1984, and the less comprehensive agreement of 1986, the Government appears to be withdrawing further from such engagements. In Spain, after the 1985-86 Economic and Social Agreement, which involved a comprehensive tripartite negotiation between the Government and the social partners for dealing with the existing economic crisis and creating jobs, it proved impossible to reach a similar understanding for 1987-88. In New Zealand it has also proved difficult to reach general agreements on policy directions for wages and related matters in the annual Tripartite Wages Conference, which has been held since 1985. In some cases (e.g. the Nordic countries), the difficulty of arriving at national agreements has arisen from increasing divisions within the labour movement, particularly differences between white- and blue-collar workers, public and private sectors, and within the latter between industries experiencing varying economic pressures.

In the absence of tripartite agreements and formal incomes policies in many countries, governments have placed emphasis on less direct means of influencing wage movements. In a number of countries pay decisions for public sector workers have played an increasingly important role in this regard. Thus, in Italy a 1986 agreement on pay indexation in the public sector set the pattern for the private sector. In France and the United Kingdom budgetary decisions on public sector wage bill increases have been the main mechanism through which government wage policy objectives have been made operational. However, while wage restraint in the public sector might appear to have the advantages of both reducing deficits and sending unambiguous messages to the private sector, eventually the cost is increasing frustration amongst public sector workers as the main victims of policies aimed at achieving greater macroeconomic stability. In those countries that have departed furthest from adherence to the "wage comparability" principle, there has been a continuation or an intensification of industrial strife in the public sector associated with efforts by various groups to "catch up".

Statutory minimum wage programmes have also been used by some governments to encourage wage restraint. Indeed, in the case of the United States there was no adjustment to the minimum wage between 1981 and 1989 with the result that it fell to its lowest-ever level relative to prevailing wages. In the United Kingdom, in 1986, the authority of wages councils to fix minimum rates for workers under 21 years of age was removed, as was their ability to fix different rates for different occupational categories and other minimum conditions of employment. In France, although the national minimum wage has continued to be regularly adjusted for cost-of-living increases, young workers employed on special training or work experience programmes, introduced with a view to reducing exceptionally high youth unemployment, are being paid at below minimum levels.

Wage flexibility

As noted in the previous *World labour report*, automatic wage indexation systems have continued to decline as a means of wage adjustment, thereby increasing real wage flexibility. A number of governments have also sought to introduce more flexibility in wage determination by encouraging "financial participation" schemes of various types (profit-sharing, employee share ownership, etc.). In the United Kingdom tax relief was granted in 1987 to "profit-related pay" schemes. To be eligible, the schemes must cover 80 per cent of the employees of a profit-producing unit. Encouragement for profit-sharing schemes has also been recently introduced in Denmark. However, in both countries the response by the social partners to the schemes appears, at least initially, to have been cautious. On the other hand, in France, where deferred profit-sharing has long been applicable to enterprises with 100 or more employees, new regulations introduced towards the end of 1986 have sought to facilitate the wider use of agreed *intéressement* schemes involving immediate pay-outs. As well as profit-sharing, such schemes may be linked to cost reductions, productivity improvements or any other "collective" measure of the performance of the enterprise or its individual units. The new simplified regulations appear to have led to a rapid expansion. By the end of 1987 there were 2,700 agreements introducing such schemes, covering over 730,000 workers, that is, about 5 per cent of all wage earners. In the United States employee stock ownership plans (ESOPs) have been growing in importance, in part owing to more favourable tax treatment introduced in 1984. It has been estimated that over 8,000 companies now offer ESOPs, covering over 11.5 million workers, a dramatic increase from under 500,000 a decade ago. Even in the absence of fiscal incentives there is a growing interest in plans that relate pay to enterprise performance. Thus, in the United States more gain-sharing plans are thought to have been introduced in the last five years than in their 50-year history.

In addition to formal gain-sharing systems, the criteria of cost-of-living compensation and wage comparability have been ceding territory to considerations of "ability-to-pay", productivity improvement and local labour market conditions. Thus, in France the central employers' federation no longer suggests to its members a specific target for annual wage adjustments but rather limits itself to some general indications of desirable wage behaviour and the recommendation that wage increases should take into account the financial situation of each sector and enterprise. In the United States there has been a breakdown in pattern bargaining and, despite the general improvement in the labour market, a continuation of such "concession bargaining" practices as wage freezes or reductions, two-tier wage structures, and lump-sum bonuses replacing wage increases.

Concluding remarks

Against the background of a favourable economic climate of recovery and sustained growth, governments in IMECs can increasingly focus their employment policies on specific labour market problems. Two broad options are available: (1) measures to improve employability, both generally and for specific target groups in the labour force; and (2) policies to facilitate the process of net job creation.

In various IMECs the quality of education has suffered over the past ten years and employers have been less inclined to train their workforces. Moreover, there is now a hard-core group of long-term unemployed who, without external assistance, will not be able to find employment. Finally, rapid changes in technologies and market conditions require an adaptable workforce. Thus, a good basic but rising level of education is fundamental for any employment-generating economy, as is shown by the examples of Finland, Japan and Sweden. There is also scope for targeted training and employment policies, which will increasingly have to focus on prime age and older workers, whose share in total unemployment is rising.

Employment policies will also have to address the problems of enterprises where most of the job generation takes place. Enterprises will only flourish if they increase productivity through better management and the introduction of new products and processes. That will require greater worker participation and responsibility and greater co-operation between enterprises and public training organisations. Since most net employment growth is concentrated in small enterprises in the services sector, it is also important that local authorities and interest groups take a greater part in generating a favourable entrepreneurial and business climate.

During the 1980s real wage increases have generally been moderate in the IMECs. While in the early 1980s many governments unilaterally intervened in the wage determination process, they have since attempted to conclude national tripartite agreements. In countries where this was not successful, some have attempted indirectly to influence the wage determination process, notably by restraints on public sector pay and minimum wages. Even though there is disagreement about the precise impact of wage moderation on employment, there is at the international level a growing consensus that, under current economic circumstances, modest real wage increases are desirable.

2. Industrialised centrally planned economies

The labour scene in the industrialised centrally planned economy countries (IPECs) has traditionally been characterised by problems of low labour productivity and inefficient use and deployment of the workforce. Recently, the emphasis has shifted to the attainment of full and "effective" employment. In addition, there is now an urgent need to correct imbalances between manpower requirements and available labour resources, as the IPECs embark on various reform programmes within an overall process of economic restructuring.

Economic reform provides both an opportunity and a challenge to overcome traditional labour market problems as well as to cope effectively with new ones that are now emerging. In the USSR, for instance, *Perestroika* has meant a substantial trimming of the workforce in both public administration and state productive enterprises, resulting in the release of hundreds of thousands of workers who need to be redeployed at higher levels of productivity. This situation is now producing shifts in employment structure and patterns as well as a change of emphasis in labour market policy towards training and retraining and more efficient utilisation of both human resources and production capacity.

The urgent need to absorb "surplus" labour into productive employment is also likely to give rise to new forms of work organisation (e.g. multi-shift work and individual work activities or self-employment), as well as facilitate labour force mobility both occupationally and geographically. The emphasis on productivity increases is also likely to result in changes in systems of wage and non-wage remuneration in order to provide necessary incentives.

State employment and the labour force

Employment growth in the state and co-operative sector was only 0.6 per cent a year for all IPECs between 1980 and 1987, compared with 2.2 per cent during the 1970s (figure 1.4). Over the same periods annual labour force growth rates dropped from 1.2 to 0.8 per cent. Thus for some countries, such as the German Democratic Republic, Hungary and Poland, there was an important turning-point in the labour market situation in the early 1980s. During the 1970s employment growth in the state and co-operative sector outstripped labour force growth and many people were drawn into state employment either from outside the labour force (women) or from the private sector (mainly agriculture). In the 1980s this pattern was reversed, with private sector employment in these countries apparently growing faster than state employment.

The slowing expansion of state employment is primarily the result of substantial reductions in public administration staff. For example, in the Russian Federal Republic of the USSR, some 263,000 public administration officials had been retrenched and/or redeployed by the end of 1988. The number of central government ministries in the USSR is also being reduced, which could lead to staff cuts of as much as 50 per cent between 1988 and 1990. In Czechoslovakia the Government has approved staff reductions at various levels of the civil service. These cuts are the result not only of an ongoing administrative reform to improve efficiency but also of reforms that aim at reducing the economic management role of the State.

The essence of these reforms is to replace the former command method of economic management by a system regulated by economic mechanisms. Enterprises will decide independently most of their inputs and outputs through wholesale trading and pricing policies that reflect supply and demand.

Various forms of socialist ownership are now being developed. These include not only the co-operative sector, but also new forms of management under existing state ownership. The rights of ownership and the right to manage are clearly distinguished, with full management autonomy being given to the enterprise. This means that the State will no longer

Figure 1.4. Annual growth rates of the labour force and employment in the state and co-operative sector: Industrialised planned economies, 1970-87 (in percentages)

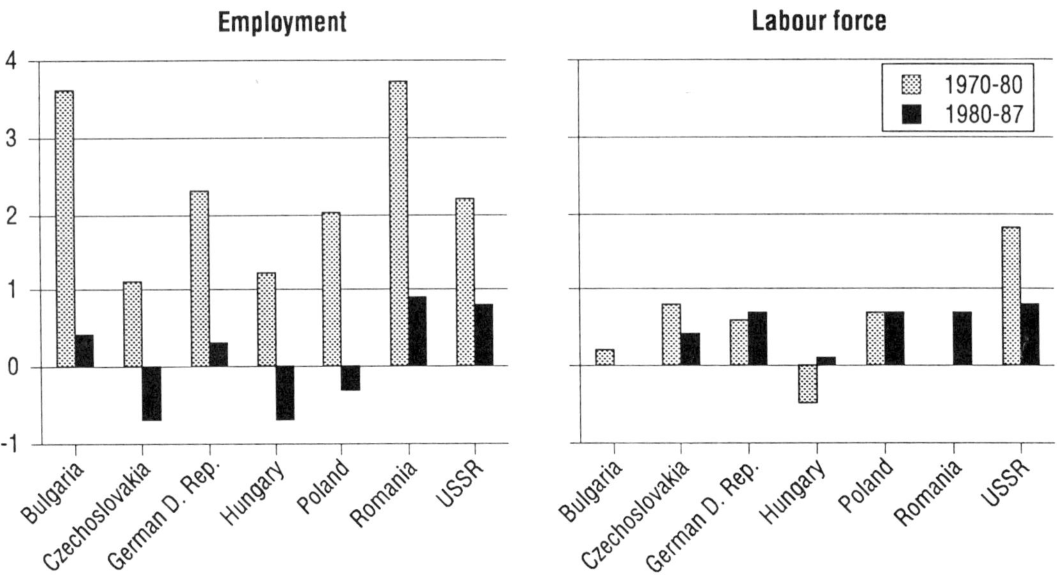

Source: CMEA: *Statistical year book 1988* (Moscow, 1988); ILO: *Economically active population: Estimates: 1950-80. Projections: 1985-2025* (Geneva, 1986).

be responsible for the financial performance of the enterprise and unprofitable enterprises cannot count on the State to bail them out of their difficulties. At the same time, enterprises no longer have responsibility for the debts of the State.

Thus, the relaxation of state domination of production and economic liberalisation associated with the reforms have provided the impetus for the promotion of *self-employment* both in the form of "individual labour activities" and within co-operatives. In the USSR, for instance, individual businesses are now permitted under amendments to the legislation on co-operatives which became effective in July 1988. Similar legislation has been adopted in Bulgaria, Czechoslovakia and Hungary. In the USSR it has recently even been suggested at the highest level that plots of land should be leased to those wishing to cultivate them for a period of up to 50 years. These changes provide new avenues for employment, especially for workers displaced in other sectors under the reform programmes. In Hungary the growth of the private sector has been significant in recent years, mainly as a result of expansion in retail trade as part of the economic liberalisation programme. In mid-1987 the sector accounted for some 33,500 private retailers and more than 23,000 employees. In the German Democratic Republic about 424,000 workers, or 5 per cent of the labour force, are handicraft workers operating as individuals or in co-operatives within the private sector. In January 1988 there were 13,921 co-operatives in the USSR, employing about 150,000 people; one year later 77,548 co-operatives employed 1.4 million. While this represents only a miniscule part of the total labour force, it is an important trend. Apart from the obvious benefit in terms of job creation, the promotion of self-employment in certain activities and services should lead to improvements in productivity and output, given the incentives that can be derived from working for oneself or for one's own benefit within a co-operative.

The structure of employment

There have also been important changes in the structure of employment by main sector of activity (table 1.5), even though they have been less spectacular. In all IPECs the share of agriculture in total employment in 1987 ranged from 10 per cent (in the German Democratic Republic) to about 30 per cent (in Poland), which is significantly higher than in the IMECs. In Bulgaria and Romania the employment share of industry increased between 1980 and 1987 but it stagnated or declined in the other IPECs. In all countries the employment share of the so-called "non-material" or "non-productive" sphere in-

Table 1.5. Distribution of employment in the material and non-material sphere: Industrialised planned economies, 1980 and 1987 (in percentages)

	Bulgaria		Czecho-slovakia		German Democratic Republic		Hungary		Poland		Romania		USSR	
	1980	1987	1980	1987	1980	1987	1980	1987	1980	1987	1980	1987	1980	1987
Material production	83.1	81.8	79.9	78.6	80.6	79.3	81.0	78.9	83.6	81.0	87.6	87.3	77.1	75.7
of which:														
Industry and construction	43.2	46.3	48.3	48.1	50.9	49.7	41.4	38.2	38.9	37.1	43.8	44.7	38.5	38.4
Agriculture and forestry	24.6	20.0	13.4	12.2	10.5	10.6	22.0	20.9	29.7	28.4	29.8	28.7	20.2	19.0
Transport and communications	6.8	6.6	6.6	6.5	7.5	7.4	8.0	8.3	6.6	6.1	7.2	7.1	9.1	8.8
Commerce [1]	8.1	8.5	10.6	10.7	10.7	10.7	9.6	10.5	7.7	8.9	6.0	5.8	8.0	7.9
Non-material sphere	16.9	18.2	20.1	21.4	19.4	20.7	19.0	21.1	16.4	19.0	12.4	12.7	22.9	24.3
Total employment	100.0	100.0	100.0	100.0	100.0	100.0	100.0	100.0	100.0	100.0	100.0	100.0	100.0	100.0

[1] Including material supply and procurements.
Source: CMEA: *Statistical year book 1988* (Moscow, 1988).

creased. This sector includes not only public services, such as public administration, education, health and welfare services, but also other services such as banking, insurance, tourism and repair. The move from "productive" to "non-productive" use of labour reflects the current concern of countries such as Bulgaria, Czechoslovakia, Hungary and the USSR to improve the non-material well-being of the population. One of the goals of economic reform is to achieve the shift in labour utilisation patterns without sacrificing output of material production. This implies higher productivity in the material sphere, based on technological changes, improved management and a more efficient use of equipment and labour.

One way of increasing the efficient use of labour is *multiple shiftwork* which, apart from increasing the labour-absorptive capacity of the economy, should also permit better and more effective use of equipment. Since 1980 many IPECs have been emphasising fuller utilisation of installed capacities, rather than expanded capacity, as a means of increasing output. Furthermore, multi-shift work makes it possible for "released workers", who otherwise would have to be redeployed elsewhere, to be retained in the same enterprise. The introduction of the two or three shift system has made it necessary in some circumstances for incentives in the form of wage differentials to be paid for working unsocial hours.

Female participation in the labour force in the IPECs has remained at about 50 per cent, which is high relative to other developed economies. This has been possible mainly through the acceptance of flexible working hours and now part-time work, and the provision of facilities such as crèches near workplaces, as well as, more recently, possibilities to work at home. However, some innovations under economic reform programmes, such as multiple shift work and retraining outside office hours, may pose a problem for women workers and could lead to a decline in female participation rates over time. This trend may even be facilitated by the rationalisation of labour use (i.e. trimming of the labour force) and higher incentive wage rates for primary income earners which would reduce the pressure for a second income within the household.

The employment problem of *youth* remains essentially that of increasing the correspondence between training and manpower requirements as well as satisfying job aspirations. In some of the IPECs there are simultaneously shortages of certain types of skills among young people entering the labour market, and an underutilisation of skilled labour. This suggests slow adaptation of training to technological innovation and economic changes.

The relatively high proportion of *older workers* (i.e. pensioners) retained in the labour force is a reflection of the traditional labour shortages in the IPECs. However, with the introduction of economic reforms aimed at greater efficiency and increased productivity, labour shortages are rapidly becoming a thing

Figure 1.5. Real monthly earnings in manufacturing: Industrialised planned economies, 1980-87 (1980 = 100)

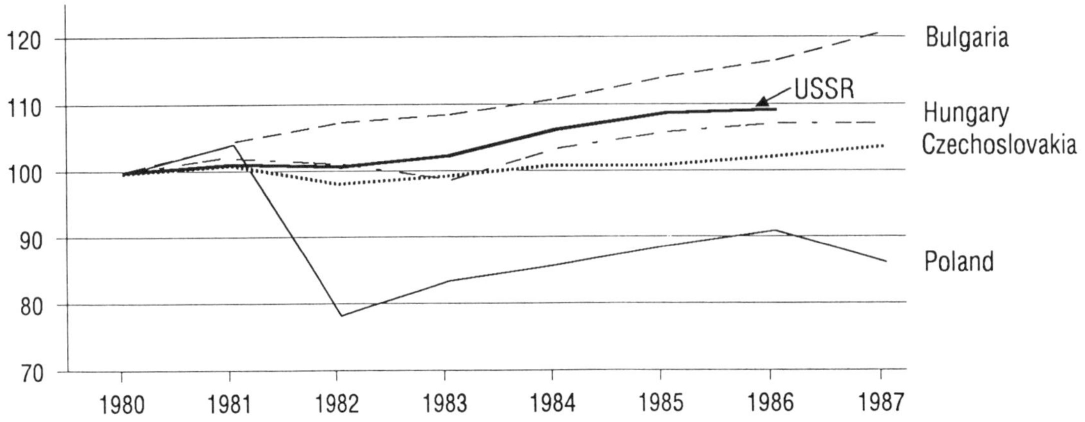

Source: ILO: *Year book of labour statistics.*

of the past. On the contrary, thousands of establishments in the USSR and some other Eastern European countries are trying to shed excess labour. For example, plants belonging to the USSR Petroleum Ministry released some 140,000 workers in 1987. In the future, as the economies of the IPECs become more efficient, there will be less need to retain pensioners after retirement, except where their experience and specialist skills are badly needed.

Real wage trends

At the beginning of the 1980s most IPECs faced similar economic difficulties to the rest of the world. Economic growth fell to historically low levels, while in some countries foreign trade deficits and external debt problems became the major concerns of policy-making. Exogenous factors, such as high interest rates and the evaporation of new sources of international finance, led to the correction of trade balances supplanting economic growth as the top economic priority. This resulted in 1982 in a slight fall in real wages in some countries, such as Czechoslovakia, Hungary and the USSR (figure 1.5). A very steep drop of about 25 per cent was recorded in Poland, mainly because of domestic social and political upheavals.

Between 1982 and 1987 real wages rose in the IPECs by between 1 and 2.5 per cent a year, which is lower than the increases recorded in the 1960s and 1970s. An acceleration of output growth in 1983-86 was not maintained in 1987. Since there were only small increases in employment, labour productivity growth increased in all countries, except Hungary.

Employment and wage policy issues

It is difficult to foresee what the eventual employment impact of the current economic reforms will be. Initially, as enterprises and public administration trim their workforces, workers will become redundant. The authorities consider that with the placement, training and retraining services provided by employment offices, unemployment and labour scarcities can be avoided. But in the long run, everything will depend on the pattern and extent of economic growth and on the consistency with which reforms (in particular, in the area of prices and enterprise autonomy) are pursued. In most IPECs there is considerable pent-up demand which is reflected in high savings on which low interest rates are paid. These savings now finance a considerable part of the state budget. If they could be used for stimulating demand, and if enterprises were able to satisfy this increased demand, then the resulting economic growth could bring about full employment with a moderate rate of inflation. The problem is how to make the transition, without large-scale unemployment or rampant inflation.

With the introduction of economic reforms in Hungary, followed by those in some other countries, particularly in the USSR, there have also been significant changes in the practice of and the debate on wage determination. In the USSR, for example, there are efforts currently under way to rationalise the various resources from which bonuses may be paid into one unified material incentives fund (thereby reportedly increasing its size by up to 15 per cent of the wage bill on average); to replace individual bonuses as far as possible by bonuses calculated for the work collective; to refine and rationalise the success indicators against which bonuses are payable; and above all to increase the role of the work collective in evaluating and rewarding the contribution of each individual. Special efforts are being made to promote a more intensive use of resources; for each percentage point by which production costs decline, the material incentive fund is increased by up to 4 per cent, depending on the sector of the economy. Enterprises can use for bonus purposes up to 50 per cent of the savings achieved in material resources, and up to 75 per cent in energy resources. Furthermore, it is the enterprise that specifies the resources in respect of which savings should be especially encouraged and that determines the amount of bonuses to be paid accordingly. Bonuses for managers and other top administrative staff in industry are increasingly linked to whether or not the enterprise meets contractual obligations. In case of non-fulfilment, for these as for other categories, bonuses are held back.

The notion of contracts plays an important role in revising the principle of wage bill formation and in enhancing the role of basic wages in stimulating performance. It is currently being argued in the USSR that this is best effected through a system of collective contracts covering the entire workforce of the enterprise. Under this system, the enterprise receives, on meeting contractual obligations, an income from which it deducts its costs, taxes, interest payments, and so on, as well as the amounts to be allocated to investment and other development and consumption funds. The remainder constitutes the income of the workforce. Thus every extra worker means a smaller per capita share of the income and the purchase of underutilised material and equipment reduces that total to be shared out. It is argued that, under such a system of enterprise self-financing, where the wage bill depends on "cost-accounting" income, all enterprises would be placed on an equal footing; the more efficient would earn a larger income and pay higher wages. The introduction of a system of this kind faces many problems. In particular, without a realistic pricing policy, any cost-accounting system lacks credibility. But it is being contemplated as a way to avoid the drawbacks of excessive central control of wage policy under which many enterprises depended on state budget allocations for wage increases. The central authorities would continue to formulate and apply a common wage policy by establishing basic rates of pay for various worker categories, elaborate principles governing output levels and issue guide-lines for the payment of incentives.

The debate regarding central wage regulation has gone beyond this point in Hungary, where those leading enterprises which comprise a so-called "special wage club" are already effectively released from the usual central wage regulation restrictions in return for meeting certain minimum conditions regarding profit and foreign exchange earnings, exports, tax payments, and so on. Indeed, it may be argued that Hungary is a test case for the IPECs. Long before the others, policy-makers in Hungary moved towards efficiency indicators for wage bill growth. For many years, and until very recently, wages could be increased by a certain percentage for every percentage point increase in gross income per employee, provided that the enterprise could afford to pay a tax amounting to a certain proportion of increased wage costs. However, this form of central wage regulation was diluted over the years by a variety of ad hoc wage policy measures to grant pay increases to different branches of the economy and categories of workers. Non-wage benefits from social consumption funds were sometimes used to complement wages and overcome the low level of basic wages. Secondary employment opportunities expanded rapidly, enabling many workers to gain much higher earnings outside the limitations of wage regulation. These factors contributed to the undermining of the perceived link between pay and performance and gave rise to widespread informal wage and performance bargaining, effectively circumventing to a large extent the official central wage regulation system.

Hungary's economic difficulties in the 1980s seem to have brought matters to a head. Recently, per capita real wages have fallen significantly, while the foreign debt burden has doubled to reach US$15 billion. In what might be regarded as a transitory emergency measure, in 1988 the pre-1968 form of wage bill regulation was reintroduced for some enterprises, purportedly allowing a greater control over wage inflationary tendencies in the short run.

Meanwhile, another major debate has been initiated in Hungary regarding the possibility of eventually removing almost all central wage regulation in the competitive sphere of activities. Wage management would be integrated into enterprise cost-accounting and central wage regulation would be largely replaced by a system of wage agreements elaborated through collective bargaining. Among the proposals is the establishment of wage increases at the highest level through tripartite national agreements, which would also set sectoral differentials. These would be binding at sectoral and enterprise levels, thereby retaining an aspect of central regulation. Another proposal would go further, limiting top-level tripartite decisions to setting maximum and minimum wage limits and to the formulation and implementation of general wage policy. While sectoral level bargaining would be tripartite, the State's role would be limited to elaborating appropriate conditions for bargaining and ensuring the application of top-level decisions. Enterprise-level bargaining, which would be the main locus of wage decisions, would be bipartite, within a context that would require considerable changes in the roles of the social partners. Such proposals have obvious very far-reaching consequences.

They are as yet tentative within a difficult and often polarised national debate. But the fact that they have been raised is a good indication of the potential depth of the reform measures now being considered.

Figure 1.6. Growth rates of GDP per head: Asia and North Africa, 1980s (in percentages)

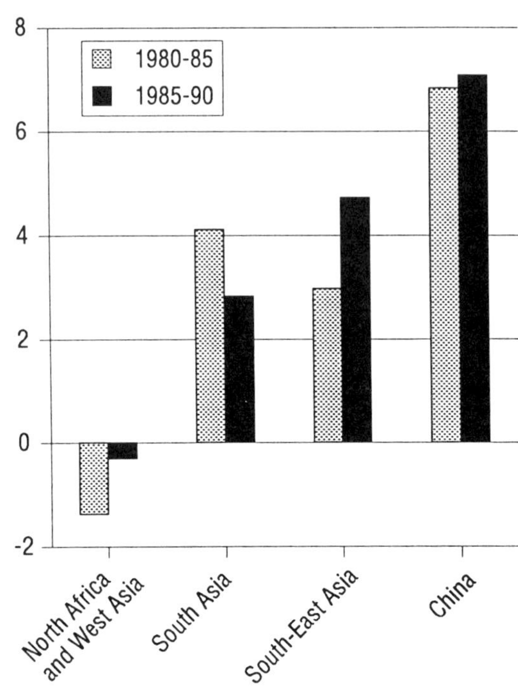

Source: Calculated from UNCTAD data files and projections.

3. Asia including North Africa

With more than 2.5 billion inhabitants Asia is by far the most populous continent, and its size and variety of growth performance make it helpful to split the region into various subregions. Employment and labour income trends in North Africa are also reviewed in this section, because the economic characteristics of these countries have more in common with West Asia than with sub-Saharan Africa. As noted earlier, China is experiencing rapid economic expansion, with an annual growth rate of GDP per head of about 7 per cent during the 1980s (see figure 1.6). It is followed by South-East Asia (about 4 per cent) and South Asia (3 per cent).

Recently, the growth performance of the South Asian economies has been adversely affected by both drought (northern India, Pakistan and Sri Lanka) and floods (Bangladesh and eastern India). Growth rates were negative in West Asia and North Africa because of falling oil revenues.

Balance-of-payments pressures have not been as intense in most of Asia as in other parts of the Third World. China and India are not sufficiently open economies to be much affected by international trade, price and capital movements. Elsewhere in South and East Asia, the deterioration in the terms of trade caused by declining commodity prices, and the rise in interest rates, had less impact than in sub-Saharan Africa and Latin America, because exports were more geared towards manufacturing and government budget deficits were lower. In addition, developing countries in South and East Asia are generally less reliant on European markets for their exports than other developing countries; they are more oriented to Japan and North America whose relatively rapid economic growth has provided Asia with opportunities to expand trade. Moreover, South and East Asian countries typically have quite diversified trade sectors; this is the case even where there is a relatively high dependence on the export of primary commodities.

The changing structure of employment

The variety of growth rates in the Asian and North African countries has been accompanied by differing changes in the structures of their economies and of employment (see table 1.6). Hong Kong and Singapore are being quickly transformed into service economies based on a growing sector encom-

Table 1.6. Share of industry and services in total employment: Asia and North Africa, 1979, 1983 and 1987 (in percentages)

	Agriculture			Industry			Services		
	1979	1983	1987	1979	1983	1987	1979	1983	1987
North Africa and West Asia									
Bahrain	3.1	2.7 [1]	...	40.0	34.8 [1]	...	56.9	62.5 [1]	...
Egypt	42.5	39.7 [1]	...	22.0	22.2 [1]	...	35.5	38.1 [1]	...
Israel	5.9	5.5	5.2	31.9	30.3	29.4	62.2	64.2	65.5
Syrian Arab Republic	32.8	30.6	...	31.2	29.2	...	35.9	40.1	...
Tunisia	35.5	32.9 [1]	...	34.3	35.9 [1]	...	30.2	31.2 [1]	...
South and East Asia									
Hong Kong	1.2	1.2	1.5	50.6	45.0	42.9	48.2	53.8	55.5
Korea, Rep. of	35.8	29.8	21.9	30.1	29.1	34.0	34.1	41.1	44.1
Malaysia	37.2 [2]	30.6	31.8	24.1 [2]	25.9	23.2	38.7 [2]	43.5	45.0
Pakistan	55.0	52.9	50.9 [3]	18.5	19.5	20.3 [3]	26.5	27.6	28.9 [3]
Philippines	51.9 [2]	52.0	47.8	15.4 [2]	13.8	14.6	32.8 [2]	34.2	37.6
Singapore	1.5	1.0	0.9	35.3	36.0	35.1	63.2	63.0	64.0
Thailand	...	63.1	63.8	...	13.0	12.5	...	23.8	23.7

... = not available.
[1] 1982. [2] 1980. [3] 1985.
Source: ILO: *Year book of labour statistics.*

passing financial institutions, trading, insurance and the like. The Republic of Korea and Taiwan, China, are still increasing the employment share in industry. Their rapid growth, which accompanied rapid structural changes in the economy, was achieved through a sustained spell of accelerated industrialisation (temporarily halted during the recession of the early 1980s); essentially labour-intensive in the initial phase, it later became capital-intensive.

The ASEAN countries (such as Indonesia, Malaysia, the Philippines and Thailand) followed a mixture of export-oriented as well as import-substitution industrialisation policies, but continued to depend on a successful performance of the agricultural sector for most of their employment and export earnings. Thus, in ASEAN countries for which data are available, the employment share of industry stagnated and that of agriculture declined less rapidly than in the newly industrialised countries. A large part of the growing services sector may well have been informal sector petty services and trading which essentially sustain a subsistence living for the poor.

A similar pattern can be observed for the Middle Eastern economies that are not predominantly dependent on oil. They have not significantly increased their employment share in industry, because of stagnating exports to other countries of the Middle East. As noted in the previous *World labour report*, remittances from workers in oil-dependent countries have also fallen steeply.

In the South Asian economies and China structural changes, in terms of relative sectoral shares, were generally much less striking than in the NICs or ASEAN. Agriculture remained the mainstay of the economy, providing the bulk of the population with livelihood and employment and generating a substantial part of foreign exchange earnings with primary commodity exports. The only exception is Pakistan, which experienced a rapid decline in the share of the agricultural sector and a marked increase in the manufacturing sector. In China there was a strong drive towards industrialisation, particularly in the Special Economic Zones, but industrial output also expanded rapidly in the countryside. The major policy focus in most of the South Asian countries, during the period under review, was increased food self-sufficiency and reduction of food imports.

Employment and unemployment

It can be extremely difficult to measure a country's employment performance for several reasons. Apart from problems of definition, the data base on employment, especially in countries with a vast rural population, is often weak. The unemployment figures, which are readily available, usually refer to open unemployment. It is well known that such figures do not properly reflect the employment conditions in economies where self-employment is predominant and permits high disguised unemployment.

Between 1975 and 1985 the labour force increased substantially in most of the Asian economies, especially in ASEAN where the average growth rate exceeded 3 per cent a year in the past decade. The NICs generally performed rather well, with an increase in wage employment which surpassed the addition to the labour force over the entire period. However, this was not true for Singapore for the period 1980-85. In 1985 Singapore experienced a net reduction of 90,000 jobs, 46,000 in the construction sector and 35,000 in manufacturing (60,000 of these jobs belonged to foreign workers), and unemployment figures have steadily risen.

Other South-East Asian countries show a more mixed picture: Indonesia and Thailand's wage employment growth has kept pace with increases in the labour force, while in the Philippines and Malaysia it has lagged behind, particularly in the period 1980-85. Both Malaysia and the Philippines have large plantation sectors which did not fare well in this period of depressed primary commodity prices and falling export demand. For example, in the island of Negros (Philippines) alone, 200,000 sugar workers were laid off in 1984.

Since underemployment is usually highest among the self-employed and family workers, it is possible to obtain some idea of a country's urban employment performance by comparing the growth of non-agricultural wage employment with that of the labour force outside agriculture (see figure 1.7). In some countries, such as Algeria, Jordan and the Republic of Korea, wage employment growth has outstripped labour force growth outside agriculture. But in most others wage employment creation has lagged behind the increase in labour supply (India, Philippines, Sri Lanka, Syrian Arab Republic and Tunisia). Thus, there is indirect evidence that in these countries employment in the urban informal sector has grown faster than that in the formal sector.

This is confirmed for India, where twice as many jobs have been created in the unorganised manufacturing sector as in the organised part of the sector over the past two decades. A similar tendency for small and informal sector manufacturing to absorb more workers has been noticeable in the 1970s and 1980s in several other Asian countries, such as Bangladesh, Pakistan and the Philippines. One explanation is the tendency for medium and large enterprises of South and South-East Asia to subcontract an increasing part of their production to smaller enterprises, often in the informal or unorganised sector, and to women working at home (under so-called putting-out arrangements).

This trend towards informal sector employment may be the result of several factors, such as:

(*a*) more rapid productivity increases in large-scale enterprises than in small-scale;

(*b*) more self-employment due to growing surplus labour;

(*c*) small enterprises being more efficient in adjusting to market demand than large-scale ones;

(*d*) small enterprises having competitive advantages over large-scale enterprises by paying lower wages and giving less employment security.

Moreover, there is a trend – documented in particular for India – towards the use of temporary and casual workers who replace permanent staff. In many medium- and large-scale enterprises, a growing share of the workload is being entrusted to workers who are either engaged on short-term contracts or who are not employed directly by the enterprise, even though their place of work may be on its premises. Their employer is a subcontractor, whose responsibilities to employees are much more limited than those required under a permanent employment contract. Similarly, the number of permanent employees is reduced by transferring their duties to casual workers, retainers and apprentices, who are engaged by the enterprise but are not counted among its staff. Together with the workers engaged on subcontracts, they constitute a growing number of so-called "working non-employees".

Table 1.7 shows the trends in open unemployment for a number of Asian countries. Unemployment has been on the rise in some countries since the beginning of the 1980s, particularly in Malaysia, the Philippines, Singapore and Thailand, and has stagnated or dropped in others, such as China, Indonesia and Pakistan.

In the NICs (except Singapore), however, open unemployment rates have been low throughout the 1980s, reflecting tight labour markets resulting from strong labour demand from export-led industrialisation. These countries, which have now launched a

Figure 1.7. Annual growth rates of wage employment and the labour force outside agriculture: Asia and North Africa, 1979-87 (in percentages)

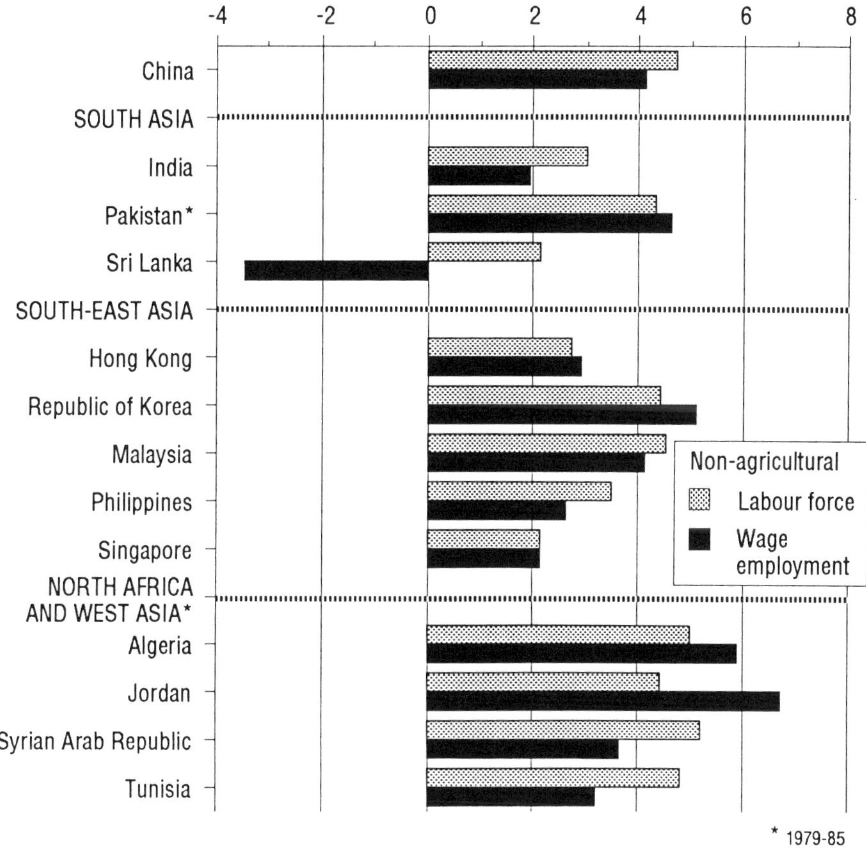

Sources: ILO: *Year book of labour statistics*; *Labour force projections*.

more capital-intensive path of industrialisation, have experienced labour shortages in certain occupations, as witnessed by the influx of low-skilled foreign workers. Among the ASEAN economies both Malaysia and the Philippines suffered a decline in living standards and reduced employment as a result of a major derailment in export prices. Not only did rural employment decrease but employment in manufacturing was also affected by the slump in demand. Industries in the export processing zones passed the burden on to their workers, resulting in shorter working time, lower earnings and retrenchments. Thailand, through diversification in agriculture and promotion of agro-based industries, has attained high rates of production and employment in the rural sector, although benefits are unequally distributed among regions.

In the low-income South Asian countries the figures on unemployment probably understate the effect of the recession on employment. There can be little doubt that the fall in prices of several major export crops in Asian countries led to a deterioration of employment and earnings for both peasant cultivators of these crops and wage labourers on plantations. For instance, in Malaysia and also Sri Lanka, a deterioration in export demand hits estate labour directly in the form of reduced work and lower earnings.

One emerging feature in the Asian region are the high rates of youth unemployment which are causing concern to parents and governments alike. Young people constitute a sizeable proportion of the total unemployed in each country. In India they account for over 80 per cent of chronic male unemployment in rural and urban areas. The problem is especially acute in the case of educated youth. The young educated category (with secondary schooling, graduates and above) who constituted 12 per cent of the labour

Table 1.7. Unemployment rates: Asia, 1981-87 (in percentages)

	Rate of unemployment						
	1981	1982	1983	1984	1985	1986	1987
Afghanistan [1]	5.5	5.5	3.8	3.3	3.0	...	...
Bangladesh [1]	...	...	...	11.5	11.9	12.1	...
Burma [1]	4.3	4.4	2.9	2.7	2.2	1.7	...
China [2]	3.8	3.2	3.2	1.9	1.8	2.0	2.0
Fiji [1]	...	15.7	16.6	17.6	18.6	...	...
Hong Kong	4.0	3.6	4.5	3.9	3.0	2.8	1.8
Indonesia [1]	2.7	3.0	2.0	2.0	2.1	2.6	...
Korea, Republic of	4.5	4.4	4.1	3.8	4.0	3.8	3.1
Malaysia	4.7	4.6	5.2	5.8	6.9	8.3	8.7
Pakistan [1]	3.6	3.5	3.9	3.9	3.9	3.7	...
Philippines [1]	5.3	6.0	5.4	7.3	6.8	6.7	...
Singapore	2.9	2.6	3.2	2.7	4.1	6.5	4.7
Sri Lanka [1]	17.9	...	...	...	...	...	...
Thailand [1]	0.8	3.5	2.4	2.3	3.8	3.5	...

... = not available.

[1] Reference years vary as follows: Afghanistan, 1978-85; Bangladesh, Burma, Indonesia, Pakistan and Thailand, 1976-86; Fiji and the Philippines, 1982-85; and Sri Lanka, 1974-81. [2] For China, indicates people waiting for a job as percentage of total urban labour force.

Source: ADB: *Key indicators of developing member countries of ADB*, Vol. XIX (Manila, July 1988).

force in India accounted for almost one-third of unemployment. Rates of unemployment also increase with rising educational attainment, putting immense pressure on governments to provide productive and durable jobs. This feature is not confined to India.

Over the past decade, overseas migration from Asian countries mainly to the Middle East has had a far-reaching impact on their domestic economies. Indeed, for a number of countries, no factor has more dramatically affected their domestic employment and the balance-of-payments situation than the outflow of mostly skilled workers to and inflows of workers' remittances from these countries. The major labour-exporting countries include Bangladesh, India, the Republic of Korea, Pakistan, the Philippines, Sri Lanka and, more recently, Indonesia. Lately, however, the slowdown in economic activity in the major labour-receiving countries has led to a decline in the outflow of contract migrant workers and a quickening pace of return migration. Similarly, remittance flows have fallen considerably. There is a broad consensus that the peak of the Middle East "boom" is over and that the safety valve that the Middle East economies provided to the growing labour force of a number of Asian countries will not be available in the future. The labour-sending countries will need to find employment opportunities for the increase in their labour force mainly in their domestic economies. To these will be added the permanent return migrants who will also have to be absorbed.

Wages and productivity

Wages play an important role in structural adjustment, first because labour costs are an important factor in determining competitiveness of the goods and services produced and, second, because of the political repercussions of wage changes, particularly in urban areas. The ability of industries to adjust is determined to a large degree by the capacity to meet changes in world market demand, in prices or in technology by restructuring employment and wages so that production units remain competitive. Some have argued that the relatively high degree of success that the East and South-East Asian economies have had in restructuring, tiding them over the two oil shocks and the subsequent recession and protectionist problems, has been aided by the unusually high degree of flexibility of their wage structures and the ease with which workers can be laid off or redeployed. According to this line of reasoning, the weakness of the trade unions, and the absence of a politically organised urban middle class, are factors which partly explain why the more liberal Asian economies have managed not only to maintain but actually to increase both production and employment in spite of world market conditions which have caused considerable damage to economies in Latin America and Africa.

If wages were entirely flexible, workers would accept a reduction in wages when productivity – output per worker – decreases as a result of shrinking markets or when the value of production declines because of falling prices. Even though there are cases in South-East Asia when workers have in fact accepted pay cuts to protect employment, this is not common. What usually happens is that wages are not adjusted for the rise in consumer prices, so that the real purchasing power of the wage is reduced. Changes in real wages – wages measured in constant consumer prices – are shown for manufacturing industry in the countries for which such data are available in figure 1.8.

In manufacturing, being the sector most sensitive to external shocks and structural changes, it is notice-

Figure 1.8. Real earnings in manufacturing: Asia, 1980-87 (1980 = 100)

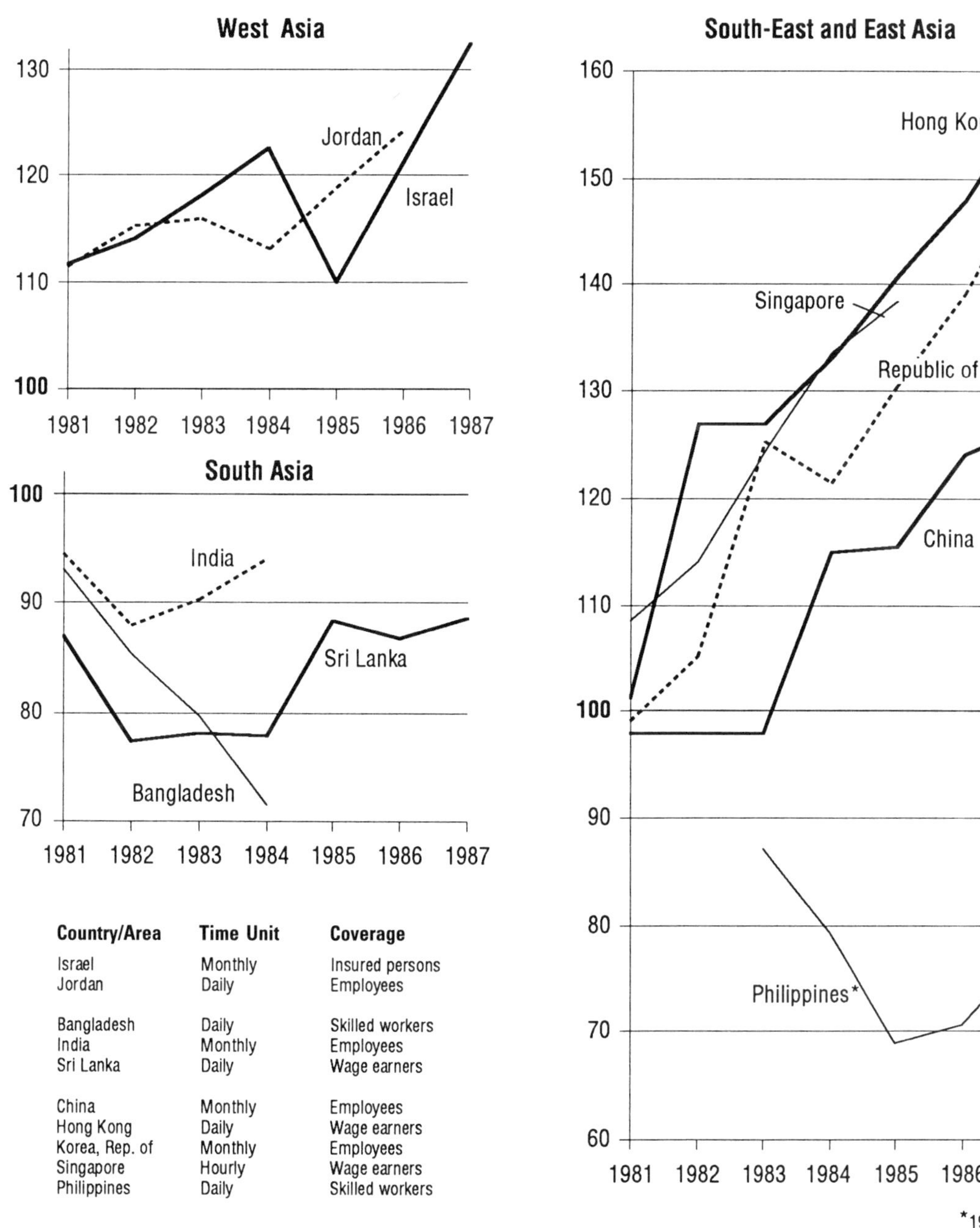

Country/Area	Time Unit	Coverage
Israel	Monthly	Insured persons
Jordan	Daily	Employees
Bangladesh	Daily	Skilled workers
India	Monthly	Employees
Sri Lanka	Daily	Wage earners
China	Monthly	Employees
Hong Kong	Daily	Wage earners
Korea, Rep. of	Monthly	Employees
Singapore	Hourly	Wage earners
Philippines	Daily	Skilled workers

Source: ILO: *Year book of labour statistics.*

able that real wages in most cases have increased during the 1980s. Only Bangladesh, India, the Philippines and Sri Lanka show falls, mostly as a result of restructuring problems. But a number of economies which have undergone rapid restructuring, such as Hong Kong, the Republic of Korea and Singapore, have experienced a rapid rise of real wages in manufacturing even in the 1980s.

Why has the rate of wage increase gone up, when the general economic environment has hardened? A recent study by ARTEP published in 1987 compares trends in productivity and earnings for the periods

1975-80 and 1980-85. It appears from this study that productivity increases have been quite substantial in 1980-85 in all countries, except Bangladesh and the Philippines, where they were zero or negative. In Hong Kong, India, Malaysia, Pakistan and Sri Lanka productivity increased faster in 1980-85 than in 1975-80, more due to a negligible employment increase than to rapid production increases. The rise in employment slowed in the Republic of Korea, Singapore and Thailand as well, but production growth declined faster.

A comparison of productivity and real wage changes for the period as a whole gives the impression that wages have generally kept pace with productivity, except in the Philippines and Thailand, where they have fallen persistently behind. In the 1980s Pakistan has experienced a faster rise in productivity than in wages, while in Singapore it has been the other way around. Malaysia has followed a pattern similar to that of Singapore, with real wages running further ahead of productivity in the 1980s, in spite of economic difficulties which affected manufacturing industries during this period.

It thus seems that the use of "wage flexibility" as a means of maintaining or increasing the competitive position of manufacturing industry has been applied only in the Philippines and Thailand during the ten-year period covered by the data. In some of the NICs which in earlier periods may have successfully used this instrument, such as Hong Kong, the Republic of Korea, Malaysia and Singapore, labour markets started to tighten during the second half of the 1970s and, even if recession and stagnation in world markets caused difficulties in the 1980s, the momentum of wage increases during the good years could not be immediately halted. Industry adjusted by slowing down employment growth rather than by suppressing wage increases. It is possible that slow growth in export demand and reduced migration to the Gulf countries may dampen wage increases in coming years, but so far there is no conclusive evidence that the suppression of wage increases in manufacturing has been a major reason for the success of Asian economies in adjusting to external shocks.

In the agricultural sector external adjustment problems have mainly affected the plantation crops, such as sugar, palm oil, coconut oil, rubber and tea. Plantation workers are generally among the lowest paid in the organised sector of Asian economies, and they have often been more negatively affected by adjustment problems than factory workers. The sugar workers in the Philippines have been mentioned as an example of loss of employment. There are also serious cases of reduced real wages, and deteriorating housing and social services in estates in many parts of South and South-East Asia. In Malaysia the wages of rubber tappers are partially related to the market price of latex. This unique arrangement for using wages as an instrument for adjusting to external shocks has placed the rubber workers in a difficult situation. After some years of rapidly rising real wages towards the end of the 1970s, the 1980s have brought a fall in real wages of about 4 per cent per year. A similar trend can be seen from the data on plantation wages in Sri Lanka.

In traditional food-crop agriculture real wages have increased much less than in manufacturing and in many cases they have been falling over long periods of time. While real wages have increased appreciably in Japan and the Republic of Korea, they have fallen or stagnated in most of South and South-East Asia. This is not only true of countries and regions where agricultural production has stagnated, such as Bangladesh, Nepal and the state of Bihar in India. It is also true of areas of high agricultural growth such as the Philippines and rural Java (Indonesia). Only in Pakistan have real wages increased. Pakistan has a relatively small hired agricultural labour force, which has been significantly affected by out-migration to the Gulf countries in the late 1970s and early 1980s. It is quite clear that the reason for wages being depressed in the agricultural labour markets of most of South and South-East Asia is not structural adjustment as such, but oversupply of labour.

Industrial relations

Although the economic performance in the 1980s of most countries in Asia has compared favourably with the rest of the world, many countries are still characterised by a labour surplus. The trade union movement in labour-surplus countries, such as Indonesia, the Philippines and Thailand, appears to have been weakened owing to changes in industrial structure (e.g. growth of small firms and white-collar jobs in the financial and service sectors), the expansion of various forms of precarious employment (casual, part-time, etc.), declining union consciousness amongst workers entering the labour force and more hostile employer attitudes. In some Asian countries there has been an increase in recognition disputes and a spread of "house" unions. Another contribut-

1.2 Flexible wages – Singapore style

Singapore wage policies have undergone a number of sharp changes of direction in recent years, reflecting the shifting preoccupations of the national authorities. After many years of wage restraint, the emergence of labour shortages led the authorities to adopt "a wage correction" policy from 1979 to 1981 to facilitate economic restructuring. Through the tripartite National Wages Council (NWC) large increases for low wage workers were recommended in order to discourage unskilled, labour-intensive activities and to shift labour into more capital-intensive, higher productivity operations. However, between 1982 to 1984, the gap between wage and productivity increases widened. A gradual deterioration in Singapore's unit labour costs, plus the slump in demand for exports, resulted in 1985 in Singapore's first recession in two decades.

In 1986 the NWC recommended a wage standstill until international competitiveness could be restored. Later in the year, a Subcommittee on Wage Reform issued a report advocating more flexible wage determination practices as compared with the prevailing pattern of national wage adjustment recommendations linked to seniority-based wage structures within enterprises. The principles endorsed by the reform were that overall wage increases should lag behind productivity growth, wage increases should take into account company and individual worker performance, such wage adjustments should not always be given on a permanent basis, there should be a measure of stability in workers' incomes, and wages should reflect job ratings. The suggested approach envisaged: (1) a structure of basic wages that would reflect job content and provide stability of income; (2) an annual wage supplement of one month's pay that might be adjusted under exceptional circumstances; (3) a variable wage component based on company productivity or profit performance that would be paid annually or bi-annually; (4) salary ranges with ratios of maximum to minimum of about 1.5; (5) a small seniority increment in recognition of workers' loyalty and experience. Collective agreements implementing wage reforms of this kind have been negotiated by an increasing number of companies.

ing factor to declining trade union militancy has been the concern of governments and employers to reduce conflict and improve labour-management co-operation (through a variety of strategies) with a view to boosting productivity and competitiveness. Where labour disputes have developed they have often been about such issues as termination of employment or privatisation linked with structural adjustment programmes. However, heightened labour militancy aimed at basic changes in labour relations has been evident in newly industrialised countries and areas which are experiencing increasing shortages of labour (Hong Kong, the Republic of Korea, Singapore and Taiwan, China).

In some countries structural adjustment has led to intensified inflationary pressures. Thus in China the extension of reforms in the system of economic management has been associated with an acceleration of price increases. Although real earnings on average have improved, there has been increased social tension, in part owing to the absence of general mechanisms for adjusting wages for inflation. In other countries the concern has been to establish a closer link between wages and productivity. Thus in Singapore a wage reform aimed at introducing greater wage flexibility is now being introduced in place of the system of national wage adjustment recommendations which has been operated for many years (see box 1.2). The development of wage adjustment practices that link pay with some measure of enterprise performance has also been a concern in India and a number of other Asian countries.

Concluding remarks

The economic strategies adopted by Asian countries have produced differing results in growth and employment. The response of Asian governments to external shocks, as well as to internal structural problems, has been relatively quick and quite effective, at least compared with other regions of the world. The performance of the NICs and the ability of their outward-oriented economies to adjust to turbulences in international trade and financial flows and to regain growth in output and employment within a very short period is outstanding.

The NIC paradigm of growth and adjustment is often contrasted with the inward-looking strategies of China and India, which have been relatively untouched by the vagaries of the international trade environment. Although India's GDP growth rate has not been as high as in some of the NICs and ASEAN, it remained fairly stable during the recession period. China and India have been able to protect themselves against external shocks by relying on their huge internal markets.

Neither the outward-oriented strategy of the NICs nor the inward-looking policies of China and India offer any readily imitable lessons of adjustment for the rest of Asia, which has been more seriously affected by the recession. Adjustment in these countries will largely depend on the structure of the economy and the strategy of growth.

Who has borne the brunt of the burden of adjustment? In the worst affected country, the Philippines, large numbers of people including modern sector wage employees have suffered a loss of real income. At the extreme are the sugar workers in Negros Occidental, who lost their jobs and their means of livelihood. In most countries those outside the modern or organised sector have suffered the worst set-backs. Youth, women and migrants from depressed rural areas have been unable to find jobs in the organised or formal sector and have increasingly resorted to insecure and low-paid jobs in the informal sector or to subcontracts or casual employment on the fringes of formal sector enterprises. In traditional agriculture hired workers have experienced a decline in real earnings, in some countries over very long periods of time. These are not direct consequences of structural adjustment, but they are the indirect results of a slowing-down of growth and decreasing degree of labour intensity in formal sector industries.

4. Latin America

The present economic crisis in Latin America, which goes back to the recession of the early 1980s, has substantially reduced growth of output and income relative to population growth in the majority of countries in the region. Between 1980 and 1988 GDP grew at an average annual rate of 0.7 per cent, while the rate of population growth was 2.5 per cent a year. This resulted in a 6.6 per cent decline in per capita GDP.

Debt problems and the consistently inhospitable international environment have propelled most Latin American economies down a path of continuous economic decline. In 1988 Latin America transferred almost US$30,000 million abroad, representing almost a quarter of total exports and about 4 per cent of GDP. Most of these transfers were debt payments made by governments to private sector creditors. Since governments could not collect sufficient taxes to finance these payments, they resorted to monetary financing, which largely explains the surge in inflation to a level of 470 per cent in 1988, compared with almost 200 per cent in 1987. As a result, government expenditure on social services and investment fell precipitously and the inflationary context prevented any significant private sector investment.

The sluggish growth of Latin American economies since 1980, especially in the earlier years of the decade, has been translated into a substantial slowdown in the rate of job creation. Furthermore, the economic downturn has affected the quality of employment: jobs generated in the 1980s have been largely low-paid temporary or casual employment, mostly in agriculture and in self-employed activities of the urban informal sector. At the same time, the employment problem in Latin America during the past eight years has been compounded by an average rate of inflation in excess of 130 per cent a year, which has led to a continuing decline in real wages and an erosion of living standards.

Table 1.8. Trends in non-agricultural employment: Latin America,[1] 1980-87 (in percentages)

	1980-83	1983-85	1985-87	1980-87
Non-agricultural employment	10.2	7.8	9.3	29.8
Unemployment	51.7	–8.0	–17.0	16.1
Urban informal sector	24.1	13.9	10.5	56.1
Urban formal sector	5.4	5.2	8.8	20.7
Public sector	13.6	9.3	6.6	32.4
Private sector	3.2	4.1	9.5	17.6
of which:				
Large enterprises [2]	(–6.9)	(5.1)	(5.6)	(3.3)
Small enterprises	(30.0)	(2.3)	(16.9)	(55.4)

[1] Weighted average of data for seven countries (Argentina, Brazil, Colombia, Costa Rica, Chile, Mexico and Venezuela). [2] Establishments with more than ten employees.

Source: PREALC: *Evolution of the labour market during 1980-87* (Santiago, Chile, 1988).

Unemployment

Between 1980 and 1987 non-agricultural employment grew almost 30 per cent or by 3.8 per cent a year (see table 1.8). This growth rate was significantly lower than that during the 1960s and 1970s and was insufficient to absorb the steadily increasing workforce. As a result, unemployment grew at about 15 per cent a year between 1980 and 1983, though it later declined; the urban unemployment rate rose from 6.2 per cent in 1980 to 8.9 per cent in 1985 and dropped to 6.6 per cent in 1987 (figure 1.9). Recorded open urban unemployment is low in the large countries of the region, such as Argentina, Brazil and Mexico, but is fairly high in the smaller countries of Central America and the Caribbean. The preliminary data for 1988 show that unemployment is probably on the increase again, particularly in Bolivia, Brazil and Panama.

Figure 1.9. Urban open unemployment rates: Latin America and the Caribbean, 1980-88 (in percentages)

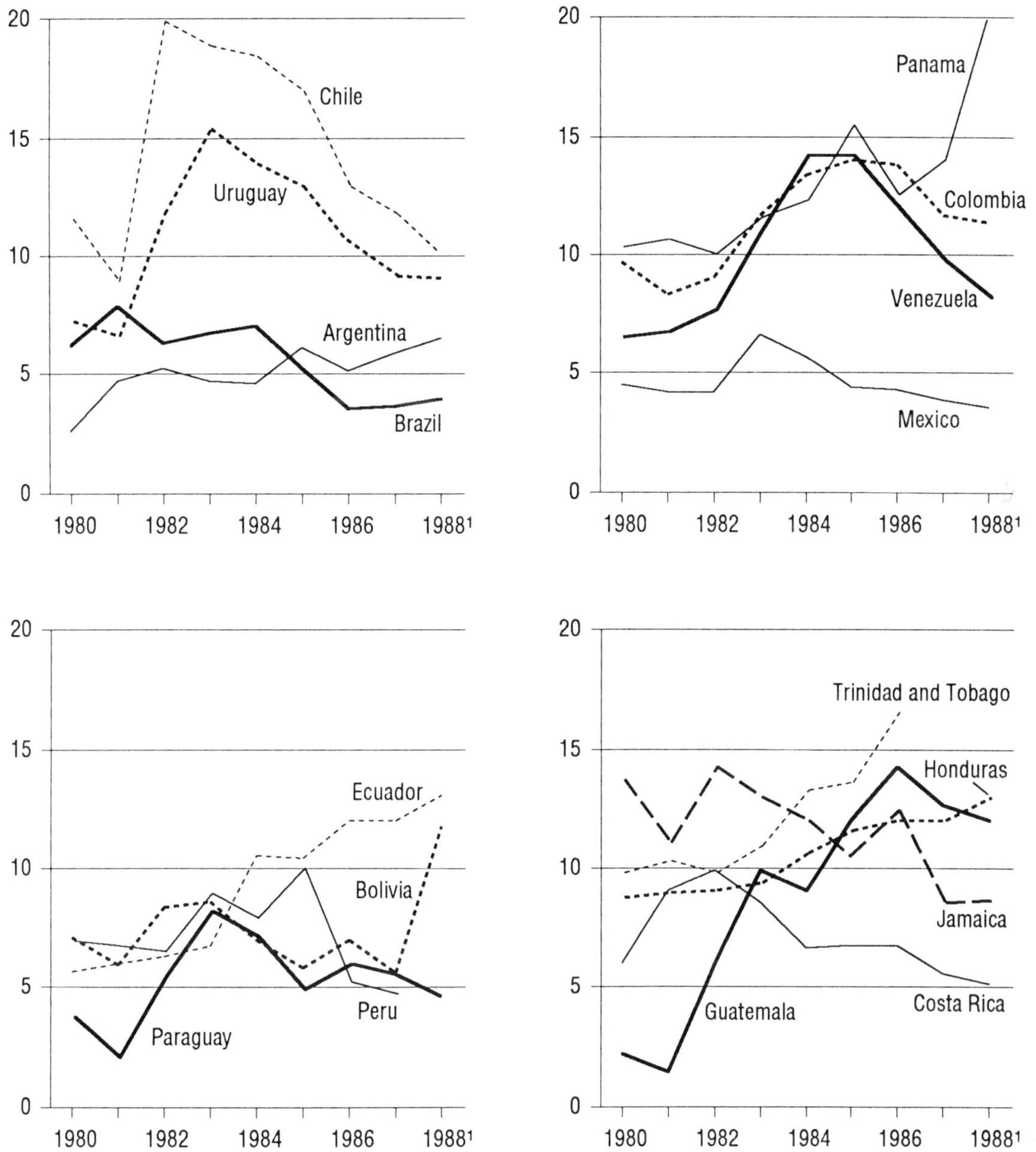

[1] First semester.
Source: PREALC.

Certain aspects of the unemployment trend are not reflected in the statistics. The first is the "discouraged worker" phenomenon: observed changes in participation rates suggest that a significant proportion of the unemployed are withdrawing "voluntarily" from the labour force in the face of high unemployment and the depressed state of the labour market. Thus the "true" rate of open unemployment is much higher than recorded, especially during the recession. The fact that some of these discouraged workers re-enter the labour force as active jobseekers during the recovery helps to explain why expansion in economic activity has not been accompanied by any significant reduction in the recorded unemployment rate.

The second concerns the distribution of unemployment over time (1980-85). Evidence from available data for Chile, Costa Rica and Venezuela indicates a sharper increase in the incidence of unemployment among those who contribute most to family incomes – that is, males and heads of households, prime age workers (24-44 years) with previous work experience, secondary and university education. Thus, increased unemployment is likely to have been accompanied by a worsening of poverty. At the same time, the incidence of unemployment among young people (15-24 years), with an unemployment rate of between 25 and 30 per cent, and women in Latin America has been consistently and disproportionately high. Within these two socio-economic groups, the unemployment rate is higher among those with secondary education and above than those with lower educational attainments, especially among youth.

Sluggish employment growth in the formal sector

The recovery which several Latin American countries experienced after 1985 was generally short-lived and obviously fragile in nature. By 1987 the rate of economic growth was again stagnant or declining and, even where the growth rate was increasing, per capita GDP in 1987 was still less than at the beginning of the decade.

Furthermore, declining and negative growth rates before 1983 severely depressed investment to the extent that economic recovery was not accompanied by any significant addition to capital accumulation in the form of new investments. Instead, growth of output in many Latin American countries after 1983 was almost entirely due to increased utilisation of *existing* capacity, which resulted in hardly any increase in *net* job creation overall.

Evidence derived from an analysis of the employment-output elasticity (responsiveness) in the manufacturing industry of nine Latin American countries for which data are available revealed a significantly higher elasticity during the recession period (1980-83) than during the post-1984 recovery (see table 1.9). This implies that in the recession employment was sustained at a much lower level of productivity, enabling companies to boost output later with the same workforce. Thus the rate of labour absorption

Table 1.9. Employment-output elasticity [1] in manufacturing industry: Latin America, 1970-85

Periods	Employment-output elasticity	Growth rate (%) per annum	
		Output	Productivity
Normal	0.45	6.2	3.3
Recession	1.10	–4.0	0.8
Recovery	0.06	6.3	5.7

[1] Percentage increase in employment for a 1 per cent increase in output.
Note: Calculations made on the basis of the information available for nine countries during the period 1970-85. Refers to simple averages of the coefficients of each country, assigning weighted averages according to the number of years included in each subperiod.
Source: PREALC, based on country information.

in the modern sector has not increased during the recovery.

In fact, the employment-output elasticity during this period was found to be significantly lower than normal. This confirms that a cautious approach has been adopted by business to investment, with reliance on a more efficient utilisation of available human and material resources, rather than new investments, to increase output. There has therefore been a trade-off between employment and levels of productivity.

The public sector, which traditionally has sustained a higher rate of labour absorption within the formal economy, grew at an average annual rate of 4.5 per cent between 1980 and 1985 and increased its share of total non-agricultural employment slightly from 15.8 to 16.8 per cent. This is in contrast to the decline in total private sector employment (in both large and small enterprises) as a proportion of total non-agricultural employment from 58.1 per cent in 1980 to 52.5 per cent in 1985. Because of social and political considerations, several governments in the region have continued to assign a major job-creation role to the public sector, and therefore have avoided retrenchment of public sector employees even in times of economic crisis. Thus, while the private sector increased output during the recovery period by rationalisation of labour inputs and increased utilisation of existing capacity, employment in the public sector of most Latin American countries has continued its upward trend throughout the 1980s.

Expanding low-productivity jobs

The rapid expansion of the urban informal sector in Latin America in the 1980s – as compared with the previous three decades – has resulted in a shift in employment structure from regular wage employment to casual informal sector-type jobs. It is estimated that informal sector employment grew at about 6.6 per cent a year between 1980 and 1987 or about 56 per cent over the whole period (see table 1.8). Formal sector employment was estimated to have grown by 2.7 per cent annually or 20.7 per cent over the whole period. The dynamic growth of the informal sector in Latin American cities and towns has thus made it a bulwark against open unemployment, especially during the recession of the early 1980s. For example, in 1980 the informal sector provided employment for about a quarter of the non-agricultural labour force in Latin America, but by 1987 this proportion had increased to one-third. Unlike formal sector employment, which was less sensitive to the recovery and output growth post-1983, informal sector employment growth has maintained an upward trend and has been more commensurate with growth of output in the sector.

A study of job creation by size of private enterprise, covering two countries, suggests not only that the private sector has generated fewer jobs, but also that most of the job creation took place in small enterprises. This is confirmed by PREALC estimates which show that in seven large Latin American countries employment in large enterprises grew by only 3.3 per cent between 1980 and 1987 (see table 1.8). However, the expansion of employment in small enterprises was a formidable 55.4 per cent, almost as great as that for the urban informal sector. The contrast between both types of enterprises was most pronounced during the recession of 1980-83 when employment in small enterprises expanded by 30 per cent while it dropped by almost 7 per cent in large enterprises.

Finally, there is a trend towards the "tertiarisation" of employment which, added to the already mentioned expansion of employment in the informal sector and small enterprises, reinforces the hypothesis that low-productivity service activities have increased during the crisis. Information on industrial employment provides an indirect indication that increasing numbers of jobseekers have been absorbed in service activities. Between 1980 and 1985 industrial employment fell by 2.2 per cent a year, with the result that in 1985 the level of employment in manufacturing was more than 10 per cent lower than in 1980. This is in sharp contrast with the three previous decades when industrial employment consistently grew at annual rates of 2 to 3 per cent.

Table 1.10. Real wages by sector of activity: Latin America, 1980-87 [1] (in percentages)

	1980-83	1983-85	1985-87	1980-87
Agriculture	−7.8	−6.6	3.6	−10.8
Manufacturing	−6.6	−4.1	0.6	−9.9
Construction	−6.3	−9.6	−0.7	−15.9
Public sector [2]	−13.8	−3.8	...	(−17.1) [3]
Minimum wage	−8.8	−7.2	2.1	−13.6

... = not available.

[1] Based on the official data of 17 countries. [2] Based on nine countries. [3] 1980-85.

Source: PREALC: *Evolution of the labour market during 1980-87* (Santiago, Chile, 1988).

Falling labour incomes

Another effect of the economic crisis on the labour market is the general deterioration of wages (see table 1.10) and other labour incomes. Between 1980 and 1987 real wages fell on average by between 7 and 16 per cent, and it is noteworthy that these declines did not occur only during the recession phase of 1980-83, but continued during the subsequent expansion. However, there is considerable variation in wage trends between countries. In Argentina, Brazil (Rio de Janeiro), Chile, Costa Rica and Uruguay average real wages remained more or less constant between 1980 and 1988, while they actually increased in Colombia (20 per cent) and São Paulo, Brazil (almost 50 per cent). On the other hand, real wages dropped in Mexico (about 30 per cent) and in Peru (about 50 per cent). In some smaller countries real wages in manufacturing also fell – in Bolivia and Ecuador (50 and 20 per cent respectively between 1980 and 1984), in El Salvador and Guatemala (more than 30 per cent between 1980 and 1985) and in Venezuela (more than 25 per cent between 1980 and 1987).

There are various factors that can help explain this pattern. First, accelerating inflation leads to deteriorating real wages in spite of various indexation mechanisms. Second, rising unemployment and the expansion of the informal sector weakens the bargaining power of organised labour. And, finally, the decline of real wages constitutes one of the basic elements of the adjustment policies followed by most Latin American governments. Behind such policies lies the assumption that reduced labour costs improve the country's competitive position and the economy's capacity to create employment. However, evidence from the manufacturing sector seems to contradict this assumption, because the employment-wage elasticity is estimated at 1.26 for 1980-83 and 0.07 for 1983-85. Thus, the employment-wage elasticity for manufacturing is positive (in other words, reductions in employment go together with reductions in real wages), which seems to suggest that lack of demand rather than uncompetitive labour costs was the cause of reduced employment levels.

The 1980s have also been characterised by increased dispersion of wages between sectors of activity. Between 1980 and 1987 real wages for the better organised workers in manufacturing lost, on average, only 9.9 per cent of their purchasing power, while losses were about 11, 16 and 14 per cent, respectively, for workers in agriculture, construction and on minimum wages. However, in the shorter period between 1980 and 1985 public sector workers lost more than 17 per cent of their purchasing power, in spite of their high degree of organisation.

There is no direct information available on labour incomes in the informal sector. In principle, one could assume that between 1980 and 1987 real incomes in this sector have fallen by at least 14 per cent (the decline in real urban minimum wages) or by at most 56 per cent (the increase in informal sector employment). The latter assumption would be plausible if the demand for informal sector goods and services had followed the same static trend as non-agricultural output as a whole. In other words, the informal sector would have faced a stagnant market, adjusting to the raised level of employment by means of reductions in average incomes. A recent estimate by PREALC, based on the national accounts of seven Latin American countries, lends support to this assumption. It shows that, between 1980 and 1987, average labour incomes in the informal sector dropped by more than 40 per cent in real terms.

In recent years there has been a great deal of discussion in the region about the distribution of the costs of the process of structural adjustment. The available data suggest that labour incomes (wages and self-employment incomes in the informal sector) have seen their share in national income decrease quite sharply. Taking 1980 as a base year, the ratio between the index of total labour earnings and the index of gross national income plummeted to 85 in 1987 (see figure 1.10). In 1985 and 1986 there was a partial recovery, but in 1987 the deteriorating situation of recession and inflation in Brazil resulted in a sharp decrease in the regional average.

Figure 1.10. Trends in labour income and GNP: Latin America,[1] 1980-87 (1980 = 100)

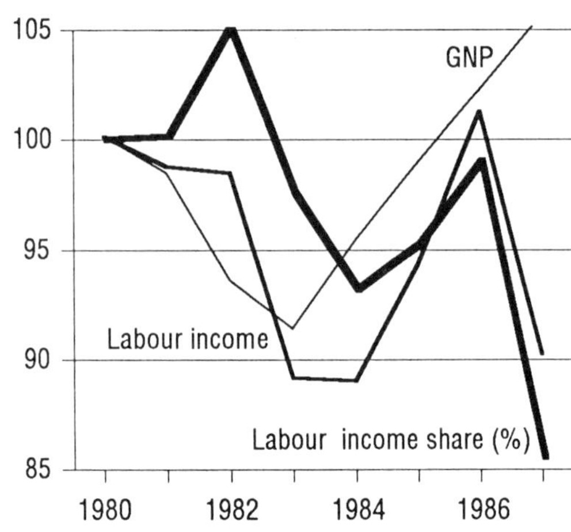

[1] Based on official data from Argentina, Brazil, Chile, Colombia, Costa Rica, Mexico and Venezuela.

Source: PREALC: *Evolution of the labour market during 1980-87* (Santiago, Chile, 1988).

Industrial relations

The economic pressures of the 1980s have affected patterns of industrial relations in the region in diverse ways. First, the contraction of employment in the large-scale modern sector relative to employment in the small-scale informal sector has eroded the traditional base of strength of the trade union movement and the relevance of the main forms of labour market regulation. Though some new approaches to the organisation and regulation of the growing segment of unorganised workers have been considered in the region, no widespread progress has been evident.

Second, the pursuit of wage restraint as part of austerity programmes has intensified government intervention in wage determination. Traditionally, governments in Latin America have played a major role in this regard, owing to the importance of the public sector, extensive legislative protection of individual workers' rights, and an active involvement in collective labour relations (limitations on negotiated wage increases, controls on negotiating procedures, restrictions on the level of negotiations, imposition of settlements). Pressure on governments to control inflationary forces and limit domestic demand has resulted in all these channels of influence on wage determination being more fully exploited. In some instances, however, the democratisation of political structures or other pressures for change have permitted, to a greater or lesser degree, the introduction of more independent collective labour relations practices. In other cases, where the trade union movement appears too weak to engage in fully independent collective bargaining, there has been a growing interest in tripartite machinery for fixing wages that leaves at least some scope for collective negotiations between the social partners.

Third, labour relations have been more unstable as a result of the sacrifices that have had to be made and the politicisation of the external debt issue. To build a greater degree of consensus and avoid social conflict, there has been much discussion in the region of the possible benefits of tripartite social concertation through social pacts, framework agreements, and so on, but to date there are few concrete developments. In December 1987 an "economic solidarity plan" was signed by the Government of Mexico and the leading organisations of employers and workers in an effort to deal with escalating inflation and the country's debt crisis. It involved minimum wage hikes, a monthly wage adjustment system, rises in prices of public goods and services, measures to stabilise certain other prices, the removal of subsidies and the privatisation of public enterprises, tax changes and measures to control public expenditures and the deficit.

It remains to be seen whether the Mexican pattern will be followed by other Latin American countries. Attempts to establish national pay and prices guide-lines through tripartite consultations have failed in countries such as Argentina, Brazil and Uruguay. However, in Uruguay efforts to set up guide-lines on an industry-wide basis were successful. Shortly after the re-establishment of democracy in March 1985, the Uruguayan authorities revived the wage council machinery which had been buried 17 years before. As a result, real wages have increased modestly and inflation has not increased further though it has continued to range between 50 and 70 per cent a year.

5. Sub-Saharan Africa

Sub-Saharan Africa is going through the longest and most severe crisis in living memory. Standards of living and real wages have fallen precipitously since 1980 and the end of the eight-year-long recession is not yet in sight. Despite the implementation by many sub-Saharan African countries of wide-ranging adjustments in economic policies – to cope with depressed export earnings and crippling debt burdens – the prospects for recovery and development in the region remain gloomy.

Until the late 1970s the looming employment crisis remained to a large extent invisible because of the relatively rapid expansion of employment opportunities in both the modern and informal sectors. But the 1980s have witnessed a sharp deterioration in the region's employment situation. The main causes of the deterioration are: (1) the growing impact of the demographic tide on labour supply; (2) a phenomenal expansion of educational enrolment which has led to a substantial mismatch between supply and demand for skills on the labour markets; (3) lack of transformation of the economy; and (4) sluggish economic growth.

Declining real wages

One of the most obvious adjustments in sub-Saharan labour markets has been the rapid fall of real wages. Table 1.11 documents real wage trends in the modern sector. Out of 18 countries for which comparable and recent data are available, only two have reported modest increases in real wages and the other countries have all registered considerable losses. The decline has been steepest in Madagascar, Sierra Leone, Somalia, the Sudan, the United Republic of Tanzania and Zambia, where the average wage rate has dropped by 10 per cent or more every year since 1980. On average, real wages have declined by approximately a quarter between 1980 and 1985.

Available information on real minimum wages in 28 countries point in the same direction. Minimum wages are more volatile than average wages because the intervals at which they are adjusted tend to be much longer. Burundi is among the countries that has given minimum wage earners full compensation for inflation, whereas Somalia, the Sudan and the United Republic of Tanzania are among the countries that have given them the least compensation. On average, the minimum wage in sub-Saharan countries declined by about a quarter between 1980 and 1986 (excluding the untypical cases of Ghana and Somalia).

Two facts deserve special attention. The first is that the decline in real wages pre-dates the economic downturn which occurred after 1980. Between 1975 and 1980 non-agricultural wages in real terms dropped by 56.1 per cent in Nigeria, by 57.8 per cent in the United Republic of Tanzania, by 47.4 per cent

Table 1.11. Real wage trends in sub-Saharan Africa, 1980-87 (1980 = 100)

Country	Coverage	Year	Index (1980 =100)	Annual change (in percentages)
Botswana	Public sector	1984	85.3	-3.9
Burundi	Non-agricultural sector	1987	105.5	0.8
Cape Verde	Public sector	1984	71.7	-8.0
Ethiopia	Civil service	1984	84.1	-4.2
Gambia	Modern sector	1984	80.5	-5.3
Kenya	Non-agricultural sector	1987	77.4	-3.6
Madagascar	Public sector	1984	54.8	-14.0
Malawi	Non-agricultural sector	1986	67.1	-6.4
Mauritania	Civil service	1984	76.4	-6.5
Mauritius	Non-agricultural sector	1986	93.6	-1.1
Senegal	Civil service	1985	70.0	-6.9
Seychelles	Non-agricultural sector	1985	110.6	2.0
Sierra Leone	Non-agricultural sector	1987	25.5	-20.6
Somalia	Civil service	1986	28.4	-18.9
Sudan	Civil service	1985	52.2	-12.2
Tanzania, United Republic of	Non-agricultural sector	1987	26.1	-17.5
Zambia	Non-agricultural sector	1984	63.7	-10.7
Zimbabwe	Non-agricultural sector	1984	88.9	-2.9
Average		1985	70.1	-6.7

Source: Compiled from ILO: *Year book of labour statistics*, government statistical abstracts, various JASPA and World Bank country studies.

in Swaziland, and by 10.0 per cent in Burundi. In Ghana the non-agricultural wage earner lost two-thirds of his purchasing power between 1975 and 1979. The data on minimum wages show a similar sharp decline before 1980 and confirm that the employment crisis preceded and was exacerbated by the economic crisis of the 1980s. The second noteworthy trend is that the annual decrease in real wages seems to have decelerated over time. This is probably related to the falling rate of inflation. Indeed, real wages have fallen in the past because nominal wages have lagged behind price increases. Real wages dropped fastest in the period 1980-84 when the median inflation rate in sub-Saharan Africa averaged 12 per cent per annum, and more slowly after 1984 as the median inflation rate in the region declined to 9 per cent.

It is important to note that real wages have fallen more rapidly than income per head since 1980. This means that wage earners have borne the brunt of the recent economic crisis. Their income position has worsened relative to that of other socio-economic groups. As documented in the previous *World labour report*, the privileged income position which they enjoyed in the 1960s and early 1970s has been substantially eroded, so that they no longer constitute a "labour aristocracy". On the contrary, real earnings have fallen to such low levels that they often need to be supplemented by other income sources to make ends meet. Hence, a rising proportion of wage earners have a secondary job. There is growing evidence of civil servants practising their profession on their own account or supervising a micro-business in the informal sector during normal working hours. It is not uncommon to find an urban household whose head is a wage earner with agriculture as a secondary income-generating activity.

Traditionally, many governments in Africa have played a dominant role in wage determination, resulting from their position as by far the largest employer in the formal sector and their extensive intervention in collective bargaining through incomes policies and other means. This dominance has been augmented further in recent years as economic conditions have provided a ready justification for more state intervention in industrial relations. Thus, under declared emergency conditions, existing laws regulating industrial relations have often been suspended. Moreover, the State has sometimes prohibited trade union activities, detained trade union leaders and interfered in trade union organisation. A number of governments have, by law, restructured and consolidated trade union organisations. Although in some instances these measures reduced a multiplicity of trade unions they have also facilitated greater control over trade union activities.

Faltering wage employment growth

Governments in most sub-Saharan African countries have followed a restrictive wage policy so as to maximise the growth of modern sector wage employment. The available data indicate that the elasticity (responsiveness) of wage employment with respect to GDP has indeed increased in a few countries. In Kenya, for example, the elasticity increased from 0.47 in the 1960s (i.e. 0.47 per cent growth in wage employment for each 1 per cent increase in GDP) to 0.69 in the period 1975-79 and 0.85 between 1980 and 1987. But the improved labour-intensity in the modern sector has not been able to offset the rapid deceleration of economic growth. Thus wage employment growth in the modern sector has declined

Figure 1.11. Non-agricultural wage employment and the labour force outside agriculture: Sub-Saharan Africa, 1979(80)-86(87) (annual growth rates)

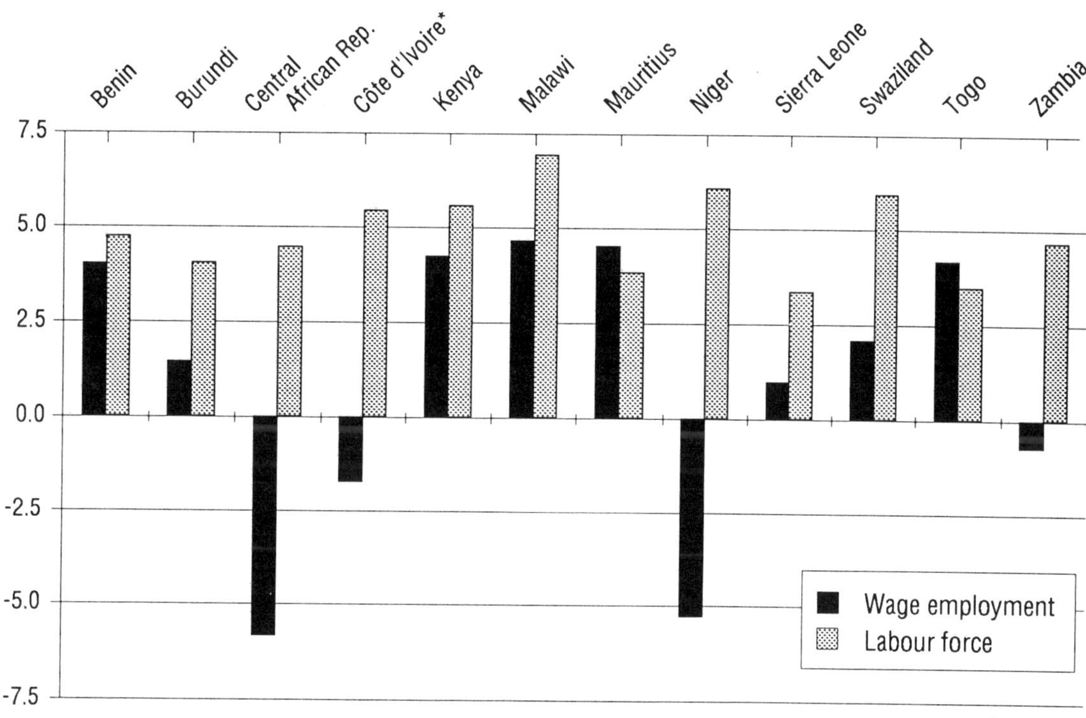

Sources: ILO: *Year book of labour statistics*; *Labour force projections*.

significantly since the early 1980s, despite the substantial drop in labour costs.

In the 12 countries for which data are available, the average rate of increase slowed from 2.8 per cent a year in the period 1975-80 to 1.0 per cent between 1980 and 1985. The decline was even steeper in the industrial sector where employment growth decelerated from 2.6 per cent to a mere 0.1 per cent a year between the respective five-year periods. Hence, a process of "de-industrialisation" appears to have started in the region. More recent information shows that since 1970 non-agricultural wage employment has grown more slowly than the labour force in most sub-Saharan African countries (see figure 1.11). The annual increase of the non-agricultural labour force is in many countries well above 4 per cent a year, because of rapid population growth and a continued high rate of rural-urban migration. Of the 12 countries for which data are available, there are only two (Mauritius and Togo) where during the 1980s non-agricultural wage employment has risen faster than the labour force outside agriculture. In some other countries, such as the Central African Republic, Côte d'Ivoire and Zambia, the gap between the two annual growth rates has been more than 5 per cent.

In many countries the public sector is the most important wage employer and is often responsible for 50 per cent or more of total wage employment. During the 1970s – and until the early 1980s – governments in the region to a large extent played the role of employer of last resort (see also Chapter 2). The growth rates of public sector employment that prevailed in the past were often unsustainable and did not always correspond with the expansion in demand for government services. For instance, employment in the Ghanaian civil service expanded by a rapid 15 per cent a year between 1975 and 1982, whereas manufacturing employment declined by 2.3 per cent over the same period. Employment in public administration in the Congo increased by 10.0 per cent a year between 1979 and 1983. In Swaziland public sector employment increased by 5.4 per cent a year between 1977 and 1983, compared with a 2.2 per cent growth rate for private sector employment. The disparity was even more pronounced in Kenya, where public and private employment expanded respectively by 6.4 and 0.6 per cent annually between 1977 and 1982.

But the situation has changed radically since the early 1980s. The tight fiscal position has forced many governments to exercise a stricter control on recruitment. Hence, the slowdown in modern sector wage employment in recent years is essentially due to the fact that the public sector – as the engine of employment growth – has become increasingly unable to sustain the high rates of labour absorption of the 1970s and early 1980s. Instead, some countries have been forced to retrench public sector workers.

Retrenchment – which can be based on voluntary departures – is usually accompanied by compensatory measures in favour of the retrenched workers, as is the case in Benin, Ghana, Guinea, Mali, the Niger and Senegal. In essence, the compensatory measures consist of (1) substantial redundancy payments; (2) the establishment of special credit schemes; and (3) the provision of technical assistance to would-be entrepreneurs. But such measures suffer from a number of weaknesses. First of all, they touch upon a minute fraction of the total labour force. Second, their impact on the creation of new jobs is extremely limited because the eligible candidates seldom possess the technical and managerial skills to set up new enterprises. Finally, the measures generally lack cost-effectiveness and often constitute a new drain on the government budget.

At the same time, it appears that the cost of retrenchment for the individual is lower than is usually thought. In Senegal, for example, a tracer study of retrenched workers found that nearly two-thirds of those who were laid off had found a job at the time of the survey. Those who remained unemployed had been laid off within the six months that preceded the survey so that their job search had been relatively short. Moreover, the unemployed were relatively young and members of families with at least one other active person. These results confirm that someone who has been employed in the modern sector – and who received on-the-job training and was able to develop a network of social contacts – has a real advantage on the labour market over a new labour force recruit. No information is available on the extent to which retrenched workers who found jobs have displaced other persons in the labour market.

Rising unemployment

Decelerating wage employment growth in the context of a rapidly expanding labour force and an accelerating rural exodus leads to the third phenomenon observed in sub-Saharan labour markets, namely the growing extent of open unemployment, especially in urban areas (see table 1.12). Admittedly, unemployment in countries where there are no social security benefits for the unemployed may constitute a poor indicator of the overall employment situation. But the general trend towards a growing prevalence of unemployment in the region is undeniable. Therefore, unemployment can no longer be dismissed as a marginal phenomenon in sub-Saharan Africa.

The unemployed population in the region has some common characteristics that are worth mentioning. First of all, a substantial proportion consists of young people. Typically, youth represent between two-thirds and three-quarters of the unemployed population in the region. Available information indicates that their unemployment rate is universally higher and averages about three times the adult unemployment rate.

Second, women appear to run at least twice the risk of being unemployed as men. For example, the female/male unemployment ratio averaged 2.2, 2.1, 2.0 and 1.8 in the urban areas of respectively Zambia (1980), Kenya (1986), Botswana (1984-85) and Ethiopia (1984). In general, high female unemployment rates extend well beyond the age of 25 years, whereas unemployment rates for adult males drop sharply. Hence, female unemployment seems to be as much an adult as a youth problem, whereas male unemployment appears to be predominantly a youth problem.

The third characteristic of joblessness in sub-Saharan Africa is that the unemployment rate for the educated labour force tends to be higher than for the workforce without any formal education. In Addis Ababa, for instance, more than half the urban unemployed population in 1984 had post-primary education. In urban Kenya nearly half the unemployed males had completed secondary education in 1986. In Botswana the urban unemployment rate was highest for those with a junior secondary school certificate. Traditionally, the unemployment rate for university graduates has been very low in the region because of an implicit or explicit guaranteed employment policy pursued by most governments. But since the early 1980s many countries – including Somalia and Benin – have been forced to discontinue this policy because of budgetary constraints. The inevitable result is an emerging problem of

Table 1.12. Unemployment rates: Sub-Saharan Africa, 1970s and 1980s (in percentages)

Country	Coverage	Year 1	Percentage	Year 2	Percentage
Botswana	Urban areas			1984-85	31
Côte d'Ivoire	Total country	1980	4	1985	14
Côte d'Ivoire	Abidjan	1978	8	1986	23
Kenya	Urban areas	1977-78	11	1986	16
Liberia	Total country	1980	13	1984	13
Madagascar	Urban areas	1975	6	1982	13
Mauritius	Total country	1977	7	1984	17
Nigeria	Urban areas	1980	6	1986	10
Senegal	Total country	1980	17		
Seychelles	Total country	1980	5	1985	21
Somalia	Mogadishu	1982	15		
Tanzania, United Republic of	Dar es Salaam			1984	22
Zambia	Urban areas	1980	31		
Zimbabwe	Males	1982	11		

Source: ILO: *African employment report 1988* (Addis Ababa, JASPA, 1989).

graduate unemployment. Some countries are trying to limit the extent of graduate unemployment by reducing the annual intake of institutions of higher learning.

Expanding labour absorption in the informal sector

Even though open unemployment is on the increase, this does not mean that those who fail to secure a job in the modern sector of the economy all join the ranks of the unemployed. Casual observation indicates that a considerable proportion of urban labour force recruits is absorbed in the informal sector. Indeed, it is not a coincidence that the informal sector was first "discovered" in a sub-Saharan African country. In recent years, moreover, the sector is increasingly playing the role of an "urban labour sponge".

Measurement of the sector's importance in terms of employment is fraught with difficulties, both conceptually as well as quantitatively. Estimates of informal sector employment are normally based on ad hoc surveys which have a limited geographical and/or sectoral coverage. Estimating informal sector employment residually is the only way to obtain an idea of its overall size. This method, of course, requires reliable data on the labour force, wage employment and unemployment in urban areas. Table 1.13 attempts to estimate the importance of informal sector employment in sub-Saharan Africa for the years 1980 and 1985.

Table 1.13 suggests that informal employment has increased by a respectable 6.7 per cent a year between 1980 and 1985, which is higher than the urban labour force growth and the labour absorption in the modern sector. By 1985 the informal sector employed about 60 per cent of the urban labour force, more than twice the modern sector, and equivalent to about 15 per cent of the total labour force in the region. Table 1.13 also indicates that the informal sector created some 6 million new jobs between 1980 and 1985, while the modern sector added only 0.5 million new jobs on the urban labour market. The modern sector absorbed a mere 6 per cent of the new labour force recruits, whereas almost three-quarters of them were absorbed in the informal sector.

The ultimate impact of the recent economic crisis on the informal sector in the region is difficult to gauge. It is beyond doubt that the sector has been adversely affected by the declining purchasing power of the urban population. However, the contraction of formal sector activities has created new opportunities for micro-enterprises. Indeed, there is evidence of substitution of informal for formal production, especially of simple everyday consumer goods.

Moreover, the official attitude in the region towards the informal sector has changed dramatically

Table 1.13. Estimated urban informal sector employment: Sub-Saharan Africa, 1980 and 1985

	1980	1985	Change (percentage)
	Millions		
Wage employment	9.6	10.1	5
Unemployment	2.8	4.5	61
Informal sector employment	15.7	21.7	38
Labour force	28.1	36.3	29

Source: ILO: *African employment report 1988* (Addis Ababa, JASPA, 1989).

since the early 1980s. Whereas, in the past, governments' position varied from benign neglect to outright harassment, the informal sector is now being considered as a lead sector for the creation of new jobs in an increasing number of countries. Measures are being proposed to promote self-employment for youth. One important measure that has been adopted by many countries relates to the introduction of vocational subjects in the curricula of elementary schools, in an attempt to make primary education more meaningful for self-employment. In the United Republic of Tanzania the Parliament passed the Human Resources Deployment Act in 1983 which established a scheme to encourage productive employment in rural and urban areas. In 1982 Kenya appointed a Presidential Committee on Unemployment and set up a National Employment Bureau in 1987. Nigeria appointed a National Committee on Strategies for Dealing with Mass Unemployment in 1986 which proposed the establishment of a new Directorate of Employment. The Directorate operates a National Open Apprenticeship Programme designed to promote self-employment of youth. In its first year of operation, the programme has reached some 100,000 school-leavers. Côte d'Ivoire initiated a National Employment Policy for the decade 1985-95 within which a programme in favour of the informal sector has been launched.

However, characterising the informal sector as a labour sponge that has virtually no saturation point could be very misleading. There are already clear indications of a growing prevalence of underemployment, low productivity and poverty. Therefore, a substantial increase in the labour productivity of informal sector workers appears to be a *sine qua non* for confronting the employment challenge in Africa.

Improving prospects for rural employment

Although the changing attitude of many governments in favour of the informal sector is a welcome development, there is a growing consensus that efforts targeted on the urban poor, without parallel policies and programmes focused on the rural poor, will be self-defeating and will merely accelerate the rural exodus. Hence, any fundamental solution to the problems of unemployment and poverty in sub-Saharan Africa will require a radical transformation of the rural economy – from a stagnant subsistence activity into a dynamic and productive sector.

Two very distinct models of agricultural production coexist in rural Africa. The predominant mode is small-scale, which is often called traditional because of its low level of productivity. The second mode is large-scale and comprises essentially private estates, plantations and ranches while state farms and production co-operatives are also relatively important.

As noted in *World labour report 3*, the development strategies of the 1960s and 1970s sought to extract the agricultural surplus to finance the development of the industrial and urban sectors. Recent economic policy reforms have been relatively favourable for the rural sector, so that the enabling environment for agricultural development has improved markedly. Distribution channels for agricultural implements and credit have become more effective; a larger share of total investment is being allocated to the agricultural sector; domestic trade and marketing channels are gradually being liberalised; participative modes of development are being promoted; and producer incentives are becoming more attractive. Agricultural producer prices in particular have increased more rapidly than wages and prices in general so that the long-term decline in the domestic terms of trade (the ratio between agricultural and industrial prices) has been halted in most countries and reversed in some.

The agricultural sector alone, however, is unlikely to absorb productively all new labour force recruits in the rural areas, particularly in land-scarce countries such as Burundi, Ethiopia, Kenya and Rwanda. Households in most agrarian societies have multiple income sources, including farm operating surplus, wage labour, cottage industry, trade and other non-farm activities and urban-rural remittances. Rural non-farm activities will have to play a lead role in the creation of new jobs in rural Africa. The importance of rural non-farm activities in terms of employment in sub-Saharan Africa is extremely difficult to quantify because they are generally carried out as a secondary occupation. But it can safely be assumed that their importance is increasing over time due to the growing population pressure on arable lands in many countries. This is confirmed by recent information on Rwanda and Kenya. In 1983 rural households in Rwanda obtained nearly 40 per cent of total income from trading and service activities. Moreover, the income derived from these activities was inversely and significantly correlated with the size of the landholding. In Kenya non-farm enterprise income increased from 9.7 to 16.9 per cent of total household income (cash and kind) between the mid-1970s and early 1980s, whereas the contribution of farm operating surplus decreased from 57.0 to 48.1 per cent. According to the 1981-82 household survey, non-farm income stemming from wage labour was also inversely and significantly correlated with size of landholding.

Hence, rural households allocate a substantial and growing proportion of their labour to non-farm activities. The recent improvements in agricultural pricing policies in sub-Saharan Africa are likely to have a beneficial impact on the rural non-farm sector in the future. Indeed, it is well established that the most important constraint on the development of rural non-farm activities is the low level of local purchasing power.

Concluding remarks

Structural adjustment has become the watchword of the 1980s in sub-Saharan Africa. At present, more than 30 countries in Africa are at different stages of implementing IMF and World Bank supported programmes of economic stabilisation and structural adjustment. Evidence is accumulating that such programmes are not making satisfactory progress towards renewed growth and development in the region. Although the need for structural adjustment is beyond discussion, it is the design of the programmes, the speed and sequencing of the reforms that are causing the present-day controversy. Adjustment programmes should not overlook distributional implications and their short-term effects on the living standards of vulnerable groups. The social costs of adjustment programmes have been extremely high for the poor in Africa, even in countries where such programmes have restored respectable rates of economic growth.

Overall, the economic prospects for sub-Saharan Africa remain anaemic and the employment situation is likely to worsen in the foreseeable future, if no further national and international action is taken. In order to arrest and reverse the downward employment trend it will be necessary to achieve a rate of economic growth of at least 5 per cent a year. Thus, with a labour force that is doubling in less than 25 years the regional economy would have to treble in size every 23 years. However, at the recorded annual growth rate of 1.7 per cent between 1973 and 1987, it would take the sub-Saharan economies 65 years to treble in size.

Part **2**

Government and its employees

Chapter 2

Structural adjustment and public service employment

The main causes and social consequences of the structural adjustment process during the 1980s have been examined in part one of this report and in the Director-General's Report to the ILO International Labour Conference in 1989. Part two takes a closer look at trends in employment conditions of public service employees and their determination. Over the past decade many governments have had little or no financial scope to improve these conditions; lower economic growth reduced tax revenues and higher debt payments pre-empted other government expenditures, including the wage bill (section 1). Lower or slower growing public spending affected employment in the public service (public administration and other government services) and – even more so – in public enterprises (section 2). But the pattern of public service employment has also been shaped by other, longer-term factors, such as increased demand for education, health and other social services and trends towards decentralisation and greater employment participation of women (section 3). The chapter concludes with a short section on some policy issues.

1. Structural adjustment and public expenditure

Since the early 1980s, almost all governments have been obliged to devote a larger part of their budgets to interest and capital repayments on debt. During the 1970s, many governments borrowed extensively in international capital markets, encouraged by the negative real interest rates offered during the second half of the decade when the markets were awash with surplus funds from oil-producing countries. When, at the beginning of the 1980s, real interest rates rose sharply and the terms of trade for many developing countries (DCs) deteriorated, government revenues failed to keep pace with rising expenditure, particularly on interest payments.

The expenditure statistics used in this section refer mainly to central government, because no comparable statistics are available for total government expenditure including local authorities. In most countries, however, central governments control more than 80 per cent of total expenditure (see box 2.1).

2.1 Interpreting statistics on government expenditure

There are two ways in which government expenditure can be analysed: by economic category and by function. The first classification shows the kinds of transactions and their impact on various markets and on the distribution of income. The second classification shows the purpose of government expenditure: general services, defence and public order, social and economic services.

There are also various definitions of expenditures. The widest relates to government outlays, comprising all payments made by the government. This is the concept used in tables 2.1 and 2.2. A large proportion of outlays may not be financed by taxation, but by social security contributions, in which case the government acts mainly as an intermediary. Government outlays are divided into current and capital expenditure; current expenditure is further subdivided into payments for goods and services (mainly wages and salaries) and interest, and subsidies and other current transfers (mainly social security).

Finally, there are different levels of government: central, state or provincial and local. In principle, it would be best to examine general government expenditure, which is the consolidation of all three levels. In practice, central government expenditure is normally used, even though that does introduce a bias in comparability, both between countries and over time. In most countries, the central government accounts for more than 80 per cent of total tax revenues. But in some (in particular industrialised and large) countries, this percentage can be as low as 50 per cent. In addition, over the past 15-20 years, many governments have decentralised their operations.

Figure 2.1. Central government deficits as a percentage of GNP, 1980-88

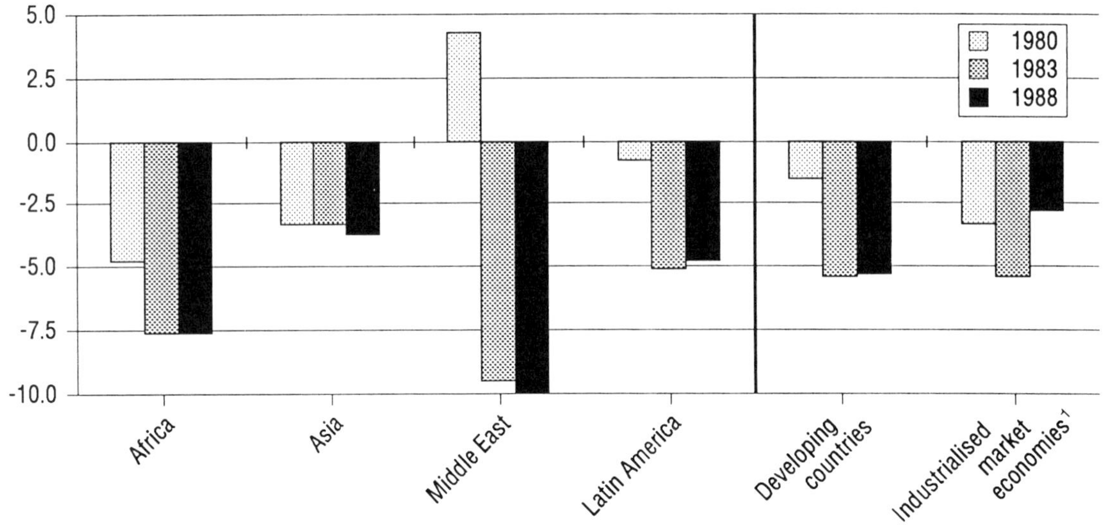

[1] Seven major countries.
Source: IMF: *World economic outlook* (Washington, DC, Oct. 1988).

Government budget deficits during the 1980s

Central government deficits soared in the Middle East, from a surplus of 4.3 per cent of GNP in 1980 to a deficit of 9.4 per cent in 1983, while in Latin America, deficits increased from 0.7 to 5.0 per cent in the three years (figure 2.1). Over the same period, deficits increased by almost 2 percentage points in industrialised market economy countries (IMECs) and nearly 3 in Africa, though they remained stable in Asia. Real long-term interest rates for the seven major IMEC currencies jumped from 0.3 per cent in 1979 to 5.6 per cent in 1983, and remained at an historically very high level of 4.8 per cent in 1988. Thus, given high real interest rates and slow economic growth, African, Latin American and Middle Eastern countries have not been able to reduce their central government budget deficits. Only governments in the IMECs were able to bring their deficits down to the level of 1979.

Interest payments represent the most rapidly increasing proportion of central government expenditure. They have grown fastest and are highest in

Table 2.1. Structure of central government expenditure, by economic category: 1980 and 1986 (in percentages)

	Wage bill		Other current expenditure		Interest payments		Social security subsidies and other transfers		Transfers to other levels of government		Capital expenditure	
	1980	1986	1980	1986	1980	1986	1980	1986	1980	1986	1980	1986
Africa	19.6	20.6 [1]	19.9	15.9 [1]	7.0	15.9 [1]	15.4	17.9 [1]	...	...	23.4	23.6
Asia	14.1	15.4	17.0	15.9	7.2	12.7	24.3	23.3	18.2	18.5	19.6	17.4
Latin America	20.8	14.3	6.5	6.7	7.7	27.3	36.0	31.3	7.4	9.5 [1]	16.8	9.6
Middle East	31.4	38.4	18.0	18.2	2.4	3.4	20.3	16.1	...	...	20.2	17.8
DCs	20.3	18.4	12.6	11.9	6.3	16.6	30.2	27.6	10.4	11.9 [1]	18.6	14.9
IMECs	12.5	11.5	14.4	15.0	7.5	11.8	56.1	54.9	13.3	11.7	5.9	5.6

... = not available.
[1] 1985.
Note: percentages do not add up to 100, because the spending category "lending minus repayment" is not included and because percentages may be based on different samples of countries.
Source: IMF: *Government finance statistics yearbook*, 1987 and 1988 (Washington, DC, 1987 and 1988).

Table 2.2. Structure of central government expenditure, by function: 1980 and 1986 (in percentages)

	Defence		Social security and welfare		Education		Health		Economic services	
	1980	1986	1980	1986	1980	1986	1980	1986	1980	1986
Africa	...	11.4 [1]	...	...	...	12.4 [1]	...	3.4 [1]	...	26.2 [1]
Asia	20.4	18.2	...	...	9.0	9.6	2.7	2.8	28.6	24.9
Latin America	6.1	4.5 [2]	25.4	20.4 [2]	11.4	8.8 [2]	4.9	4.4 [2]	24.2	17.8 [2]
Middle East	23.8	24.4	7.4	11.2	14.5	14.7	5.3	5.1	18.6	14.5
DCs	14.6	12.8	15.2	13.7 [2]	10.6	9.3	4.1	4.0	25.2	20.7
IMECs	13.3	14.9	37.5	33.4	4.8	3.9	11.6	12.7	10.1	9.3

... = not available.
[1] 1984. [2] 1985.
Note: Percentages do not add up to 100 because interest payments and expenditure on public administration are not included.
Source: IMF: *Government finance statistics yearbook, 1987 and 1988* (Washington, DC, 1987 and 1988).

some Latin American countries: more than 25 per cent on average in 1986 (table 2.1). In highly indebted Brazil and Mexico, the respective proportions were 50 and 34 per cent in 1986 and have increased since. However, in most other Latin American countries (except Panama and Peru), this share was below 10 per cent. In Africa, it reached about 16 per cent in 1986, while governments in Asia and IMECs kept the share of debt service down to about 12 per cent.

Adjusting public expenditure

High budget deficits have led all governments to cut down on two main items (see table 2.1): social security, subsidies and other transfers, and public investment. In many countries, subsidies to both consumers (food, rent, etc.) and public enterprises were reduced. The share of social security expenditure also declined, particularly in Latin America and the Middle East. This was due to reduced government subsidies and to falling or slow-growing wages which diminished the base for social security contributions. In addition, as noted in *World labour report 3* (Chapter 2), social security regulations were changed so as to reduce benefits and/or coverage.

Government priorities on other expenditure categories varied more widely. The massive increase in interest payments obliged central governments in Latin America to cut back sharply on the wage bill share, which fell by 6.5 percentage points from 20.8 per cent in 1980 to 14.3 per cent in 1986. The wage bill share, also dropped in IMECs from 12.5 per cent in 1980 to 11.5 in 1986, but rose sharply in the Middle East. Finally, central governments in Asia and Africa reduced the proportion of other current expenditure (purchases of goods and services).

It is worth noting fundamental differences in the structure of central government expenditure between IMECs and DCs. In IMECs, central governments spend more than half of their budgets on transfers, while in DCs these average no more than 30 per cent. On the other hand, central governments

Table 2.3. Trends in per capita current expenditure on government services (CEGS): Market economies, 1970s and 1980s (in percentages)

	Share of CEGS in GDP	Annual growth rates		
	1980	1970-75	1975-80	1980-85
Sub-Saharan Africa	13.7	3.9	–0.1	–1.0
North Africa and West Asia	17.2	14.7	2.3	0.0
Latin America and the Caribbean	11.2	4.3	2.9	–1.2
South and South-East Asia,	10.6	3.9	6.0	4.3
of which: India	(10.2)	(1.5)	(5.8)	(8.6)
Developing countries	13.0	9.8	3.5	0.7
Developed countries,	17.0	1.8	1.8	2.4
of which: United States	(17.6)	(–0.8)	(0.8)	(3.6)

Calculated from: *UN national accounts statistics: Analysis of main aggregates, 1985* (New York, 1988), table 11.

2.2 Resources for labour administration during the 1980s

The economic recession at the beginning of the 1980s has had a profound impact on resources for labour administration. In many developing countries these resources have suffered more than other areas of public administration from budget cuts, being seen as of low priority and already underfinanced. As a result, the relative impact of labour policies has weakened.

By contrast, in many industrialised countries, this impact has increased. The industrialised market economies (IMECs), particularly in Western Europe, have allocated increasing resources to combating unemployment. And in the industrialised centrally planned economies (IPECs), one of the main economic objectives is to overcome the problem of labour shortage by using the existing supply of labour more efficiently. Most IPECs are either in the process of equipping their labour administrations to meet this new challenge, or are studying ways of doing so.

Box table 2.2.1 summarises information on the labour ministry's share of the total central government budget in a number of developing countries, with one industrialised country – the United Kingdom – included for comparison. The percentage change in the budget share between 1980 and 1987 is shown where available. Unfortunately, it is not possible to give information on resources for labour policies carried out by other ministries, but the data available for labour ministries show that the proportion of government resources allocated to labour administration is generally extremely low. In 1987, the labour ministry's share of the national budget was below 1 per cent in all but two of the developing countries for which data are available and below a quarter of 1 per cent in the majority of them. While a few countries showed an improvement in the relative allocation of resources to the labour ministry, in most there was a substantial decline between 1980 and 1987.

In most IMECs, action against unemployment has become the first priority of labour administration since the mid-1970s, clearly shown by the steep increase in resources devoted to this purpose, often against the trend of other government and labour administration expenditures. In France, for example, the GDP share of public expenditure on employment measures went up from 1.1 per cent in 1974 to 3.5 per cent in 1983, since when the share has remained constant. In the Federal Republic of Germany, expenditure on employment measures rose from 9.1 billion Deutschmarks in 1982 to DM14.2 billion in 1987.

Most public expenditure on labour market programmes in IMECs is devoted to income maintenance that is, unemployment compensation and early retirement (box table 2.2.2). The proportion of GDP spent on unemployment compensation is highest in Ireland, the Netherlands, Denmark, Spain and Belgium – where (except in Denmark) unemployment rates are among the highest, and where (except in Spain) benefit levels and conditions of access are relatively favourable. Four of the same five countries (not including Spain) also stand out as leading spenders – after Sweden – on "active" measures (employment services, labour market training, youth measures, direct job creation, employment subsidies and measures for the disabled).

In general, the outlay per person served is relatively high for income maintenance and direct job-creation schemes, while it is relatively low for placement services. These differences do not necessarily imply that one labour market programme is more efficient than the other. But it is inefficient to spend large sums on costly programmes – be they "active" or "passive" – unless the chances of job placement that exist with less expenditure have first been exhausted.

Table 2.2.1. The labour ministry's share in the central government budget: 1980-87 (in percentages)

Country	1980	1987	Percentage change
Latin America			
Argentina	0.31	0.12	–61
Barbados	0.52	0.62	+19
Bahamas	0.20	...	...
Colombia	3.61	2.21	–39
Cuba	0.07	0.06	–14
Ecuador	0.44	0.16	–64
El Salvador	1.11	0.34	–69
Grenada	0.22	0.08	–64
Honduras	2.32	1.31	–44
Jamaica	0.33	0.24	–27
Peru	0.11	0.17	+55
St. Lucia	0.29	0.24	–17
Venezuela	0.66	0.77	+17
Asia			
Bangladesh	...	0.24	...
Malaysia	0.20	0.30	+50
Pakistan	...	0.31	...
Philippines	0.23	0.53	+130
Sri Lanka	0.21	0.14	–33
Thailand	0.10	0.09	–10
Other countries			
Côte d'Ivoire	...	0.21	...
United Kingdom	...	2.30	...

... = not available.

Source: ILO Regional Labour Administration Centres; United Kingdom: *White paper on public expenditure* (London, HMSO, 1988).

Box continued on page 47.

Table 2.2.2. Public expenditure on income maintenance and "active" labour market programmes: IMECs, 1987 (as a percentage of GDP)

	Income maintenance	"Active" labour market programmes	Total		Income maintenance	"Active" labour market programmes	Total
Australia	1.2	0.3	1.5	Japan	0.4	0.2	0.6
Austria	1.1	0.4	1.5	Luxembourg	1.0	0.5	1.5
Belgium	3.3	1.1	4.4	Netherlands	2.9	1.1	4.0
Canada	1.7	0.6	2.2	New Zealand	1.1	0.6	1.7
Denmark	3.9	1.1	5.0	Norway	0.4	0.4	0.8
Finland	1.6	0.8	2.4	Portugal	0.4	0.5	0.9
France	2.3	0.7	3.1	Spain	2.5	0.8	3.3
Germany, Fed. Rep. of	1.4	1.0	2.3	Sweden	0.8	1.9	2.7
Greece	0.4	0.6	1.0	Switzerland	0.2	0.2	0.4
Ireland	3.7	1.5	5.1	United Kingdom	1.7	0.9	2.6
Italy	0.8	0.5	1.3	United States	0.6	0.2	0.8

Source: *OECD Employment outlook 1988* (Paris, 1988)

in DCs take a much more active part in economic development, through investments not only in infrastructure but also in public enterprises.

Higher debt service payments have also led to readjustments in central government spending by function (table 2.2). Again, the average Latin American response shows the most dramatic changes, with all expenditure categories affected. Between 1980 and 1986 the share of expenditure on economic services (to enterprises) dropped by 7 percentage points, that on social security and welfare by 5 percentage points and that on education by 2.5 percentage points. In the Middle East, a sharp fall in the share of economic services was offset by a corresponding increase in the share of social security and welfare.

Comparing expenditure patterns in IMECs and DCs, between 1980 and 1986, central government defence expenditure increased by 1.6 percentage points in IMECs but dropped by the same amount in DCs. Expenditure on health in IMECs went up by 1 percentage point while it remained stable in DCs. Central governments in both IMECs and DCs have reduced the share of spending on social security and welfare, education and economic services. But – as box 2.2. shows – governments in IMECs strongly increased expenditure for employment measures, while many in DCs did the reverse.

Levels of government services

In most developing countries, current expenditure on government services (called officially government final consumption expenditure) is the largest part of general government expenditure (i.e. at the central, state and local levels). In 1980, it constituted about 13 per cent of GDP in the developing market economies and about 17 per cent in the developed market economies (table 2.3). It is not possible to make a comparison with the planned economies, because they have a different system of national accounts.

It is surprising that shares of current spending on government services in GDP are so similar between countries at different levels of economic development. The provision of public administration, defence, health, education and certain economic services would appear to be so basic that no country can afford to do without. In 1980, sub-Saharan countries spent almost 14 per cent of national income on these services, while those in Asia and Latin America spent about 11 per cent. Developed countries and the oil-rich countries of West Asia and North Africa spent 17 per cent on government services.

Over the past 15-20 years, current expenditure on government services per head of the population has risen in practically all countries. But it has been declining from peak levels in sub-Saharan Africa since the mid-1970s and in Latin America since the 1980s. Only in Asian developing countries has there been steady improvement. For instance, in India, current expenditure on government services per capita increased by nearly 9 per cent a year between 1980 and 1985. In the developed market economies, these expenditures have also risen consistently, even accelerating during the 1980s. This has mainly been due to the rapid build-up of spending by the federal Government in the United States.

In most countries, the wage bill for public service employees accounts for the lion's share of current expenditure on government services, usually between 70 and 90 per cent. The level and distribution of public service wages play a crucial role in determining both the size of the government wage bill and public service employment. Many governments have used public service wages as an important adjustment tool to maintain or even increase public service employment at a time of rising unemployment in the private sector.

2. Public sector employment levels

The size of a country's public sector depends on various factors, such as its level of economic development, its political system and changing perceptions of what activities the public sector should undertake. In all societies, governments have a core responsibility for public administration, defence, the provision of basic social services and infrastructure. The complexity of economic, social and political life makes it necessary to assign an important role to public administration. Moreover, the free provision of basic education, health and infrastructure is a necessary condition for increasing a country's level of economic, social and political development. Finally, in many developing countries, governments have been the employer of last resort, which has led to overstaffing in various parts of the public sector. There is much less uniformity in the government's role in the production of goods and services. In the planned economies, governments own and manage practically the whole enterprise sector, while in most DCs and some IMECs governments have an important stake in the production of goods and services. But recently, there has been a trend towards liberalisation and privatisation which has reduced the government's involvement in the enterprise sector, and its role as the employer of last resort.

Definition and statistical sources

Published employment statistics for public administration and defence are easily comparable between countries, because these services are usually only supplied by the State. This is not the case for social services which can be – and often are – provided by the private sector. In the grey area between government and the private sector lie non-profit institutions, which – according to the United Nations definition – should be considered public if more than half of their current expenditure is financed by the government and if they are under the active control of the public authorities. It is sometimes difficult to draw the borderline for hospitals, schools and universities which are mainly financed by the government but managed and controlled by non-profit institutions.

The variety of institutional arrangements is even greater in the case of public enterprises. Ownership and control are the two relevant criteria for deciding whether an enterprise is public or private. While the definition of ownership is fairly straightforward, the meaning and measurement of "control" is more complicated. The government is considered to be in control if it can intervene in the investment and price policies of the company and can determine the goods and services it produces. For financial institutions, government control should extend to the acquisition of assets and the incurrence of liabilities and, for banks, to policies on interest rates.

The most reliable statistics on public sector employment are produced by special censuses. It is often financially not possible to organise them on a regular basis. But they may sometimes be necessary to provide a reliable benchmark. (Censuses have recently been carried out in a number of African countries.)

Government budgets usually do not provide adequate information on employment levels even though they may provide some indication on trends. The problem is that, for various reasons, the number of budgeted posts does not correspond to the number of people employed. One person may, for example, draw a salary from more than one budgeted post; or budgeted posts may be vacant. Moreover, many public service employees are paid from budget items other than wages. Thus, payroll or other administrative information is more reliable than budget data.

Information from labour force surveys has the advantage that employment is measured according to a uniform definition so that comparisons can be made between sectors and over time. The disadvantage is that household respondents may not be aware of all the intricacies of defining what constitutes the public sector. This lack of awareness may bias, in particular, the statistics on employment in public enterprises and some social services. However, this bias does not exist for statistics from administrative sources (mentioned above) and establishment surveys, because the statistical office itself can determine whether an enterprise or institution belongs to the public or private sector. The statistics in this chapter are drawn mainly from administrative sources and labour force surveys.

Employment in the public service

During the 1960s and 1970s, public service employment expanded strongly in almost all countries. In the developing countries, this was mainly due to rapidly growing demand for education and health services but, increasingly, governments also assumed the role of employer of last resort. In the industrialised countries, the welfare state was the engine of public service employment growth. At the beginning of the 1980s, the public service share of non-agricultural employment was particularly high in Africa at 33 per cent while it was around 20 per cent in Asia, Latin America and the industrialised market economies. The public sector shares (including public enterprises) were even higher – at respectively 54, 36, 27 and 24 per cent. This means that governments have a substantial direct impact on wage determination in many developing countries – an issue which is examined in greater detail in Chapter 4 (on remuneration).

A rough comparison of the importance of public service employment during the 1980s is made in figure 2.2. Even though it includes only a limited number of countries and areas, some general observations can be made. The share of government employment in the labour force is much lower in developing than in industrialised countries. In most developing countries, this share does not exceed 6 per cent, while in most industrialised countries, it is above 15 per cent. There are, however, significant variations within these two groups. In some developing countries, such as Botswana, Egypt, Panama and Venezuela, the share is more than 10 per cent. This is probably explained by high government revenues from mining (Botswana, Venezuela) or foreign earnings (Egypt, Panama). On the other hand, the share of government employment in Japan is very low (6-7 per cent) compared with other industrialised countries. This may be partly due to the fact that an important part of social services is provided by the private sector. There is also a difference between the industrialised market and centrally planned economies. In the latter, a higher proportion of the labour force is engaged in the so-called non-material sphere, which includes not only government services but also tourism, retail trade and financial services.

During the first half of the 1980s, the public service employment share in the labour force increased in some, but decreased in other developing countries for which information is available. However, it rose consistently in all IPECs and in most IMECs, with the exception of Japan, the United Kingdom and the United States. During the same period, public sector employment grew at an annual rate of more than 3 per cent in four Asian countries (India, Malaysia, the Philippines and Thailand). According to recent information from the World Bank, government employment in sub-Saharan countries increased by 4 per cent a year between 1981 and 1983 and 2.8 per cent a year between 1984 and 1986, in both periods exceeding the 2.4 per cent annual growth of the labour force between 1980 and 1985. An ILO study based on a sample of eight Latin American countries found that, with the exception of Chile, government employment grew faster than total employment until 1984, but that afterwards its growth was equal to or lower than that of the private sector.

Since the mid-1980s many developing country governments have attempted to contain public service employment growth with freezes on hirings and lay-offs of temporary staff. In sub-Saharan Africa, for example, freezes on hirings were adopted in Benin, Gambia, Mauritania, Sierra Leone, Somalia and the United Republic of Tanzania. Since 1987, Kenya has allowed hiring only if it does not result in net creation of civil service posts. Automatic hiring has been discontinued in countries which previously guaranteed government jobs to school graduates (Benin, Central African Republic, Congo, Guinea, Mali, Rwanda, Somalia and Sudan). Lay-offs of temporary staff took place in Congo, Côte d'Ivoire, Ghana, Nigeria, Rwanda and Somalia. Since 1985, various Latin American governments, such as Bolivia, Brazil and Mexico, have started to cut back (federal) government employment.

Figure 2.2. Share of public service employment in the labour force, 1980s (percentages)

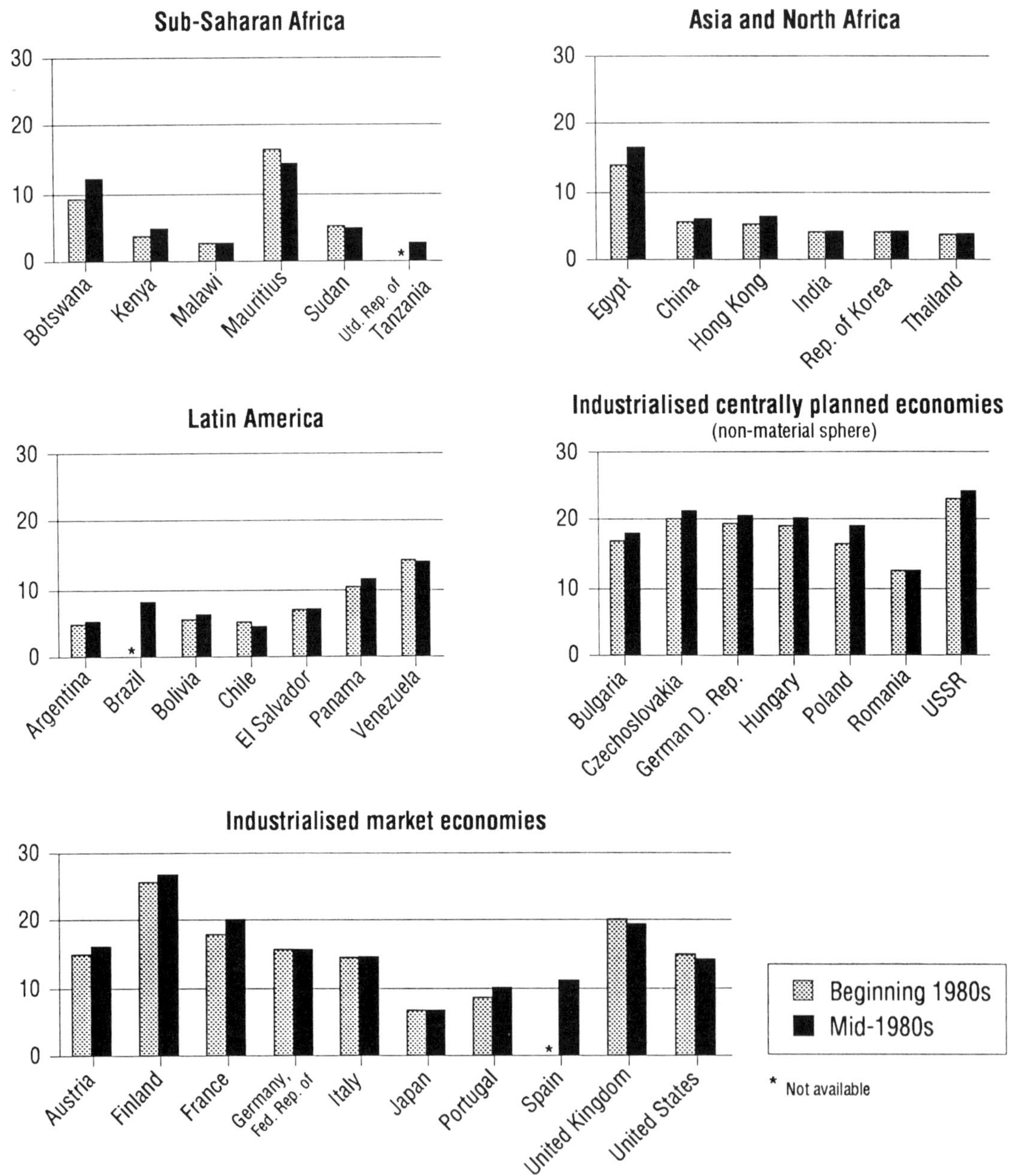

Sources: ILO estimates; CMEA: *Statistical year book 1987* (Moscow, 1987).

During the first half of the 1980s, IMECs too followed various policies to curb public service employment growth. Many – mainly European – governments encouraged reduction of working time (such as Belgium, France and the Netherlands) and part-time employment. Some also experimented with early retirement, although this has turned out to be an expensive and not very effective measure. Moreover, in many countries, employment in education is slowing as a result of the falling birthrate. Employment in the health sector is still growing rapidly – partly as a result of the ageing population – but an increasing part of this employment may be generated by the private sector in the future.

Despite attempts at restraint, government employment has continued to grow after 1985 and this trend is expected to persist. In the United States, for example, employment at the federal, state and municipal level, after a slight decline in 1985, increased at all levels in subsequent years, particularly in state and local government. The upward trend is predicted to continue until 1995, as a result of an increase in the elementary school population, with employment in public education reaching 7.2 million in 1995 and accounting for three out of every seven new jobs in state and local governments.

In the IPECs employment in the so-called "non-material" sector is certain to grow most rapidly. This is mainly due to an expansion of health services and some other services which do not fall under our definition of public service. However, it is likely that employment in public administration will rise much more slowly or stand still. In the USSR, for example, the staff of all central ministries and departments are to be reduced by as much as 50 per cent between 1988 and 1990, and this is to be followed by similar reductions at the regional and district level.

Government as the employer of last resort

During the 1960s and 1970s, many African governments followed – explicitly or implicitly – a policy of guaranteeing jobs for graduates with university-level education.

The Government of Sudan, for instance, began a policy of guaranteeing employment to all graduates of universities and post-secondary institutions in 1966. By 1970, this policy had extended to the graduates of secondary schools. In 1974, the policy was revised to exclude university graduates in such fields as arts, humanities, law, general science and mathematics, but it continued to apply to those with a technical degree, and to non-degree tertiary-level technicians. Guaranteed employment for university and secondary school graduates fuelled rapid expansion of the civil service in Senegal; attempts to contain its growth were made as early as the mid-1970s but had very little effect. Mali also had a policy of automatic hiring of university and secondary school graduates.

In some African countries, governments also tried to perform a "counter-cyclical" role, recruiting in periods when private sector employment growth was slowing down. In Egypt in 1973-74 the Government decided to recruit demobilised military conscripts, in spite of reduced public expenditure following the Arab-Israeli war. (For a more complete description of Egypt's policy of guaranteed public employment, see box 2.3.) In the Nigerian Federal civil service, employment tripled between 1973 and 1983, rising at an annual rate of 11 per cent, while aggregate GDP declined by about 14 per cent over the same period.

In Asia, there are also various examples of rapid public service employment growth, prompted initially by swiftly increasing government revenues but then maintained in spite of reduced resources.

In the Philippines, the number of government workers rose from half a million in 1963 to 1.7 million in 1983, an average annual growth rate of 5.4 per cent. There was a marked upturn in public employment in the mid-1970s, following a commodity boom which raised the country's foreign exchange earnings and government revenues. This increase in public revenues was only temporary; nevertheless, public spending levels were not reduced subsequently and employment continued to expand.

In Indonesia, the civil service grew from 2.6 million in 1983 to 3.2 million in 1986, at an average annual rate of 6.4 per cent. This compares with an estimated 2 to 3 per cent annual employment growth for the economy as a whole. The increase in civil service employment was made possible by the oil boom at the beginning of the 1980s and was mainly inspired by the Government's desire to reduce unemployment.

In some cases, public employment was provided to counter seasonal unemployment. In Bangladesh, for example, the public sector provided large-scale seasonal employment in construction, agricultural projects and the food-for-work programme. Between 1972 and 1983-84, such employment increased by about 34 per cent and stood at 1.75 million in 1983-84. Most of this employment, however, was financed by aid and grants and did not prove to be a burden on the government budget.

In the 1960s and 1970s, various Latin American governments attempted to provide a buffer against unemployment, for example, by subsidising public sector enterprises to avoid bankruptcy and redundancies. They also created public employment in regions and areas where private sector employment growth was low. Thus, in the metropolitan area of Recife (north-east of Brazil), 40 per cent of formal sector employment is generated by the public sector.

2.3 Egypt's policy of guaranteed public sector employment

In the late 1950s, Egypt's public sector expanded significantly through a series of Egyptianisation decrees (1956-59) which gave the Government control of foreign-owned assets, such as the Suez Canal. This was followed in the early 1960s by the adoption of a highly centralised development policy approach and a massive wave of nationalisations of Egyptian-owned enterprises in industry, banking, trade and transport. At the same time, the Government embarked on an employment drive whereby state-owned enterprises were forced to include among their annual targets the creation of significant numbers of new jobs, while the administrative apparatus of the State was also expanded rapidly both at the central and local government level. Equally important was the objective of spreading health and education services in urban and rural areas with a corresponding growth of government employment in these services. Between 1952 (the year of the revolution) and 1965, primary school enrolment rose from 45 to 75 per cent of the relevant age group and the ratio of population per doctor fell from 4,000 to 2,260.

During the first Five-Year Plan (1960-65), government employment grew at 8.6 per cent a year. The growth rate fell to a lower, but still respectable, 4.5 per cent a year between 1966-67 and 1971-72. However, the Government's resources were becoming strained, following the 1967 Arab-Israeli war which brought development expenditure to a virtual standstill.

After the 1973 war, the Government absorbed a new wave of military conscripts, leading to annual government employment growth of more than 10 per cent between 1971-72 and 1974. With accelerating private sector activity from the mid-1970s and rapidly increasing migration to other Arab countries, the Government made no attempt to retract its costly pledge to employ all diploma and university degree holders. As a result, during the 1970s, government employment, together with migration, together absorbed close to 90 per cent of the total increase in labour supply in Egypt.

During the second half of the 1970s, the State was accumulating funds on the strength of the oil boom (from remittances of migrant workers), enabling it "to maintain its extravagant recruitment policy". By the mid-1980s, its new-found revenues from petroleum, the Suez Canal and generous aid levels were stagnating. More recently, in the face of severe budget deficits, the Government has had to cut back on new employment. In contrast to an annual growth rate for government employment of 6.9 per cent in the ten years from 1975 to 1985, the budgeted growth rate for 1985-86 to 1986-87 has declined to 4.2 per cent.

While forced employment policies have been abandoned in the public enterprise sector, there is continued pressure on central and local government to employ new graduates. A difficult issue now facing policy-makers is how to reduce the Government's commitment to job creation in the face of severe recessionary conditions in the economy. With a record level of 15.5 per cent overall (open) unemployment, according to the 1986 population census (up from 7 per cent in the 1976 census), and with poor prospects for either the domestic productive sectors or the Arab oil-rich markets to create significant job opportunities for Egyptian workers, the State cannot reform its employment policies without reviewing the system of supply and demand that has ruled Egypt's labour market for more than two decades.

The combined policies of free higher education, together with guaranteed government employment, have been the major cause of an abnormally high rate of growth of production of new graduates from intermediate schools and universities. This averaged 7.4 per cent a year over the decade 1976-77 to 1986-87. The number of university degree applicants through the Ministry of Manpower rose from 20,786 in 1976-77 to 25,298 in 1982-83 (the latest class employed), while the number of diploma applicants increased from 81,656 in 1977 to 114,038 in 1981, implying annual growth rates of 4 per cent and 8.7 per cent respectively. The recruitment of teachers, doctors, dentists, pharmacists, nurses and graduates of some branches of the arts is the responsibility of the relevant ministries but there continue to be chronic shortages in public service for most of these professions.

Applicants for government jobs have not been discouraged by deteriorating government salaries and growing delays in government recruitment – from two-and-a-half years in 1977 to five years in 1987 for university graduates and from three years in 1977 to six years in 1987 for diploma holders. The lack of attractive jobs outside the Government probably explains a major part of the large-scale unemployment recorded in the 1986 census. It is only within the framework of a comprehensive employment policy, embracing all sectors, that a solution can be found.

Subsequently, some governments in Latin America have attempted to compensate for cyclical falls in employment. This is most clearly demonstrated in Chile, where special unemployment programmes have become a permanent feature of labour market policy as a result of the continuing economic crisis. The Brazilian Government also followed a clearly counter-cyclical public sector employment policy during the recession of 1981-83.

Public enterprises

The size and structure of the public enterprise sector vary significantly within groups of otherwise comparable industrial and developing countries. For example, in the IMECs, the share of public enterprise output in GDP in the mid-1970s varied from 4 per cent in the Netherlands and Spain to 15 per cent in Austria. Similarly, among DCs, the shares varied from 1 per cent (Nepal) to 14 per cent (Taiwan, China) in Asia; 7 per cent (Liberia) to 38 per cent (Zambia) in Africa; 1 per cent (Guatemala) to 38 per cent (Guyana) in Latin America. This heterogeneity, in structure as well as size, reflects the range of considerations that led to the decision to undertake a particular activity in the public sector.

Initially, the assertion of national independence and the creation of employment were important factors. Thus, after independence, many African and

Asian countries began to nationalise industries and/or replace expatriates by nationals. In Africa, many governments, as in Tanzania and Zambia, directly nationalised plantations, mines, manufacturing industries and various services. In addition, several governments, as in Uganda, created new state-owned enterprises to spearhead industrialisation. In Asia, nationalisations were generally limited to manufacturing industries and some services such as banking.

In Pakistan, a sudden expansion of public sector employment took place in 1972, when 31 large manufacturing enterprises and all insurance companies were nationalised. Two years later, they were followed by commercial banks and five years later by rice and cotton processing and exporting companies. These companies were mostly operated by bureaucrats with little training or aptitude in the running of commercial enterprises. As a result, many were run inefficiently and became a burden on state funds. The first reorganisation measures adopted in 1977 had some success: between 1976-77 and 1981-82 production in public enterprises increased by 62.2 per cent and labour productivity by 16.2 per cent. However, employment declined by 7.5 per cent.

In India, the parastatal sector's share in total public sector employment was around 11 per cent in 1961. This rose to about 18 per cent in 1971 and by 1985 it stood at 32 per cent. The growth rate of employment in the parastatals was extremely high in the 1970s when it averaged 13.7 per cent a year. It has since declined to about 5.0 per cent annually between 1981 and 1985.

In Latin America, many governments nationalised private mining companies in the 1930s and 1940s. Examples are the nationalisation of oil companies in Mexico and Venezuela and of copper and tin mines in Bolivia, Chile and Peru. Latin American and some South-East Asian governments adopted a more indirect approach towards manufacturing enterprises. They supported them with various incentives and protectionist measures within the context of an import substitution strategy.

All parameters for public enterprises changed drastically during the 1980s. Increasing budget deficits and changes in the world economy forced governments to recast their priorities. They were not able to carry the burden of loss-making public enterprises and many governments changed their economic strategy from import substitution to export promotion. As a result, employment in public enterprises grew more slowly (or dropped more severely) than in the public service.

A number of African countries are planning to sell off public enterprises. The Government of Côte d'Ivoire has drawn up a list of more than 100 businesses in which it wants to sell its shareholdings. Ghana has decided to divest itself of 30 parastatals. Mozambique has privatised more than 20 industrial plants since 1985. Congo, Guinea, Nigeria, Senegal, Togo and Zaire are among those implementing or considering privatisation. Plans by Nigeria, the largest economy in Black Africa, range from full privatisation of parastatals to measures to streamline those that remain under state control. However, privatisation in Africa faces many obstacles. Potential buyers of state enterprises are few in number and may be politically unacceptable.

Privatisation measures have also been taken in various Asian countries. In Bangladesh, a privatisation policy was initiated in 1975. Between then and 1982, some public enterprises were divested, but since they were small units, this had little impact on total employment in public enterprises. However, the de-nationalisation programme appears to have picked up momentum from 1982. From the very limited information available, it seems that total public sector employment grew by around 5 per cent from 1972-73 to 1977-78, but by only around 3.2 per cent between 1977-78 and 1983-84. With the tendency towards de-nationalisation, restrictions on government employment and encouragement of the private sector, the share of public sector employment in Bangladesh is likely to decline in the future.

Public sector employment in Malaysia increased sharply after 1971, with growth peaking at 11.4 per cent in 1980. Between 1983 and 1984, the growth rate fell to 2.8 per cent and in 1985 to 1.1 per cent. This is said to reflect attempts by the Government to reverse previous expansionary policies on public sector employment, attempts which include privatisation of certain government functions. In Pakistan, a divestment committee was established in 1985-86 to sell off RS2 billion in shares of public enterprises. Public sector employment is likely to be affected adversely by these measures.

In some Latin American countries, the decline of employment in public enterprises was already visible in the 1970s. This was particularly so in Argentina, Chile and Uruguay, where many public enterprises were restructured and privatised (figure 2.3). In most other countries, the first steps towards privati-

Figure 2.3. Share of public enterprises in public sector employment: Latin America, 1970s and 1980s (percentages)

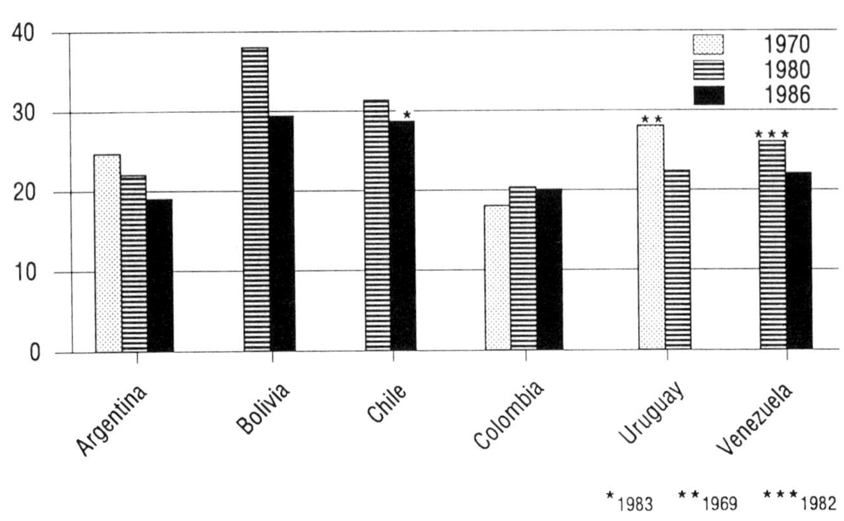

Source: A. Marshall (ed.): *El empleo en el Estado en América Latina* (Geneva, International Institute for Labour Studies; forthcoming).

sation of large state monopolies were taken during the 1980s, largely as a consequence of the debt crisis and the need to reduce the public sector deficit.

The drive towards privatisation during the 1980s has been strongest in Europe and the United States. Both conservative and socialist governments in Austria, France, the Federal Republic of Germany, Italy, the Netherlands, Spain, the United Kingdom and the United States are pursuing privatisation policies. In Europe, the most radical policy has been espoused by the British Conservative Government which, in eight years, raised more than US$31 billion by selling state-owned industries, such as British Airways, British Telecom and British Gas. As a result, the workforce in public corporations was reduced from more than 2 million full-time equivalents in 1980 to less than 1 million in 1987. Privatisation in the United States, contrary to the European pattern, has been implemented mainly at the state and local levels, and has typically taken the form of contracting-out of public services, such as refuse collection, sewage treatment, solid waste disposal, public transport and fire protection.

In planned economies, such as China, Bulgaria, Hungary, Poland and the USSR, similar trends are reflected in the increasing independence of public enterprises from government bodies, the introduction of cost-accounting, creation of financially autonomous service co-operatives and the legalisation of self-employment.

3. The changing structure of public service employment

The structure of public service employment has been affected by various long-term factors, such as increased demand for education, health and other social services. Moreover, the trends towards decentralisation and feminisation have continued to have a strong impact. Finally, the long-term trend towards greater stability of employment for civil servants has been called into question during the 1980s.

Growing employment in the social services

Heller and Tait (1983) have done much pioneering work in the analysis of government employment. They found that cross-country comparisons of employment can be biased by the degree of federalism in a country. Federal countries usually delegate much of the administrative, health, education and policy functions to government units below the central level. For some, mainly OECD countries, Heller and Tait were able to make estimates of state and local government employees in health and education, which were added to health and education workers at the central level. They found that the average number of employees in adjusted central public administration was about the same in OECD and in developing countries, at 0.30 and 0.29 per 100 inhabitants, respectively. However, the number of employees per capita in the education sector of the

Table 2.4. Share of education and health in central government employment: selected developing countries, 1980s (percentages)

Country	Year 1	Percentage	Year 2	Percentage
Sub-Saharan Africa				
Burundi	1983	53.2	1986	58.6
Côte d'Ivoire		...	1987	40.9
Gabon		...	1986	31.5
Malawi	1982	24.3	1984	23.8
Niger		...	1986	52.0
Togo [1]		...	1986	59.7
Other developing countries				
Korea, Rep. of [2]	1983	31.9	1985	32.6
Syrian Arab Republic [1]	1983	29.0	1985	30.6
Trinidad and Tobago [2]	1982	28.5	1986	29.2
Tunisia	1982	54.0	1985	56.7
Venezuela [2]	1978	50.3	1987	54.2

... = not available.
[1] Central public sector. [2] General government.
Source: ILO: *General report.* Report I, Joint Committee on the Public Service, Fourth Session (Geneva, 1988), p. 91.

Figure 2.4. Social and cultural services [1] in employment in the non-productive sphere: IPECs, 1980 and 1986 (percentages)

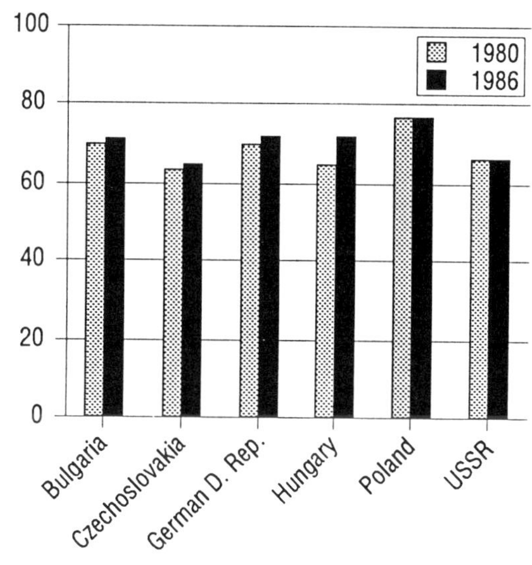

[1] Social services include: education, culture, arts, health care, social security, sport and tourism.
Calculated from: CMEA: *Year book, 1987* (Moscow, 1988).

OECD countries was almost three times that in the developing countries; for health, the ratio is four times larger in the OECD region. For both sectors, employment is considerably higher on a per capita basis in the Latin American region than in Africa or Asia.

As noted earlier, during the first half of the 1980s, government employment in most countries continued to increase faster than private sector employment. Most of this increase was due to the continuing growth of employment in the social services. As a result, the share in government employment of public administration dropped while that of social services rose.

This is highlighted in table 2.4 and figure 2.4 which cover DCs and IPECs respectively. In DCs, education and health can represent from 25 to almost 60 per cent of government employment. And in almost all countries for which statistics are available, the share of central government employment accounted for by education and health has increased by 1 percentage point or more between 1983 and 1986. The same pattern is observed for the IPECs, though the concept of public service as such does not exist. Thus, as a proxy, the non-material sector – with somewhat wider scope – was chosen. Again, the employment share of social services in most IPECs increased by more than 1 percentage point between 1980 and 1986.

For the IMECs, there are few reliable and/or comparable statistics available on the share of government employment represented by education and health. The employment statistics published by the OECD and the EEC concern either the entire sector including community, social and personal services or government services without any further subdivision. The only information available for some IMECs is the share of private education and health in total wage employment (table 2.5). Between 1980 and 1986, this share went up in all IMECs for which statistics are available. It is also worth noting that in Scandinavian countries this share is only 0-3 per cent, while it reached more than 20 per cent in Australia. The relatively high shares in Australia, the Netherlands and United States do not imply, however, that a large part of education and health is financed from private sources. As noted earlier, a social service institution is defined as private if it is managed by a private or non-profit institution. It is quite possible that such institutions are largely financed by public funds. Thus, table 2.5 provides an

Table 2.5. Share of private sector employees in education and health in total wage employment: IMECs, 1980 and 1986 (percentages)

	1980	1986
Australia	18.2	20.3
Denmark	0.8	0.8
Finland	0.3	0.3
Netherlands	6.8	7.6
Norway	2.8	2.9
Sweden	1.8	1.8
United States	9.6	10.4

Calculated from: OECD: *National accounts, 1974-86: Volume II* (Paris, 1988).

indication that privatisation has affected social services in some IMECs, but a more detailed study would be needed to determine its extent and nature.

Additional information on the education sector corroborates the trends highlighted above. The UNESCO *Statistical year book* shows, for example, that during the 1980s the number of teachers in DCs has continued to grow faster than the labour force as a whole (figure 2.5). According to UNESCO's statistical definition, teaching staff include employees from both the public and private sectors. But in practice, most teaching staff are paid directly or indirectly by public funds. Since more than half of public expenditure on education is devoted to wage payments, it is likely that real wages for teaching staff have dropped substantially.

The trend towards decentralisation

Over the past 25 years, the share of state and local government in general government has increased in almost all countries. Decentralisation may be the result of a deliberate policy to transfer certain activities or responsibilities from the central to lower levels of government. Or it may simply be that the activities already carried out by local government have grown faster than those performed by the central government. In both cases we shall speak of "decentralisation". One reason for this trend towards decentralisation is that the provision of social services has increasingly been devolved to and carried out by the state, provincial and local levels of government. However, the fact that the management of social services is now mainly in the hands of local and/or state governments does not mean that all aspects have been decentralised. For the government as a whole, the equitable distribution of social services is an important objective which may necessitate central financing. But with dwindling resources at the central level, countries have sometimes also decentralised the financing of social services or have made users pay for them. This is, for example, the case in Chile,

Figure 2.5. Teaching staff and labour force: 1970-86 (annual growth rates)

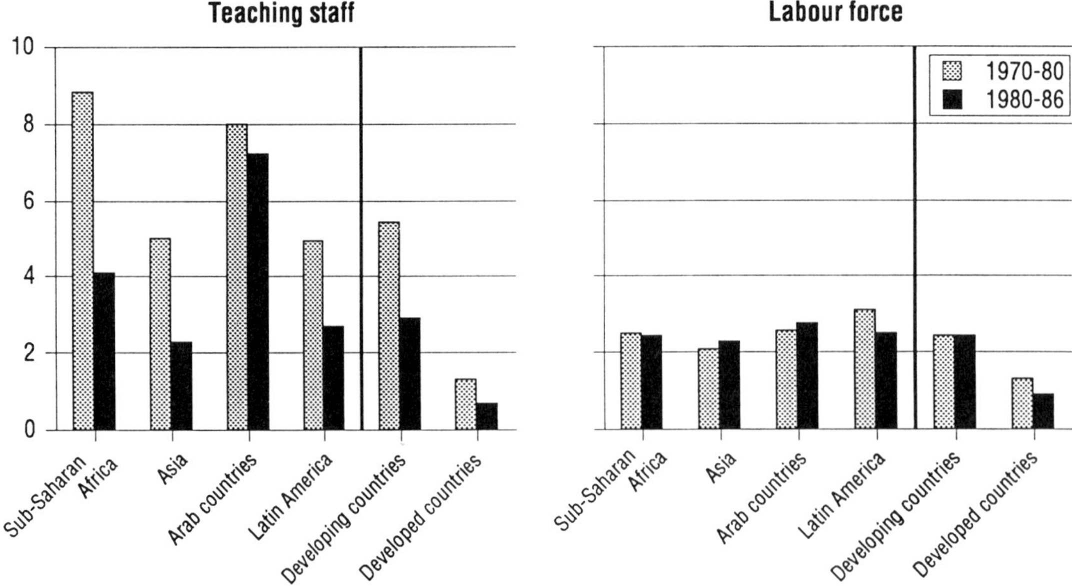

Sources: UNESCO: *Statistical year book 1988* (Paris, 1988); ILO: *Economically active population, 1950-2025* (Geneva, 1986).

Figure 2.6. Percentage of state and local government in general government employment, 1980s

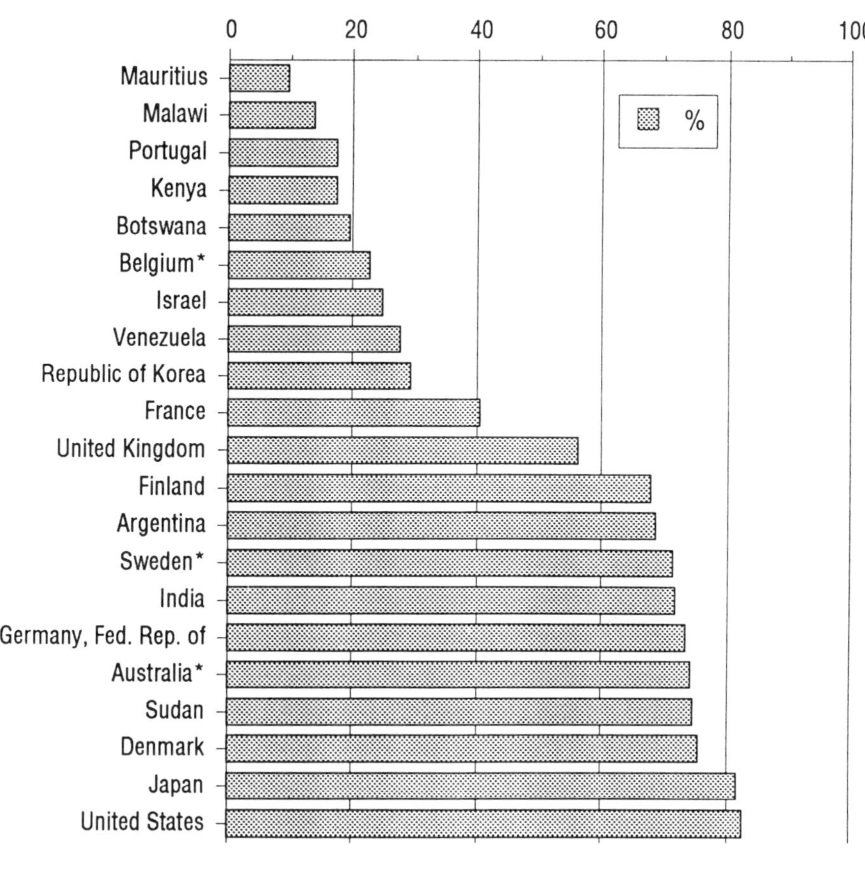

Source: ILO Secretariat.

where the trend towards municipalisation was accompanied by the privatisation of some health and education services. In the mid-1980s, the central government of Bolivia proposed transferring the financial responsibility for education and health to the regional development corporations and the municipalities. However, it had to withdraw this proposal in the face of strong opposition from the more populous regions, such as Oruro and Potosí where government revenues from mining are relatively low. In 1988, the Tanzanian Parliament accepted that, from 1989 onwards, patients will have to pay about 40 per cent of the cost of treatment in public hospitals.

The degree of decentralisation is much higher in IMECs than in DCs. Heller and Tait found that, at the end of the 1970s, local and state employment in IMECs represented almost 60 per cent of government employment, compared with only 15 per cent in DCs. African countries were least decentralised, with about 10 per cent of government workers in local and state employment. For Asia and Latin America, the proportion is around 20 per cent. Africa's high degree of centralisation is accounted for by various factors: the challenge of nation-building, the rapid growth in government size and the general weakness of local government and administrative institutions.

The extent of decentralisation depends not only on the importance of social services, but also on the size and political structure of a country (see figure 2.6). In large countries such as India, Sudan and the United States, local and state government employment represents more than three-quarters of total government employment. The degree of decentrali-

Table 2.6. Women in government and in non-agricultural wage employment: IMECs, 1980s (percentages)

	Year	Percentage of government employment		Percentage of non-agricultural wage employment
		Central	State/local	
Denmark	1981	33.8	70.7	46.7
	1983	35.2	70.4	47.2
Finland	1983	39.9	...	49.3
	1986	41.5	78.0	49.8
France	1985	51.0	56.0 [1]	42.5
Germany, Fed. Rep. of	1983	23.9	45.1	38.1
Japan	1983	20.0	...	38.6
	1986	20.0	...	39.0
Norway	1981	35.1	...	42.2
	1986	38.7	...	44.1 [2]
Sweden	1981	39.8	77.0	47.1
	1986	40.3	78.0	48.4
Switzerland	1983	16.5	...	31.7
	1986	16.6	...	32.0
United Kingdom	1986	56.8	57.5	45.2
United States	1980	31.7	51.2	42.2
	1986	35.6	53.6	45.7

... = not available.
[1] 1984. [2] 1985.
Sources: ILO: *General report.* Report I, Joint Committee on the Public Service, Fourth Session (Geneva, 1988); ILO: *Year book of labour statistics* (Geneva).

Table 2.7. Share of women in government employment: The Netherlands, 1985 (percentages)

	Women	Of whom: part-timers
Public administration (incl. social security)	26.9	8.4
Defence	0.7	...
Education	45.6	38.3
Health	72.8	17.4
Social welfare	84.1	45.4
Other social/cultural services	43.9	36.6
Total	51.1	29.9

... = not available.
Source: CBS: *Arbeidskrachtentelling 1985* (Labour force sample survey) (The Hague, 1987).

sation is also related to whether a country has a centralised or federal political structure. This is clearly demonstrated by the comparison between France and the Federal Republic of Germany, countries of about the same size at about the same level of economic development. In France, where education is a central government function, only two-fifths of government employees are employed by local or departmental governments, while in the Federal Republic this share is almost three-quarters.

In most countries for which statistics are available, decentralisation has progressed further during the 1980s. This process was particularly vigorous in France, where in 1983 some public administration responsibilities were devolved to departmental and local levels. In many DCs, particularly in sub-Saharan Africa, decentralisation was prompted by concern about deteriorating service conditions, particularly in rural areas, and determination to overcome the administrative bottlenecks resulting from overcentralisation. It is more difficult to generalise about Latin America and Asia. In Argentina, for example, decentralisation had already taken place during the 1960s and 1970s, mainly explained by employment growth at the provincial level. In countries such as Costa Rica, it is a much more recent phenomenon, while in others such as Venezuela, centralisation remains as strong as ever. It seems that in Asia decentralisation is mainly spurred by the sheer size of countries and the increasing importance attached to rural and local development. It has been particularly strong in China where, since 1978, the proportion of local and provincial staff in government employment has increased considerably.

Women in the public service

As explained in Chapter 1, the trend towards greater participation of women in the labour force has been a feature in most countries since the 1960s and 1970s. For various cultural, social, economic and political reasons, female participation rates vary widely between groups of countries (see also *World labour report 2*). Women in IPECs already participate fully in the labour force, while they are reaching this stage in various IMECs. In most DCs, the majority of women work in agriculture, and cultural and social attitudes often determine whether women's work is considered an economic activity. As a result, it is sometimes difficult to compare women's participation in public service employment with that in other sectors of the economy and, in particular, agriculture. Thus, where possible, female participation in

2.4 Part-time work in the public service of IMECs: Government and workers' points of view

Many governments of IMECs are encouraging part-time work in the public service. In passing the Federal Employees' Part-Time Career Employment Act in 1978, the US Congress took the view that part-time career employment would benefit the Government as an employer by providing management with the flexibility to meet work requirements, and would benefit society by providing an alternative for those who require or prefer shorter hours. In the United Kingdom, part-time work and job-sharing are encouraged within the context of a programme of action to increase equality of opportunity. And in the Federal Republic of Germany, the extension of part-time work in the public service is regarded as a measure to promote female employment.

According to the Swedish Municipal Workers Union (SKAF), in a report prepared for Public Services International (PSI), part-time work in Sweden has been strongly encouraged by new statutory provisions on parental leave and child-care benefits adopted in the 1970s. In particular, employees were given the right to reduce their working hours by a quarter until any child in their care is eight years' old. In recent years, part-time employees have tended to work longer hours, probably because the trend in real earnings has been less favourable. A survey found that, whereas 16 per cent of all Swedish workers wanted – if hourly pay was maintained – a shorter working week and only 8 per cent a longer one, among part-time workers as many as 22 per cent wanted to work more hours and only 5 per cent fewer hours. Also, as between a reduction in working time and higher wages, more part-time workers chose higher wages than did workers in general.

According to the German Civil Servants' Union (DBB), the number of part-time government employees increased by 120,000 between 1983 and 1986, while the number of full-time employees declined by 30,000. Part-time workers are at a disadvantage in a number of areas. Those working less than half the average working week could be dismissed at shorter notice. Part-timers, according to the German Confederation of Trade Unions (DGB), were not entitled to parental leave without pay. And since part-time employment is mainly practised in the general and clerical services, opportunities for promotion are limited. Contractual part-time employees especially have few full-time alternatives to their part-time work. However, as a result of an agreement concluded by its public service affiliate, the OTV, the provisions for part-time employees have since 1 January 1988 been consistent with those for full-time employees. This new arrangement concerns contractual employees in the OTV's area of competence, that is, parts of central and local government.

the public service will be compared with that in non-agricultural wage employment.

In most countries, there is a substantial discrepancy between women's participation in central and state/local levels of government. In IMECs, women typically represent 25 to 35 per cent of central government employment and 45 to 80 per cent of state-/local government employment, while their share in non-agricultural wage employment is between 35 and 50 per cent (see table 2.6). Central government usually pays better and requires higher-qualified personnel than the state and local government, which results in some job segregation between the two levels. In addition, women are well-represented in health services and education, which are mainly the responsibility of local government.

There are also considerable differences in the participation of women in the various sub-sectors of government employment. This is clearly shown by the example of the Netherlands (see table 2.7) which is typical of most IMECs. In 1985, women represented more than half of Dutch government employment. But in health and social welfare more than three-quarters of workers are women, while in public administration, only one-quarter and in defence, virtually none. The incidence of women in part-time employment varies greatly, from 10-20 per cent in public administration and health to 35-45 per cent in education and social welfare. In most IMECs, part-time work is much more prevalent at the state and local level than at the central level. This is partly due to the fact that education and social welfare services have often been decentralised to sub-national levels. The high incidence of part-time employment in the public service raises a number of problems, particularly in the area of worker protection. Some of these are discussed in box 2.4.

In IPECs, the participation of women in government employment has progressed even further than in the IMECs. The average employment share of women in the non-material sector is typically about 70 per cent, while in health and education services it can reach 75-80 per cent.

In DCs for which statistics are available, women's employment share in central government varies between 5 and almost 50 per cent. In most DCs, notably in Africa and the Middle East, feminisation in central government is higher than in non-agricultural wage employment, but it is lower in India and some South American countries. In Africa, feminisation of central government employment has not increased much over the past ten years but it has risen strongly in the Middle East and Latin America.

In the education sector, feminisation progressed very rapidly during the 1970s (figure 2.7), especially in sub-Saharan Africa, Arab and Asian countries, where between 1970 and 1980 female primary school teachers increased their share by 4 to 5 percentage

Figure 2.7. Share of women in teaching staff for primary and secondary education: 1970-86 (percentages)

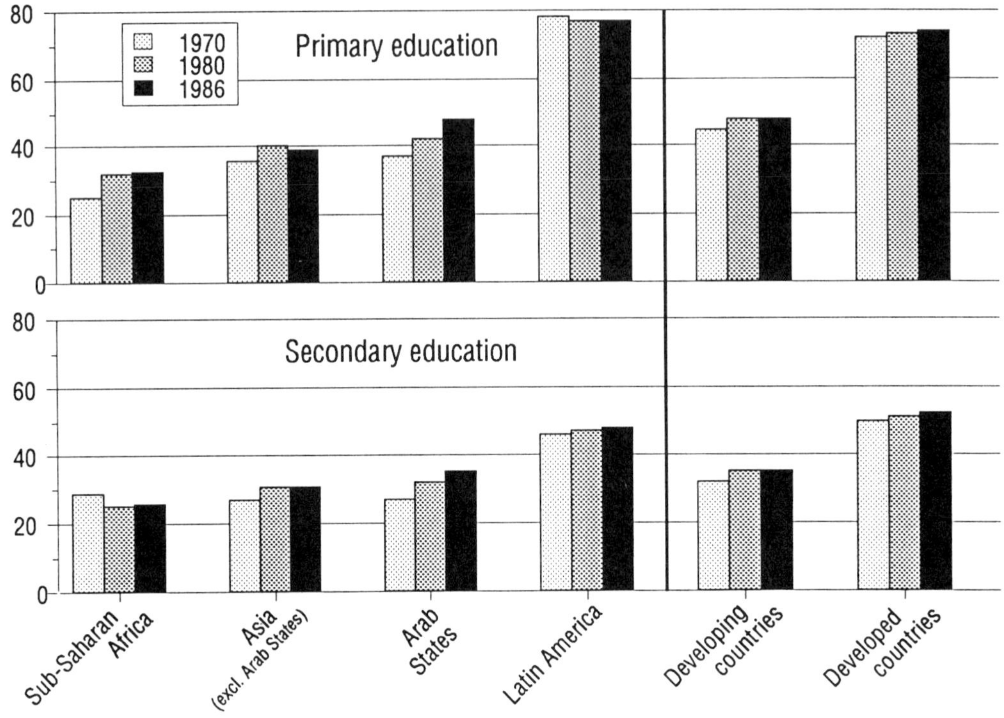

Source: UNESCO: *Statistical year book 1988* (Paris, 1988).

points. In Arab and Asian countries the share of female secondary school teachers also rose, though in sub-Saharan Africa it declined by 4 percentage points. In Latin America, women account for more than 75 per cent of primary school teachers, a higher proportion than in the developed countries; for secondary school teachers the level is about the same, around 50 per cent.

The reasons for the recruitment of temporary staff are various: government's inability to make long-term budget commitments, the need for a certain flexibility in the recruitment of staff, the need to hire people with specialised skills not normally available or needed in public administrations.

Temporary and non-established staff

Stability has been traditionally one of the hallmarks of the public service. Staff, once recruited and after a probationary period varying between six months and three years, have normally been given life tenure with grounds for termination of employment and dismissal being in most cases clearly defined and restricted in civil service laws and regulations. Tenure, however, has usually been granted only after candidates have passed rigorous selection and competition procedures. Lately, there has been a perceptible trend in several countries to circumvent these long-established procedures by recruiting staff on a purely temporary basis, with no guarantee that this employment will lead in the normal course of events to established tenure and thus with few career prospects and services. Furthermore, the specific conditions of entry into the public service, such as nationality, may also prevent the recruitment of non-national staff with certain specialisations on a permanent basis. On the other hand, if governments have to dismiss workers, they are more likely to dismiss temporary and non-established staff. This explains why the share of this category has fallen in many developing countries.

The proportion of temporary or non-established staff in total public service employment varies greatly from country to country. In some industrialised countries, temporary staff constitute about a quarter of total public employment. In Australia and New Zealand, they account for 20 per cent, in Portugal for 27 per cent and in France for some 25 per cent. In 1988 in France there were 1 million non-established staff out of a total of 4 million public employees; their share is even higher at local and departmental level (about 35 per cent). In other countries, such as Norway or the United Kingdom, their share is very low – 1.8 per cent and 2.9 per cent respectively.

In developing countries, the available statistics show that the share of temporary staff in total public service employment is on average higher than in industrialised countries, reaching a peak of almost 50 per cent in Niger and Sudan and 34 to 37 per cent in Burundi, Mauritania and Togo. A striking feature in developing countries is that, in nearly all cases for which data are available for more than one year, there has been a decline in both the proportion and the absolute number of non-established employees. The fall in numbers has been particularly steep in Burundi and Togo (where their share decreased by 12 and 13 per cent respectively between 1980 and 1986), and to a lesser extent in Bahrain, Cyprus, Ethiopia and Niger. In Burundi, the decline in the number of non-established employees has been nearly offset by an increase in the number of established officials. In the Philippines, there is an established order of dismissals: first, casual employees with less than five years of service and then those with more than five years. They are followed by temporary appointments; permanent officials are dismissed last. Within each category, those least qualified in performance and merit are laid off first.

There are exceptions to this trend. In Tunisia, for instance, there has been an increase in the share as well as in the number of non-established employees and in the Republic of Korea there has been an increase in their absolute number though a decline in their share. In a recent study on employment in the public service in Colombia and its impact on the urban labour market, it was shown that between 1976-87 temporary employment increased by 6.1 per cent whereas permanent employment in the public service rose by only 2.1 per cent. The reasons cited for the increase in temporary employment were lower labour costs and a greater flexibility in the recruitment of staff, particularly technicians and specialists.

The growth of temporary employment in the public service of developing countries has been partly a result of the deliberate policy choice of governments to be the employer of last resort. Such policies have created a number of problems, especially where the public service is under heavy pressure to create jobs to reduce unemployment, even when they are not needed to deliver services or produce goods. In many cases, these jobs have been created through the expansion of public sector enterprises, or by adding clerical and administrative posts to the civil service. In the Philippines, for instance, there has been a rapid growth of temporary and casual jobs in government service as well as in parastatal enterprises. Other countries of Asia have also adopted employer-of-last-resort practices in recent years.

It is worth noting that a number of countries have recently introduced measures to stabilise the situation of temporary staff and give them the status of permanent officials. In France, the Government granted tenure *(titularisation)* to some 150,000 contractual employees between 1983 and 1987. In New Zealand, the introduction of permanent part-time work now enables part-time temporary staff to become permanent. In Australia, the Public Service Statutory Authorities Amendment Act, 1985, includes provisions for recognising the status of long-term contractual employees; at the same time it gives management the flexibility to recruit staff to meet short-term workload fluctuations and other needs. In Canada, most temporary employees are eligible to compete for permanent public service jobs, except those recruited on an emergency basis and for whom the normal rules of selection according to merit are not applicable. Other countries, such as Italy, have restricted the recruitment of temporary staff to no more than 90 days a year; they may be given permanent status only exceptionally.

4. Concluding remarks

During the 1980s, there has been a strong political current to the effect that government is inherently inefficient and that – as far as possible – government activities should be transferred to the private sector. There are instances where governments have indeed been inefficient, but there is no need to take a dogmatic position on this issue. Some public enterprises are run well and, even if they are not, privatisation is not the only option (more autonomy and improved management being other possibilities). In addition, there are many new tasks for governments in the industrialised countries (such as management of the environment) and many unfulfilled tasks in the developing countries (such as literacy and primary health care).

But like any other economic agent, governments have to face up to the reality of their limited resources, which are the more constrained in circumstances of indebtedness and slow economic growth. During the 1980s, many governments initially chose a maximum employment strategy by maintaining the wage bill while failing fully to adjust nominal wages in line with inflation. Public investment and repair and maintenance have been neglected, which has led to various inefficiencies. Infrastructure, such as roads, electricity installations and railways, has been allowed to deteriorate. And low investment has held back the expansion of telecommunications and of viable public enterprises.

Thus, governments have often cut non-labour inputs while staffing levels are maintained. In many developing countries, this has led to a situation where, for example, agricultural extension offices can no longer function properly because there is no money for petrol or car maintenance. Another example relates to rural health-care expenditure in the United Republic of Tanzania, which was reduced in the early 1980s by cutting spending on drugs, bandages and other inputs, while preserving employment. The result was a drastic deterioration in the quality of services. In other words, labour and non-labour inputs are complementary, and it is not possible to reduce one without affecting the efficiency of the other.

More recently, some governments have begun to pursue an active retrenchment policy, particularly in sub-Saharan Africa where budget deficits have been most acute. An analytical survey carried out for Africa by Collier (1988) shows various elements of such a policy. A first step in containment of public sector employment is the establishment of a verified payroll, without "ghosts", that is, persons who receive government wages but either do not exist or are not employed in the position for which the payment is made. Secondly, it is essential, both on equity and efficiency grounds, to separate the education system from public sector recruitment. Employment guarantees provide an unnecessary extra bonus to graduates of secondary and tertiary education which in general is already heavily subsidised by the State. Thirdly, attempts to reduce the payroll by recruitment freezes, while they may have slowed the pace of recruitment, have not always achieved wage bill reduction. Frequently, some hiring remains permitted as a fraction of those leaving (such as one-for-three-rules). Under such circumstances, it is better to specify the fraction in monetary terms; otherwise, low-wage earners may be replaced by high-wage earners. Fourthly, retrenchments should precede any increase in public sector wages because the higher the wages the greater will be the opposition to dismissals. And if dismissals are contemplated, public information campaigns are necessary to explain why they are necessary and how dismissed workers will be compensated and/or helped to find new jobs.

Chapter 3

Personnel management

Key issues of personnel management in the public service include how people are selected and appointed, what criteria govern their promotion and transfer during their career and how their work and working time are organised. Procedures for recruitment, career development and work organisation may affect considerably the conditions of employment and calibre of public servants and hence staff competence as well as the quality, efficiency and prestige of the public service. Moreover, the size of the public service workforce means that the State plays a key role as a model employer in relation to working conditions, especially in promoting of equality of opportunity and treatment.

The diversity of public service systems and of staff categories as well as the multiplicity of government agencies and administrations, with their differing functions and staff requirements, greatly complicate international comparisons. There are, however, some basic principles and criteria governing recruitment and career development which are common to a majority of countries and public service systems. They are generally laid down in special public service laws and regulations and are based on principles of equity, merit, efficiency and impartiality. These principles are examined below together with some of the practical and political problems which arise in applying them.

Generally, two conflicting views of the relationship between politics and the civil service can be distinguished. The first approach emphasises the *political nature of the civil service* as an instrument of government social, political and economic policy. The other regards the civil service as a *neutral technical machine* whose part in policy implementation should be regarded as a non-political, managerial matter. This concept of civil service neutrality rests on the notion of a clear dichotomy between policy formulation and implementation, but in its extreme form it has generally been abandoned. Recently, the emphasis has been placed on complementarity between political and civil service functions. The complexity of civil service functions requires a certain degree of separation not merely between administration and politics, but also between decision-making and policy implementation. Governments should resist weakening the influence of their professional career civil servants, who are needed not only to manage complicated operations but to contribute independent and objective advice even when it runs counter to opinions or wishes of political leaders. The system should protect civil servants' views and actions from arbitrary political manoeuvring.

1. Recruitment

The State is in most countries the largest employer of skilled personnel. It may even be the only employer of professional staff in areas such as education and health. And in many developing countries the public service is the only employer of skilled workers simply because the private modern sector is small and/or employs mainly unskilled workers. Obviously, for skilled staff, specific professional pre-entry qualifications are prescribed as conditions for appointment to the public service in almost all countries. In most cases, the right to practise the profession concerned is also conditional on the possession of a recognised professional diploma or university degree.

But the State also employs large numbers of less skilled workers, such as clerical staff, shorthand typists, drivers, janitors, security and prison staff and so on, whose entry requirements may differ considerably from those of professional staff. Post-entry training may be more important, particularly where the general education and training system does not offer the necessary specialisation. In a number of countries, some kinds of staff are not required to have studied particular subjects before entry, but must undergo intensive training and pass strict professional examinations in order to progress in their careers, or even to stay in the service (i.e. in the police and customs service).

Procedures and practices

In principle, staff are recruited into the public service through open and impartial competition on the basis of merit and, in some countries, partly on the basis of merit and partly on a quota basis, as will be seen later. The competitions may take different forms. They may be general competitions intended for recruiting employees to initial career grades in a specific administration or service. In some countries, recruitment procedures vary depending on the category of staff (permanent or temporary) to be recruited or the legal system to be applied to them (special regulations governing the public service or general labour legislation). There are competitions open to both external and internal candidates, or internal competitions, reserved for existing staff. In many cases, these last two methods are combined, with a certain percentage of posts being reserved for internal recruitment, which in fact often results in a promotion. Selection is usually made through written examinations, or tests, in some cases supplemented by an oral interview or by psychological tests.

In several countries, independent bodies are responsible for applying the rules on recruitment to the public service. These bodies have broad powers with regard to competitive examinations and appointments. Most often, the decisions of these bodies need not be supported by a statement of reasons, and in many cases no appeal may be lodged against them.

Newly recruited staff are normally required to undergo a probationary period, the duration of which varies from two months to three years. In some countries, the competition for permanent appointment to the public service takes place at the end of this probationary period.

At present, most countries follow two broad patterns of recruitment at the direct entry level. The first pattern consists of recruitment from a comparatively young age group, that is, from schools or universities. Here, the emphasis is usually on the education attainment of candidates. This type of recruitment is often subject to upper age limits, since the State, and also the recruits themselves, are usually looking for a life-long employment relationship. Career advancement tends in this case to be based on seniority or merit, or a combination of both, with heavy emphasis on loyalty.

The second pattern relates to recruitment of people with professional experience in the private sector, also called "lateral recruitment". It is based on tests that bear some relationship to their work and is used in particular for recruiting persons with certain skills not normally available in the public service.

In many countries, public service legislation stipulates the level of education (primary, secondary, higher) required of candidates for different grades. Although, in most countries, these laws and regulations also specify that recruitment should be based on merit and the successful passing of an open competition, they are not always strictly observed and may be bypassed by political considerations, personal relationships, patronage or friendships. The formal recruitment procedures are also bypassed where staff are hired on a contractual basis without having to undergo the usual competition. This practice is used in a large number of countries, either to cope rapidly with shortages or as a means to combat unemployment.

Equality of opportunity

One important issue in state recruitment and promotion policies is how to reconcile the principle of merit with equality of job opportunities for underrepresented groups. Women, ethnic minorities and the handicapped are, in an increasing number of countries, given either preferential treatment to remedy imbalances or special employment promotion programmes. Some of these programmes, most of which emphasise equality between men and women, are described below.

In Australia, equal employment opportunity programmes have been developed in the public service for women and for the three groups designated in the Public Service Act – Aboriginal people, people of non-English speaking backgrounds and people with disabilities. The purpose of these programmes is to eliminate any inequality of opportunity affecting women and members of the designated groups and to introduce measures to enable them to pursue careers in the service as effectively as others. Success in achieving these objectives is expected to result in three broad outcomes for all groups – an increase in the number employed, an improvement in employment status, and an increase in the variety of jobs being performed.

The Government's approach to equal opportunity programmes is based on the view that denial of equal opportunity does not result only from particular discriminatory rules, but is a consequence of long-standing attitudes and approaches which are embodied in a network of formal and informal rules, processes, conventions and institutional structures. A similar equal employment opportunities programme exists in New Zealand. An Equal Employment Opportunities Unit was established in 1983 in the public service and is now responsible for women, Maoris, people with disabilities and ethnic minorities.

In the United States, the Federal Equal Opportunity Recruitment Program (FEORP) was established in 1978 to provide for external and internal recruitment of women and minorities within the federal civil service. This programme requires federal agencies to use recruitment to improve the representation of women and minorities in various occupations and grades. The programme is administered by the Office of Personnel Management (OPM), which assists federal agencies to improve their programmes, evaluates them and reports to Congress every year on the operation of the programme and the progress made. According to the Standards for a Merit System of Personnel Administration, set up by OPM, equal employment opportunity is to be assured by actions appropriate to overcome the effects of past or present practices, policies or other barriers to equal employment opportunity. Affirmative action may include, but is not limited to, outreach recruitment to encourage minorities, women, and other groups to apply for public service jobs, especially where they are substantially under-represented; removal of artificial barriers to entry and advancement within the system; affirmative action to eliminate exclusion of

3.1 United States: Progress towards racial and sexual equality in the federal civil service

In addition to being one of the largest employers in the country – in 1987 it employed almost 3.1 million civilian employees (including the public postal services) – the federal civil service of the United States acts as a pace-setter for the country's commitment to racial and sexual equality. Nearly 50 per cent of federal employees are women and almost 25 per cent are members of racial and ethnic minorities. During the 1980s, White males have probably been more attracted to the private sector, as a result of increasing pay differentials between the federal government and the private sector (see Chapter 6). During the last few years, substantial efforts have been made to increase representation of women and minorities and approach pay equality. Policy has slowly shifted from strategies for eliminating discrimination to affirmative action as a means to abolish inequality of opportunities by the use of numerical goals and timetables.

Though White males still hold the vast majority of highly paid policy-making positions in the federal civil service, earning far more than women and minorities at all education and experience levels, their share of General Schedule (GS)-type employment dropped from 50.2 per cent to 41.8 per cent between 1976 and 1986. All other groups (Asian, native American, Hispanic, Black non-Hispanic men and women) increased their representation in the same period, though not equally. Women's share of federal white-collar jobs rose 6.5 per cent, as women in each group made larger gains than men. In terms of numbers, Black women showed the biggest increase, filling an additional 2.8 per cent of federal jobs by 1986. Asian women, however, nearly tripled their representation. White and Hispanic women also showed substantial numerical increases. Among men, Hispanics and Asians made much larger gains than Blacks.

Progress towards representativeness has also been made in the higher grades of the federal civil service (GS 13 and above). Although White men still held 79 per cent of positions at GS 13 and above in 1986 (down from 89 per cent in 1976), women's share, although still low, more than doubled from 5.4 per cent to 13 per cent. The percentage of men from minority groups rose by nearly half, from 5.5 per cent to 8.1 per cent. White women were the biggest gainers at the management level, accounting for more than half the White male decline (5.9 versus 10.1 per cent). Black women showed the second-highest numerical increase (taking an additional 1.1 per cent of GS 13+ jobs) and nearly tripled their share. Asian men also showed substantial increases, and remained the only group besides White men to have greater representation at top levels (2.0 per cent) than in the federal workforce as a whole (1.4 per cent).

Differences in average salaries between White men and women and minorities have also narrowed over the 1976-86 period. With the exception of Asian men, however, whose average salaries were somewhat higher than those of White men in 1976 and were 5.7 per cent below them in 1986, other men from minority groups earn about one-quarter less than White men. Women earn about 35-45 per cent less.

Unexplained salary differences, that is the gap that remains after controlling for the effects of education, experience, age and other characteristics, seem to have fallen for almost all groups between 1976 and 1986. The drop was most dramatic for Hispanic men, whose salary disadvantage shrank from 17.9 per cent to 13.0 per cent, a decline that narrowed the gap by more than a quarter. It was also noticeable and statistically significant for Black men and native American, White and Hispanic women. Native American men and Asian and Black women also improved their position, but the gains were statistically insignificant.

Unexplained salary differences narrowed more than overall differences for six of the nine groups between 1976 and 1986. For White women, for instance, the average salary gap shrank 3.4 percentage points, whereas the unexplained salary difference fell 3.9 percentage points. This suggests that the salary gains of the past decade are not illusory; indeed, they may be stronger than they appear on the surface.

any person from full and fair consideration for appointment or promotion; and enforcement of prohibitions of discrimination and impartial resolution of allegations of discrimination. The progress achieved by this programme is described in box 3.1.

In Canada, the Treasury Board announced in June 1983 implementation of an Affirmative Action Program across the public service. Departments must submit annual affirmative action plans to the Board and the Public Service Commission. The Commission has conducted an extensive review and revision of all selection standards to remove the potential for systemic discrimination. Special measures have been taken to ensure that disabled people have necessary technical aids when their qualifications are being assessed for employment in the public service. Special recruitment and development programmes have been established for members of visible minority groups to improve their level of representation in the federal public service. In recruitment, preference is given first to veterans of the Korean and World Wars or their widows and then to all Canadian citizens.

In the Federal Republic of Germany, as in a number of other European countries, attention has focused on ways of encouraging and promoting women into higher-ranking positions, where they are still under-represented. This has led to the drawing-up of affirmative action plans *(Frauenförderpläne)* to promote the employment of women. The plans which have been developed at the federal level and in the states *(Länder)* differ in detail but all cover the same areas: the advertisement of vacancies, appointments, training, working time, and re-entry after a career break, especially for family reasons.

3.2 Reducing job segregation between men and women (IMECs)

Generally, women tend to be concentrated in certain public service occupations and professions, namely teaching, nursing and clerical work. Although over the past few years women have increased their share of managerial and professional posts, they are still over-represented in lower grade jobs and under-represented at higher grades.

In the United Kingdom, women outnumber men in the National Health Service, education, and social services. In the civil service, where the percentage of women was 47.7 per cent in 1986, they represented only 1.3 per cent in the professional category (167 posts out of 12,619). At the same time, they occupied 4,416 out of 9,138 messenger posts (48.3 per cent); 1,460 out of 1,741 telephonists' posts (70.3 per cent); 1,567 out of 1,655 cleaners' posts (94.7 per cent); and 24,374 out of 24,525 secretarial posts (99.4 per cent).

In the Federal Republic of Germany, more than 3 million people were employed in 1986 on a full-time basis in the public service, of whom 1.2 million were women. Only 6.3 per cent of women were in the higher categories or career groups, 21.9 per cent were in the middle categories and 71.8 per cent were in the lower categories or services; for men these percentages were respectively 13.4, 22.7 and 63.9 per cent. There have been no significant changes in this respect between 1983 and 1986.

A similar situation has been reported from France, where women made up 51 per cent of the public workforce in 1985. They were over-represented in intermediate professional occupations (57.4 per cent) and among clerical staff (62.5 per cent). Within the category of managers and higher professionals their share was particularly low among executives (8.8 per cent) and high among associate professors and in educational administration (51.6 per cent). Within the category of intermediate professionals, they were under-represented among supervisors (7.7 per cent), but their shares were very high – the highest for the 16 occupations identified – among health and social workers (78.5 per cent) and primary school teachers (71 per cent). A comparison with 1982 data does, however, show some improvement, particularly for the category of managers and higher professionals, where the percentage of women increased from 26.7 to 29.9 per cent among senior administrators and judges, and from 10.8 to 12.7 per cent among scientific professionals.

In other countries women are also increasing their share of managerial and higher administrative posts requiring a university education. This trend is likely to be sustained and strengthened as a result of a number of factors, including changes in the age structure of the population (notably fewer young people) and the elimination of age barriers, the efforts of governments and unions to initiate affirmative action programmes, and the improvement in women's educational qualifications. A growing number of women hold a university degree, which is one of the basic requirements for recruitment and promotion to higher grades.

In Australia, for instance, the number of women in the Senior Executive Service has increased from 30 (2.2 per cent) in 1981 to 99 (6.1 per cent) in 1986, and in senior clerical administrative positions (central administration) from 356 (6.6 per cent) to 1,361 (15.3 per cent) over the same period. In Canada, women have increased their share of promotions (in all categories) in the federal public service from 48.3 per cent in 1983 to 49.8 per cent in 1986. In the management category the increase was even higher – from 12.6 per cent to 15.7 per cent – and in the scientific and professional category the share of promotions went up from 23.1 per cent to 26.7 per cent over the same period. In the United States, among white-collar federal employees in general (80 per cent of all federal employees), women's share of top grades (GS 13 to 15) increased from 5.2 per cent to 12.4 per cent between 1976 and 1986. The increase was even higher in grades 9 to 12, where women's share went up from 22.6 per cent to 40.3 per cent.

On the other hand, women are often hampered by family responsibilities in their career development. In the Federal Republic of Germany in 1986 women represented 22.3 per cent of all recruits at entry grade (A 13) of the higher category of the civil service. But they made up only 2.2 per cent of the top positions in this category. This seems to be mainly attributable to the fact that women often have to interrupt their career or take part-time work, because of family responsibilities. As a result, they lose the required seniority for promotion.

In Sweden, the Government has established two national authorities, the Office of the Equal Opportunities Ombudsman and the Equal Opportunities Commission. A steering group comprising representatives of the State, in its capacity as employer, and the main organisations of state employees, together with the central staff authorities, has been set up for promotion of equal opportunities within the national administration. Activities of this steering group have included an experimental scheme whereby certain agencies and government departments have been nominated for the promotion of equal opportunities. The steering group also receives annual reports based on equal opportunities plans from various national agencies. Out of a total of 31 decisions by the Labour Court in sex discrimination cases since 1981, 26 referred to the public sector; in nine of these cases, the Labour Court found that sex discrimination had taken place.

The implementation of the various equal opportunity schemes in the industrialised market economies has had a considerable impact on the position of women in the public service (see box 3.2).

In a number of developing countries, a quota system and other measures have been introduced to ensure a balanced representation of the various ethnic and/or linguistic communities and an equitable recruitment of the various population groups in the public service. In Bangladesh, for example, 40 per cent of the posts in Classes I and II (the higher classes in the civil service) are filled on the basis of merit; 10 per cent are reserved for women and another 10 per cent for women who were affected by the liberation war. There is furthermore a 30 per cent quota for veterans of this war (freedom fighters) and a 10 per cent quota for others. In the lower classes (III and IV) the quota for posts to be filled on merit is 10 per cent, the quotas for women and war veterans remain the same and the quota for others is 40 per cent. In India, too, a fixed percentage of posts is reserved for specified groups like the scheduled castes and scheduled tribes. Provisions also exist to relax the standards on height for certain groups for recruitment to the police and similar organisations. In Fiji, the Fiji Service Commission and Public Service (Amendment) Decree 1987 states that: "The Public Service Commission shall ensure that, in so far as possible, each level of each Department in the Public Service shall comprise not less than 50 per cent of indigenous Fijians and Rotumans". Similarly, in Malaysia, the Constitution provides that a reasonable proportion of positions in the public service shall be reserved for Malays. The Government of Rwanda has adopted a policy of regional and ethnic balance in the public service in order to reduce inequalities maintained by previous administrations.

Finally, in some countries, geographical and linguistic considerations are also taken into account in recruitment to the public service. In the Federal Republic of Germany, for instance, civil servants employed in the highest federal authorities should, according to the Constitution, be drawn from all states *(Länder)* in appropriate proportion. Those employed in other federal authorities should, as a rule, be drawn from the *Land* in which they serve. Similar provisions exist in other countries with a federal system such as India and Nigeria. In Belgium, a strict parity is observed between the linguistic communities in the central administration.

Conditions of entry

In most countries, there are special criteria for the recruitment of public service employees, such as citizenship and enjoyment of civic rights (such as the right to vote), minimum and maximum age limits, physical fitness, good morality and conformity with rules on military service. A number of countries have also established loyalty towards the nation, the constitution, or the political regime in force as a general condition of entry to the public service. These criteria may be justified under certain circumstances when the posts involved concern the exercise of public authority (judiciary, police, etc.).

Citizenship

Most public service laws and regulations require public servants to be citizens of the country concerned. Although the legal provisions are generally fairly rigid, several countries have waived this requirement or made it more flexible. Thus, in some countries, non-nationals may have access to jobs in the public service after acquiring citizenship, if they have lived in the country for a specified period of years following naturalisation. In Australia, non-Australian citizens may even be appointed on probation pending the grant of citizenship. In the Netherlands, an amendment to the Recruitment and Selection Decree now under way will also allow non-nationals to be appointed as civil servants. In Egypt, the Public Service Law (Law No. 47 of 1978) stipulates that candidates for a post in the public service must have Egyptian nationality or the nationality of an Arab country, on condition that there is reciprocity.

The countries of the European Communities are at present considering the possibility of allowing citizens of the Community to take part in national competitions for jobs in some parts of the public service. Article 48, paragraph 4, of the Treaty of Rome stipulates that its provisions (which establish the free movement of workers within the Community) do not apply to employment in public administration. But the Court of Justice of the European Communities has ruled on various occasions that this derogation should be interpreted in a restrictive manner, arguing that the jobs covered by paragraph 4 are those directly related to specific activities of public administration, that is, those invested with the exercise of public authority and with the responsibility of safeguarding the general interests of the State.

The Commission of the European Communities has also taken the view that Article 48, Paragraph 4, of the Treaty of Rome does not apply to jobs which could be equally well performed outside the public sector without nationality restrictions. It has therefore recently proposed promoting employment of non-nationals in the following public services in member States: *(a)* public transport; distribution of electricity and gas; air and maritime transport; posts and telecommunications; radio and television; *(b)* operational services of public health; *(c)* education in public establishments; and *(d)* research with civil objectives in public establishments.

In some other countries the requirement of citizenship for access to the public service applies only to permanent and established posts or those vested with public authority. In Sweden, for instance, only some senior posts in the state service (for example, in the army and police force, certain jobs in the national administration and posts dealing with international relations) are reserved for Swedish citizens. In the United States, the Office of Personnel Management may, by virtue of an executive order of the President, engage aliens in the federal civil service with a view to promoting the efficiency of the service in specific cases or for temporary appointments. In other countries as well (for instance, Côte d'Ivoire, the Federal Republic of Germany and Kuwait) aliens may be recruited on a contractual or temporary basis in the public service. In New Zealand, aliens may be appointed as temporary staff to the public service, provided they hold a temporary residence permit and a work permit.

Age limits

The career principle implies that a person joins the public service at a relatively young age and, once recruited, spends the rest of his or her working life there. Lower and upper age limits have therefore been prescribed in a number of countries for direct entry into the public service.

The ILO's Committee of Experts on the Application of Conventions and Recommendations, in its recent survey on equality in employment and occupation, observed that upper age limits set for access to certain categories of employment, such as jobs as public officials, should be re-examined in order to determine the extent to which the restrictions are justified by the requirements of the job in question.

In some countries, the age range is a wide one: for example, in New Zealand it is between 15 and 54, in Côte d'Ivoire between 18 and 35, and in Madagascar between 18 and 40 years. Other countries (e.g. Argentina, the Philippines) have set fairly high upper age limits (60 and 50 years respectively). Furthermore, a number of derogations from the upper age limits have been foreseen in several countries for certain population groups or individual cases. In India, the upper age limit for direct recruitment depends upon the nature of duties, educational qualifications and experience. Upper age limits for higher posts vary between 40 and 50 years, and for middle and lower posts between 18 and 35 years. Relaxations of these age limits are, however, allowed in certain cases (officials who are in Government service, widows and judicially separated women).

In some countries, the upper age limit for entry into the public service has been raised for women who are bringing up or have brought up children. Thus, in the Federal Republic of Germany, the upper age limit has been raised to 38 years for women who have brought up children and in France, relaxations of the age limit for entry to the public service are possible in the case of people with children in charge or mothers having brought up at least three children, as well as widows and divorced women. In other countries, for example Denmark, there is no general upper age limit for public service positions. In the United Kingdom, upper age limits for recruitment to most grades were abandoned in 1983. In Sweden, under the Ordinance prohibiting age discrimination in job selection, a national authority may not prescribe an upper age limit as a condition for appointment.

Political opinion

In a large number of countries, constitutional and legislative provisions prohibit discrimination on the basis of political opinion, membership of a political party or political activities. The ILO's Convention (No. 111) on equality in employment and occupation provides protection against such discrimination. Its Committee of Experts on the Application of Conventions and Recommendations has defined its scope, noting that "the protection afforded by the Convention is not limited to differences of opinion within the framework of established principles. Therefore, even if certain doctrines are aimed at fundamental changes in the institutions of the State, this does not constitute a reason for considering their propagation beyond the protection of the Convention, in the absence of the use or advocacy of violent methods to bring about that result."

However, in some countries, the constitution, legislation or regulations ban access to employment in the public service (and in some occupations in the private sector) on the grounds of membership of political parties. In Chile, for instance, under article 8 of the Constitution, any act by a person or group that is intended to disseminate certain doctrines, including those that promote a concept of society, the State or the judicial system "of a totalitarian nature or based on class struggle" is unlawful and contrary to the institutional order of the Republic. According to the same article, those who commit the above-mentioned offences are barred for ten years from any public post or position, automatically lose any such employment or office they may hold, and may not during that period exercise an important function in education or in the world of mass media and publications.

In Argentina, entry into the national public administration can be refused and public servants can be dismissed for belonging, or having belonged, to groups advocating the denial of the principles of the Constitution or for adhering personally to doctrines of this kind. In some countries, members of the Communist party are excluded from the public service or from certain occupations. In Paraguay, this exclusion extends to all public servants; in the Philippines, it is limited to those holding an appointed public office; while in the United States, the exclusion can lawfully be applied to all employees, including those in the private sector.

In the Federal Republic of Germany, under section 7 of the Federal Civil Service Act, "no one may be appointed as an official unless he satisfies the authorities that he will at all times uphold the free democratic basic order within the meaning of the Basic Law (Constitution)". The Federal Constitutional Court considers that a breach of the duty of faithfulness to this order justifies in principle the dismissal of an official on probation or in a revocable post and may lead, after disciplinary (judicial) proceedings, to permanent removal from office.

On the other hand, in a number of countries, membership of a party, normally the ruling party, is a prerequisite for access to employment in the public service. The civil service is regarded in these countries as the main instrument for implementing the political directives laid down by the party or the government. This requires civil servants to demonstrate unequivocal loyalty towards the party or regime.

In Czechoslovakia, for example, in the selection procedure for cadres, the Communist Party assesses not only the professional qualifications, skills and moral qualities of candidates, but also their political opinions and loyalty. Moreover, employees are assigned to or withdrawn from cadre posts only after approval of the competent Party organ. In Zaire, the Public Service Regulations provide that the official "shall demonstrate in all circumstances an unfailing commitment to the ideals of the Party". In other countries, such as China, the German Democratic Republic, Mozambique and Romania, despite the existence of constitutional or legislative provisions regarding equality of opportunity and treatment, rules governing employment in a large number of jobs specify that account is to be taken of political and social attitudes, of civic commitment and moral and political qualities.

Political activities

Rules on the political activities of civil servants vary widely among countries. While in some countries such activities are permitted subject to certain conditions, in others they are either restricted for certain categories of civil servants – usually those in the higher ranks – or prohibited altogether.

In Canada, article 32 of the Public Service Employment Act stipulates that "... upon application made to the (Public Service) Commission by an employee, the Commission may, if it is of the opinion that the usefulness to the Public Service of the employee in the position he then occupies would not be impaired by reason of his having been a candidate for election as a member . . . (of the House of Commons, the legislature of a province or of the Council of a Territory), grant to the employee leave of absence without pay to seek nomination as a candidate and to be a candidate for election as such a member . . .". Deputy heads of departments, that is, the top-ranked civil servants, are excluded from such activities nor may they engage in work for, on behalf of, or against a political party.

In the United Kingdom, political activities of certain categories of civil servants are restricted to varying degrees depending on their rank. Whereas industrial staff and non-office grades are completely free to engage in national and local political activities, other categories, such as principals and executive officers, are debarred from national political activities. Some leeway exists, however, for involvement in local political activities. Certain staff, including those working in the private offices of ministers, are excluded from all political activities.

In the United States, in accordance with the Hatch Act, federal government officials are forbidden to participate actively in the running of parties or political campaigns; this Act does not affect their right to vote or to express their opinions. The states have generally adopted laws similar to the Hatch Act, covering the political activities of their officials. In Nepal, no state employee may, in any way whatsoever, take part in political activities under penalty of termination of his contract or dismissal.

2. Career development

Most public service systems have an internal career development process which governs promotion on the basis of ability, in-service and other training undergone, seniority and other factors. The procedures and criteria for promotion are very varied, depending on the employment relationship (statutory, contractual), job category and grade level. The main promotion criteria are seniority or merit. Other factors taken into account include the potential for higher duties, current performance and, in a number of countries, a health record. Merit is usually determined either by reviewing performance or sometimes through a personal interview or a promotion examination.

Generally, public servants do not move frequently and the great majority, once recruited, tend to stay within the public service throughout their career. But mobility both within the public service and between the public service and the private sector is seen increasingly as an essential element of career development of public service employees.

Performance appraisal

The evaluation or appraisal of the work performed by public employees is a crucial element of personnel management and an important information source for both management and the employees themselves. It provides essential information on such issues as the identification of personal capabilities (for example, leadership and communication skills) and job accountability (such as management of people and resources), improvement of efficiency, salary reviews, promotions and transfers, further training and also dismissals and resignations of staff. It may also help employees in their career development, providing them with information concerning their own strengths and shortcomings as well as their training and development needs. A good example of a staff appraisal system is that of the United Kingdom (see box 3.3).

Traditionally, single appraisal schemes have been used for these various purposes, but in recent years separate reviews of salary and performance have become more common, and within the general evaluation of performance there is a move towards a separation of appraisals of current and potential performance. In a number of countries a clear distinction is now made between the performance and efficiency of officials in their present grade and their potential ability and competence to perform efficiently the duties and responsibilities of a higher grade. In the Netherlands, for instance, separate appraisals are regularly carried out *(a)* for the purpose of guiding public employees in the performance of their duties, *(b)* with a view to taking certain decisions concerning their legal status, and *(c)* in order to evaluate their career prospects (potential appraisal). In Australia, the definition of efficiency in the Public Service Act, as amended in 1986, has been broadened to allow managers to take into account the career potential of staff and their ability to undertake a variety of jobs at the same level when deciding on promotions. In Canada and the United Kingdom, reporting officials are required to make an assessment in their reports of an employee's promotability to the next grade. Similar methods are used in other countries as well, including France, the Federal Republic of Germany, Nigeria, the Philippines and the United States.

3.3 Civil service staff appraisal in the United Kingdom

A revised staff appraisal scheme was implemented in the United Kingdom civil service in 1986. It covers all non-industrial civil servants up to the level of assistant secretary. Each civil servant receives an annual written appraisal of his or her performance. An annual appraisal interview is recommended but is not yet mandatory. The process consists of three components: performance assessment; promotion assessment; and assessment of potential.

Performance assessment

Performance assessment is judged in terms of job description and, where possible, set objectives. Overall performance is given one of the scale ratings set out below.

Box 1: Outstanding.
Box 2: Performance significantly above requirements.
Box 3: Performance fully meets requirements of the grade.
Box 4: Performance not fully up to requirements, some improvement necessary, or
Box 5: Unacceptable.

Box 4 has three functions: *(a)* to identify staff whose performance is expected to improve, but are new to a job or are having temporary problems; *(b)* to identify staff who may, if their poor performance continues, be open to disciplinary action; and *(c)* to draw attention to deteriorating performance. Box 5 markings automatically trigger a formal warning as a first step towards possible dismissal. All staff receiving a box 4 or 5 marking must be informed of this by their reporting officer. In general, individual officials have access to the assessment of their performance, that is, they have a right to know what has been written under this heading.

Promotability

All staff must be assessed on their potential for promotion, or "promotability", the purpose being to identify a pool of staff who are suitable for higher grade work. The ratings in this part of the assessment process are: (i) exceptionally fitted for promotion; (ii) fitted; (iii) likely to become fitted in the next two years; and (iv) not fitted.

Departments have flexibility to determine when, and how often, these assessments are carried out. The central principles do not, however, allow staff to be informed of their assessed "promotability". This restriction on openness is one of the main shortcomings of the system identified by the civil service unions. Following a recent review of the scheme, an experiment in fully open reporting has now been started in the Home Office. The administration hopes that experiments will likewise take place in several other areas. In fact, government departments now have the discretion to experiment if they so wish, in co-operation with the Office for the Minister of the Civil Service (OMCS).

Finally, departments are required to devise effective means of determining the long-term potential of staff to carry out different or higher grade work.

Training for assessment

The guide-lines include a statement on equal opportunities and remind reporting officers of their responsibility to guard against discrimination based on grounds such as sex, marital status, race, disability and religion. They also recognise the need to train reporting officers in order to ensure fairness, consistency and objectivity. The success and quality of this training has been one of the main areas of concern in subsequent negotiations and reviews of the system.

The recent OMCS report on the functioning of the new appraisal scheme found that "reporting standards were still neither as rigorous nor as consistent as they should be", and a reason for this weakness was said to be the rather low priority given to staff reporting by managers. The trade unions have suggested that lack of resources for training has been a contributory factor.

Proposed solutions in the report include better communications so that staff are aware of "the purpose and importance of the appraisal system and (management's) commitment to achieving fair, rigorous and consistent reporting standards". The report also recommends a survey of how different departments approach appraisal training, with a view to identifying "best practice".

A few departments have introduced computerised statistical monitoring systems which enable senior management to check for any evidence of discrimination on the grounds of race or sex and for overall consistency of standards. The OMCS report advocates the extension of these arrangements to all departments, a proposal which has the support of the unions. It is generally agreed that only further review will show whether these measures will improve the level of fairness and consistency in staff reporting.

Combining staff appraisal and reward

The new civil service staff appraisal scheme is now being used as the basis for assessing performance-related awards under the performance pay system agreed for three groups of civil servants – specialists, senior managers and Inland Revenue staff. In all these cases performance is measured by annual report markings. For example, in the agreement covering specialist staff, on which the other agreements were based, those in receipt of a box 1 marking are awarded an immediate extra increment within their incremental scale. For those who have reached their ceiling, further progression up an additional "range" is entirely linked to performance. A "range" increment can be awarded following receipt of at least one box 1 marking, three box 2 markings or five box 3 markings in successive annual reports.

The unions are concerned that the performance-linked pay system will put pressure on the appraisal system and have the effect of undermining it. Since the award of performance-related increments is limited by a "quota" within departments, the unions also fear that these will produce arbitrary "quotas" on box markings, with managers under-marking in order to avoid paying performance increments. The OMCS report states: "Performance pay must be related as directly and objectively as possible to performance and the staff appraisal system is the most readily available means of measuring and assessing performance". To make the system work it recommends that standards of reporting should be improved and departments should consider ways of separating the performance appraisal and pay assessment process.

Usually, the employee's work, skills and abilities are assessed in annual reports which are mostly written by the immediate superior. Although in many countries such annual reports are confidential, a number of them (Australia, Canada, the Federal Republic of Germany, Ghana, Kenya, the Netherlands, New Zealand, Nigeria, the Philippines, Portugal, United Republic of Tanzania, United Kingdom, and the United States, among others) have adopted an open reporting system in which the main results of the appraisal are communicated or shown to employees and in some cases discussed with them. In the United Kingdom, for instance, the annual report forms part of a career development programme which includes, in addition to the report, interviews with the employee about his/her work and career. Such interviews are conducted both by the employee's superiors and by members of the personnel division specially trained for the purpose. In the Federal Republic of Germany, the appraisal interview is obligatory; employees also have a right to see their personal files, including appraisal reports. In some countries, joint evaluation committees have been established in which staff representatives take part. Employees who disagree with the results of the appraisal usually have the right to appeal to the competent bodies.

There are, however, drawbacks and weaknesses in the open reporting system, largely due to the lack of training of personnel officers in the techniques and methods of performance appraisal. The system of staff reporting also requires that the supervisor be honest and straightforward; many supervisors find it difficult to criticise staff to their face and do not want to spoil established relationships. There is therefore a certain tendency to make unduly favourable reports and to omit unfavourable statements.

A recent report of the Presidential Task Force on the implementation of civil service reforms in Nigeria listed four grounds for criticism of the present open reporting system in the Nigerian civil service. These are also valid for many other countries. The report identified: *(a)* poor objectivity by supervising officers; *(b)* poor knowledge of subordinate staff and their jobs on the part of many supervising officers; *(c)* fear of reprisals in the case of adverse reports being issued on some subordinates; and *(d)* occasional refusal to sign an adverse report by subordinate staff. The Task Force recommended the retention of the principle of open reporting but also some structural changes in the system. These included replacing the present annual performance evaluation scheme for individual civil servants with one which emphasises concrete and measurable performance, with appropriate rewards and sanctions being based on performance ratings. The Task Force also recommended a new evaluation scheme based on four criteria: *(a)* actual performance compared with prescribed performance standards; *(b)* character traits; *(c)* attendance and punctuality at work; *(d)* leadership performance.

The new approaches adopted by various countries to increase public service staff participation in work evaluation procedures and in planning their career development should help improve the efficiency of performance evaluation systems. However, the fact that work evaluation in most cases is automatically carried out every year, and is often not accompanied by promotion or a rise in pay, may make staff indifferent to the evaluation process and to improving their work.

Criteria for promotion

Traditionally, promotion in many countries is based on seniority. But in recent years, there has been a shift in emphasis from seniority to merit with the result that governments have begun to develop methods of assessing merit through promotion examinations, efficiency ratings, and records of individual civil servants' past performance. Generally speaking, most higher positions are now filled on the basis of merit, whereas the seniority principle often still predominates for promotion to lower positions.

In some countries, seniority has been removed altogether as a basis for promotion. In the Australian public service, for instance, where for nearly 40 years there was a provision for seniority to be used as a tie-breaker in case of equal efficiency, relative efficiency is now the sole criterion for promotion and determination of appeals. In the United States, length of service plays no part in promotion decisions unless it is directly related to the ability to do the job. In Sweden, there has been a shift of emphasis in favour of the competence criterion.

In a number of countries, internal candidates are given priority when vacancies occur. Internal recruitment recognises good performance and training efforts, and provides both a reward and an incentive for progression within the public service. Length of service is in these cases not a criterion *per se* but is only a factor in so far as the candidate is able to demonstrate that he/she is better qualified for the job than other candidates with less experience.

Staff involvement

Staff representatives often participate or are consulted in promotion decisions or the principles governing promotions. In some cases, promotion boards or committees include elected representatives of public employees and/or their unions. In Australia, for instance, the joint selection committees, which may be set up with the consent of the relevant union(s), comprise an independent chairperson, a departmental nominee and a union nominee. They may recommend promotions which, if approved by the secretary of the department, are not subject to appeal. In Ireland, a general council deals with matters affecting civil servants generally and claims affecting the general civil service grades, while departmental councils deal with claims concerning grades within a given department and other local matters. The councils are composed of representatives of civil service unions/associations (the staff side) and the management/Government (the official side), with a chairman appointed by the appropriate Minister. They can only make recommendations. Final decisions on the implementation of these recommendations rest with the appropriate Minister and the Minister for Finance. In the absence of agreement within the councils certain claims may be brought to an arbitration board under an independent chairperson. Arrangements to minimise grievances relating to promotion have been drawn up in agreement with the unions. In France, the joint administrative committees *(commissions administratives paritaires)*, which must be consulted prior to any decision concerning individual public servants, are composed of equal numbers of members nominated on one side by the head of each ministry and elected on the other side by the staff concerned. Similar bodies exist in most French-speaking African countries.

In the Federal Republic of Germany, the staff councils under the Federal Personnel Representation Act of 1974 have wide-ranging co-decision rights. These councils are composed solely of elected staff representatives. The head of the administrative unit and the staff council must meet at least once a month to discuss the internal organisation of the service and all questions having an important effect on the staff. The staff councils have co-decision rights, first, in respect of a number of individual personnel questions (somewhat different for public servants than for salaried employees and workers) and, second, in respect of the adoption of general decisions such as distribution of working hours and the work-week, methods of payment of salaries and holiday schedules. They are also entitled to participate in the appointment, promotion and transfer of public servants and to exercise co-decision rights concerning wage and salary reclassifications and transfers of salaried employees and workers.

In other countries, for example Canada, the United Kingdom and the United States, trade union representatives do not participate in the promotion process as such, but are involved at a preliminary stage when the principles governing promotion are laid down.

Promoting mobility

An increasing number of countries are trying to promote mobility within the public service and between the public service and other sectors of the economy, and have introduced special programmes to this effect. They are, however, mostly designed for senior and highly qualified staff. The objectives of increased mobility include the development of new skills; the broadening of experience; breaking down resistance to change; fostering cohesiveness of government; deploying senior staff in a flexible manner; improving links and understanding between the administration and the public; addressing problems of promotion blockages, motivation and retention of staff; supporting the effective use of new information technology; and the development of more service-oriented organisational structures. The following are some examples of mobility or interchange programmes for public servants operating in a number of countries both at the national and at the international levels.

In Canada, the Public Service Commission is responsible for administering several programmes in which mobility is a key element. All these programmes are intended to develop potential managers and broaden the horizons of experienced executives. The so-called Career Assignment Program is an education and assignment programme for potential senior managers. Interchange Canada is a programme designed to promote, plan and administer exchange assignments between employees of the public service and persons in other employment sectors, including the private sector, other levels of government (municipal and provincial), crown corporations, academic institutions and non-profit/voluntary organisations. The Business/Government Executive Exchange aims at providing business and government executives with the opportunity to participate in decision-making with their counterparts in the public and private sectors. Under the International Assignments Program, high calibre managers and executives may be appointed to key positions in international organisations. The Labour Assignment Program is a vital component of the Labour Outreach Initiative which was announced in September 1986 by the federal Government. The purpose of this programme is to improve the working relationship and the quality of the policy dialogue between organised labour in Canada and the federal Government. This is accomplished by means of a series of individual staff exchanges financially supported by the programme. These exchanges can take place between labour organisations, joint labour-management organisations and the federal public service.

In Denmark, the Government has introduced a rotation scheme under which academic staff, during their first ten years of service, have to work on three different assignments within the sector to which they are recruited. In New Zealand, a scheme for exchanges with the private sector has been in operation since 1978. Officials are selected for the express purpose of gaining training and background experience for a period of approximately 12 months. Where an official is seconded to a private firm, he or she is treated as being on leave with pay. In Australia, the Interchange Programme is a staff exchange scheme aimed at promoting understanding and communication between the Commonwealth (federal) sector, other public sector bodies, tertiary institutions and the private sector. Participants are given the opportunity to acquire new information, skills, insights and contacts while tackling management or professional problems in a new environment. Since its inception in 1977, nearly 1,000 placements have been organised with over 300 organisations participating from outside the Australian public service. During 1985-86, agreement was reached with the Australian Congress of Trade Unions for interchanges with the trade union movement. Reciprocation from the private sector is a problem, however. To help redress the imbalance, personal letters together with details of interchange opportunities and information about the operation of the programme have been sent to a number of private sector chief executives. To ensure that staff losses are kept to a minimum, all officials are now required to sign an undertaking to remain in the service for at least three years after completing the interchange placement.

In the United Kingdom, arrangements for the exchange of staff between the civil service and outside organisations have been in operation for some years. In 1977 an initiative was launched to increase the number of secondments between the civil service and industrial and commercial organisations. In 1986 there were nearly 500 in operation with about 300 civil servants on secondments to organisations in the private sector and about 200 from the business world on secondment to Whitehall. About 170 commercial and industrial organisations are at present involved. Exchanges also take place between the civil service and other outside organisations; there were about 500 of these in 1986. In the United States, temporary assignments of personnel between the federal Government and state or local governments, institutions of higher education, Indian tribal governments and other eligible organisations for work of mutual concern and benefit are provided for by law. An assignment may be made for up to two years and in each case the assignee remains an employee of the federal agency and retains the associated benefits.

In a number of countries (including Algeria, Argentina, Bangladesh, Barbados, Belgium, Belize, Benin, Cameroon, Côte d'Ivoire, France, the Federal Republic of Germany, India, Japan, Morocco, Portugal, Tunisia), public service laws and regulations provide for the secondment of public servants to and from the central, local and/or provincial administrations and, in some cases, to private enterprises, to international organisations and to trade union organisations. Such a system facilitates the mobility of public servants, since it guarantees them reintegration in the original administration after completion or termination of the assignment.

In many developing countries, particularly those with a small private sector, movements out of the public service are rare. In some cases, there are transfers to public enterprises. In a number of countries, however, public servants, in common with other highly qualified people, have been forced to emigrate due to the domestic economic and, in some cases, political situation. This aspect of international mobility is part of the "brain drain" phenomenon which affects developing countries in particular.

Barriers to mobility

Mobility of public servants is hampered by a number of barriers. Some of these problems stem from the fact that the public service has in most countries its own pension scheme and pension rights are not automatically recognised by or transferred to another pension system (see box 3.4). This may entail loss of pension benefits. Another key question concerns the need to reconcile organisational demands

3.4 Occupational mobility and pension rights

Occupational mobility can take various forms. It can occur not only between the public service, public enterprises and the private sector, but also within the public service, for instance when a non-established official is given tenure. In most countries, it is generally assumed that civil servants spend their entire career in the public service, and as a result a fairly long period of service is usually required for entitlement to a pension. In countries with a single pension scheme covering all employees, there are no barriers to mobility. Such barriers are high when each scheme pays a pension based on actual contribution periods, where pension rights are conditional upon a qualifying period. Mobility barriers can be significantly lowered if there is proper co-ordination between the various special and/or occupational pension schemes.

There are basically two ways in which the pension rights between schemes can be co-ordinated. First, the pension rights accumulated within one scheme can be transferred to the employee's new scheme. The receiving scheme will then pay a single pension benefit. Or, second, accumulated pension rights remain within each scheme, but both pay partial pension benefits proportional to the employee's contribution period. In contrast to non-coordination, however, the level of pension benefits in this case is determined on the assumption that the employee has spent his entire career within each scheme. For example, if a person contributed to scheme A for five years and scheme B for 15 years, he or she will receive one-quarter of the pension calculated on 20 years of service within scheme A and three-quarters of that within scheme B.

Transfer of pension rights

There are various ways in which pension rights can be transferred from one scheme to another. The receiving scheme can validate, or even repurchase, the period that the person has contributed to the previous scheme. Or, the sending scheme can refund the insured person's contributions, as originally provided for under the legislation in Gabon and Niger. One problem is that the insured person may not receive a refund sufficient to purchase the same number of years within the new scheme. Another problem may be that the insured person does not use refunded contributions to buy his pension rights in the new scheme.

Thus, it is better to co-ordinate the transfer of pension rights directly between schemes. For example, when a civil servant in the Federal Republic of Germany moves to a job in the private sector, the State pays the employer's and employee's social security contributions to the relevant private sector pension fund, corresponding to the years of service. But the transfer cannot be made in the opposite direction and the insured employee remains entitled to a partial pension in the private sector only if he has completed the required qualifying period. A similarly incomplete system of transfer exists in Malaysia, where the National Provident Fund covers all private sector employees and civil servants with less than ten years of service. It is only after more than ten years' service that the civil service pension scheme validates this period in exchange for the amounts credited to the insured person in the National Provident Fund.

A more complete system applies in France, where the rights of civil servants who leave the administration with no claim to a pension are re-established under the general social security scheme (which covers private sector workers) for the period when they were in the public service. Conversely, when a non-established state employee is granted tenure, the contributions previously paid into the general social security scheme are transferred to the State; however, since they may be insufficient (the state scheme being more advantageous), the insured person must pay the extra into the state scheme to repurchase the contribution periods in question.

A special situation exists in countries such as Canada, Switzerland and the United Kingdom where civil servants come under the same general scheme as private sector workers or residents in general and where their special pension scheme merely affords them additional protection. In those countries, the actuarial value of the pension rights under the previous scheme is transferred to the insured person's new scheme – a method often practised in transfers between private schemes. The transfer normally takes place regardless of the direction of occupational mobility and there is no guarantee that the new scheme will provide benefits based on the same period of service as that completed under the previous scheme.

Pro-rata co-ordination

A system of pro-rata co-ordination applies when there are considerable differences in the rates of contribution and benefit between various schemes. Under this system, the scheme that an employee leaves normally pays pension benefits based on years of contribution, without prejudice to rights under the scheme being joined. But this unilateral solution is inadequate if an employee has not worked long enough to qualify for pension rights under one or both schemes. In such a case, the benefits due under each scheme are calculated on the basis of the total period completed under both schemes. This is the solution that has been applied in Togo, for instance, since 1977. Each scheme meets the cost of its own share of the pension and there is no refunding or repurchasing of contributions or transfer of money. If there has been a considerable currency depreciation between the date to which the earnings relate and that at which the pension is calculated, this normally entails revaluation for pension purposes of the earliest of the two sets of earnings.

Finally, there is the question of whether transferring pension rights or pro-rata co-ordination should be optional or whether they should be applied only where no pension rights have been acquired – where the minimum length of service has not been completed. The latter option would seem to be the simplest solution from the administrative point of view. However, pension benefits are sometimes not entirely proportional to earnings but guarantee minimum levels of protection. Thus, the waiving of co-ordination could result in an accumulation of minimum pension rights, leading to entitlements that no longer bear any relation to the contributions paid.

for increased mobility with individual career development needs. While in some countries mobility appears to be organised as part of a broad strategy for staff development and in terms of a reasonably well-defined career structure, this is not the case everywhere. Officials returning from secondment sometimes encounter difficulties in retrieving their previous job status. At a time when public services are under pressure to cut back on staffing levels, there may also be severe constraints on releasing staff for mobility assignments.

Geographical mobility raises problems relating to disruption of the spouse's career, variations in housing costs, availability of good quality schools, and so on. In some countries (e.g. Algeria, Canada, France), if the spouse is also a public servant, he/she may apply for leave without pay for family-related purposes, as in Canada, or for secondment, as in Algeria and France. Geographical mobility also highlights structural disparities, as in the case of Canada and France, where in the northern regions there are more jobs than candidates, while in the southern regions the reverse is true.

As regards interchange programmes with the private sector, it has often proved easier to find an adequate job for a manager from the private sector in the public service than for a public servant in the private sector. A matter of controversy in recent years has been the appointment of top civil servants to jobs in private industry after retirement. In the United Kingdom, for example, a growing number of senior civil servants leaving Whitehall at the retirement age of 60, or earlier, have moved into top boardroom jobs with salaries two or three times higher than they earned in the civil service. Similar movements have occurred in France, Japan, the United States and elsewhere. Critics argue that there is a danger that, in order to obtain a particular private sector post, a civil servant could bestow favours on his prospective employers and, after his move, use his knowledge of the department's affairs, and his contacts, to secure unfair advantages for his new employer. The danger of abuse of such appointments has long been recognised. In the United Kingdom, rules governing acceptance of outside business appointments were introduced as long ago as 1937, and were substantially revised in 1975. Senior civil servants of the rank of under-secretary and above, taking up posts within two years of leaving the civil service, must obtain prior permission from the Government. In the case of applications from permanent secretaries, the Prime Minister is advised by an independent advisory committee. Responsibility for decisions in all other cases rests with departmental ministers. Refusals are rare, however. In the period 1979-83, of 1,809 applications from civil servants and officers in seven major government departments (1,404 of them from the Ministry of Defence, over half of which involved jobs in the defence industry) only 15 were rejected. In France, public servants may, at their request, be seconded to private enterprises, under the condition that within the five previous years they neither supervised nor did business with the enterprise or another enterprise financially linked to it. In practice, however, secondments of public servants to private enterprises take place without the prescribed conditions being observed.

Mobility and decentralisation

A large number of developing countries have in the 1970s and 1980s decentralised some development and administrative as well as public service functions to regional and local authorities and have at the same time transferred personnel management functions. This delegation of power has not always been accompanied by adequate incentives, appropriate financial resources and the qualified staff needed to perform the delegated development planning and management functions. In most cases, moreover, central governments have retained responsibility for such key personnel management functions as recruitment, promotion and transfer. In some cases the structure of the civil service itself and the policies regulating it have also affected human resource development and mobility at the local level (see box 3.5 for the example of Indonesia).

3. Organisation of working time: The case of health services

The last two decades have seen major changes in the pattern of working time. The ILO's Reduction of Hours of Work Recommendation, 1962 (No. 116), which applies to all wage-earning employees, set the standard 40-hour week as the social objective to be attained, if necessary in stages. This has now been achieved or is close to being achieved in an increasing number of countries, and some industrialised countries have bettered the target. The periods of paid annual leave are being extended, so that the number of hours spent at work is diminishing. And the way in which working time is distributed over the

3.5 Decentralisation and mobility in the civil service: The example of Indonesia

In Indonesia, the Government began decentralising some development and planning functions during the 1970s and also delegated to regional governments personnel management functions, such as recruitment, dismissals, temporary lay-offs, salaries, pensions, and other matters related to the legal position of regional civil servants (Basic Law No. 5 of 1974). Subsequent laws and regulations seem, however, to have undermined the power given to regional governments in terms of personnel. Ministers have authority to appoint, promote, move and discharge all employees in their jurisdiction or functional area above a certain civil service rank, and there is a centralised approval process for all permanent appointments at central government, provincial and district level. At the end of 1985, 1.7 million (55 per cent) of all civil servants were working in regional governments. Most of these (1.3 million or 76 per cent) fell into the category of seconded central government employees paid through central, provincial or district level regular budget funds. This suggests that, whatever the responsibilities given to regional governments in the decentralisation programme, it has not included to any significant extent the development of staff who are permanently attached to regional governments.

The centralised appointment process for permanent employees is managed by the Civil Service Administration Agency, a central government agency which considers applications from, and allocates appointment and promotion quotas to, all public agencies. The regional government quotas are settled in negotiation with the Ministry of Home Affairs, which acts on the regional government's behalf. In addition to setting the quotas, the Agency's role is to check that the proposed appointments satisfy all the regulations as to minimum qualifications appropriate to the post and grade, age limits and so on, and to enter them into the central staff records. An appointment is confirmed by the issuing of a permanent or lifetime civil service number (NIP). Appointments cannot be made prior to the confirmation of the NIP. Political and security clearances have been an additional requirement since 1983.

One of the implications for decentralised management of this cumbersome and centralised control over numbers of civil servants is that it is very difficult to staff new development projects at the district level. Even if the present freeze on hiring any new permanent employees were withdrawn, the complexity and centralisation of the appointment process means that new appointments take years. Thus projects are often staffed with temporary employees whose training and experience thus acquired fail to accrue to the public agency concerned.

Another problem linked to the centralised appointment process and the present structure of the civil service is that it favours employment in central government and leads to a "brain drain" into central government agencies with a resulting negative impact on development and mobility of human resources at the regional level. A person entering the civil service is given either a central-functional (lower digit) or a regional (higher digit) NIP. Though central public works employees may be placed in a region at the start of their career, they have greater chances of upward and lateral mobility than regional public works employees by virtue of the fact that lower digit NIPs may occupy a position at any administrative level in any region. Higher digit regional NIPs can only occupy positions in a regional agency – where the number of administrative levels does not exceed two. There are, moreover, four grades in the central service, four extra steps within the top grade and many more senior positions in central government agencies. For these reasons, the "best and brightest" generally aspire to enter the civil service as central rather than regional employees.

Local authorities are naturally anxious to prove to central government that they are capable of shouldering added responsibilities in decentralisation and use a number of strategies to maximise their resources. As already mentioned, there is significant reliance on temporary employees, paid with project funds rather than through the regular budget. Furthermore, they also obtain employees on loan from higher (central, provincial) levels. These employees, however, although usually better trained and in possession of a greater degree of technical know-how, are placed in positions subordinate to permanent district employees with long tenure. Thus some local civil servants, while suffering from the stultifying effects of overall civil service policies on career prospects and ambition, are in a position to compensate by long and broad knowledge of local conditions for the lack of opportunities for mobility and advancement.

day, the week, the year or even over the entire working life is becoming more diversified and more flexible in response to a number of factors, including technical progress, the demographic structure and the aspirations of the active population, and the economic imperatives of efficiency and competitiveness. This trend, which affects the gamut of economic activities, is equally discernible in the public service and in the private sector.

Many public services operate on a continuous or prolonged basis for reasons of public health, safety, utility or convenience; this, of course, complicates greatly the organisation of their work and places the staff concerned under special constraints. Like all workers, they naturally need proper safeguards regarding working hours. This section is concerned with the regulation and organisation of working time in one specific public service, the health and medical services, where the working time constraints are probably the most onerous and the organisational problems most complex and delicate. Staff not only have to provide care, mostly on a round-the-clock basis, but their work involves a great deal of responsibility, because the health, well-being and sometimes the life of patients can be at stake.

Because most health services operate for long hours or round the clock, they necessarily require shift work, night work, and work on public holidays and weekends. They may also involve irregular work schedules, require workers to be on stand-by or on call, and necessitate many hours of overtime. This is particularly the case where the staff complement is relatively small, where the resources at their disposal are limited or insufficient, or where there is a shortage or unforeseen absence of staff, so that the workload has to be spread among fewer people. As a result, medical, and in particular hospital, staff frequently work long and irregular hours, in spite of the fact that normal hours of work have often been reduced and holidays increased.

Normal working time

The standard 40-hour week has by now become the rule in the health services of many industrial and developing countries, though there are marked exceptions (see table 3.1). Some progress – in some cases very distinct progress – has been reported in recent years towards a reduction of normal working time of health service personnel, in particular as a result of collective bargaining. For example, in Australia normal weekly working hours for most hospital staff were reduced from 40 to 38 in 1983; in France, weekly working hours in all health services were reduced in 1982 from 40 to 39; in the Netherlands from 40 to 38 hours as from 1985; and in 1987 from 38 to 37½ hours in Norway, from 40 to 37 hours in Barbados and from 38 to 37 hours in Italy. Working hours were gradually scaled down from 44 to 40 hours a week in Sierra Leone, from 44 to 36 hours for nursing personnel and from 41 to 37½ hours for other paramedical staff in Saint Lucia, and from 44 to 35 hours for nursing personnel in Uruguay.

For some groups of workers – staff exposed to special hazards such as X-rays – the normal working time is shortened in several countries (Bulgaria, Czechoslovakia, Hungary, USSR, United Kingdom). Another peculiarity of the health sector is that in many cases the normal working time is not fixed on the customary weekly basis but is calculated as an average of several weeks – as, for example, in Finland, France, the Federal Republic of Germany, the Netherlands, Sweden, Switzerland, the United States and Uruguay. As a consequence, hours of work vary from week to week and some working weeks may be very long. Thus it is important to fix the maximum number of hours that may be worked in any one day or week and to specify the period taken into account in calculating average working time (two weeks in France and the Netherlands for the purpose of qualifying for the weekly rest, and three weeks in Finland and the Federal Republic of Germany, for example).

Paid holidays

In general, health personnel have the same paid annual holidays as employees in other sectors of the economy. Some health staff qualify for extra leave by reason of the difficult and arduous nature of the work or of the way in which the work is organised (e.g. shift work, as explained later). In Austria, for example, under the provisions of agreements applicable to the public sector, additional days of leave are granted according to the intensity of the workload. In Benin, staff employed in the radiological services are entitled to an additional four weeks' leave; an extra two weeks' leave is granted to these workers in Finland, and an extra eight days' leave in France to private hospital workers exposed to the hazards of radiation. Similarly, in some of the countries of Eastern Europe – Bulgaria, Czechoslovakia, Romania and the USSR – staff working under difficult conditions are entitled to additional leave; in the USSR, some categories of workers – for example, in charge of paediatric hospitals or services – are entitled to 36 working days' paid annual leave.

In many cases, however, health service workers run into difficulties over timing of leave. Their freedom of choice may be limited by staff shortages, lack of replacement staff and unforeseen absence of colleagues, which may mean that they have to stagger their holidays and take leave at awkward times or at a time that does not fit in well with family and social life, outside school vacations or the good-weather season. To alleviate this situation, more effective measures are being sought to recruit replacement staff during leave periods and to avoid last-minute staffing changes. These were included in the collective agreement concluded in France in autumn 1988 following a protracted strike by health and medical staff called to protest against inadequate pay and poor conditions of employment.

Overtime

Overtime work and work beyond scheduled hours are the rule rather than the exception, particularly in the specialised and emergency services and in small health-care units, and are not always reckoned very precisely.

The most common form of compensation for overtime is payment at a higher rate. The rate may vary greatly from one country, sector, health service or establishment to another. It may also vary according to the amount of the extra workload and whether overtime is worked during the day, at night, on a

Table 3.1. Normal weekly hours of work in the health services, mid-1980s

Normal weekly working hours	Country
50-54	Switzerland (statutory maximum in pharmacies).
50	Madagascar (ambulance staff), Switzerland (statutory maximum in hospitals, clinics, old-age and disabled persons' homes, medical and dental consulting rooms – except for office staff: 45 hours, but shorter hours in practice under agreements).
48	Bolivia (ambulance staff), Central African Republic, Costa Rica (ambulance staff), Guatemala, Guyana (ambulance staff, doctors), Jordan, Malaysia, Mexico (nursing personnel), Peru, Zaire.
46	Cyprus (ambulance staff), Romania.
45-46	Republic of Korea.
45	Bangladesh (nursing personnel, physiotherapists, X-ray technicians, ambulance staff), Botswana (ambulance staff), Cameroon (dentists), Chad, Côte d'Ivoire (ambulance staff), Madagascar (X-ray technicians, nursing personnel), Niger (deemed equivalent to 40 hours in hospitals and treatment centres and for sales personnel in pharmacies), Rwanda, Sri Lanka (private sector), Turkey (public sector), Zambia (ambulance staff).
44	Algeria, Angola, Cuba, Fiji (ambulance staff), Guatemala (dentists), Honduras.
42½	Czechoslovakia (but reduced to 36 hours in certain localities and for certain occupations).
42	Fiji (auxiliary nursing personnel, ambulance staff), Nepal, Saint Lucia (doctors, dentists), Yugoslavia.
41	Botswana (nursing personnel), Cape Verde, USSR (but reduced to 38½ hours for certain occupations).
40	Argentina, Austria, Benin (doctors, dentists, nursing personnel, physiotherapists, X-ray technicians), Bermuda, Burkina Faso, Cameroon (doctors, dentists, nursing personnel, physiotherapists, X-ray technicians), Comoros, Côte d'Ivoire, Federal Republic of Germany, Grenada, Guatemala (nursing personnel), Guyana (nursing personnel), Indonesia (nursing personnel), Ireland (doctors: 33 hours), Kenya (doctors, nursing personnel), Mali, Mauritius, New Zealand, Nigeria, Pakistan, Philippines (doctors, nursing personnel), Sierra Leone (since 1987; previously 44 hours), Suriname, Sweden (shorter hours for shift work and if the service involves work on Sundays or public holidays), Trinidad and Tobago, United Kingdom (in general, but shorter hours for certain grades and occupations in the National Health Service), United States (in general, but 38½ hours for nursing personnel in certain hospitals and in some states), Venezuela, Zambia (other occupations), Zimbabwe.
39½	Belize (since 1985 for nursing personnel and since 1986 for ambulance staff; previously 48 hours).
39	Bangladesh (doctors, dentists), Denmark, Equatorial Guinea, France (normal service fixed per half-days for doctors).
38	Australia (in general; 40-48 hours according to occupational category, sector and state).
38¼	Netherlands (ambulance staff since 1985; previously 40 hours; up to 50 hours for doctors in hospital training).
37½	Norway (since 1986, previously 38 hours), Saint Lucia (physiotherapists, X-ray technicians, since 1985, 40 hours in 1984 and 41 hours in 1983; ambulance staff since 1985, 40 hours in 1984).
37	Barbados (since 1987, previously 40 hours), Canada (in general, but 38 hours for ambulance staff), Fiji (doctors, dentists, certificated nursing personnel), Finland (plus on-call duty for doctors), Italy (since 1987, previously 38 hours).
36¾	Papua New Guinea.
36½	Guatemala (physiotherapists, X-ray technicians).
36	Bahrain, Bolivia (nursing personnel, X-ray technicians), Egypt (state employees), Saint Lucia (nursing personnel since 1985, previously 44 hours).
35	Bahamas (nursing personnel), Burma, Seychelles, Uruguay (assistant nursing personnel since 1987; 36 hours in 1986, previously 44 hours).

Sources: ILO: *Employment and conditions of work in health and medical services*, Joint Meeting on Employment and Conditions of Work in Health and Medical Services, Geneva, 1985; ILO: *Bulletin of labour statistics*, October Inquiry results, various years (1983-87); the Inquiry gathers data concerning the following occupations of the medical service: general physician, dentist (in general), professional nurse (in general), auxiliary nurse, physiotherapist, medical X-ray technician, ambulance driver; US Department of Labor, Bureau of Labor Statistics: *Industry wage survey: Hospitals, August 1985* (Washington, DC, Feb. 1987).

public holiday or on a traditional day of rest (e.g. in Colombia 125 per cent for overtime worked during the day, 175 per cent at night; in France, 125 per cent from the 79th to the 94th hour of work during two consecutive weeks, 150 per cent thereafter, in private hospital establishments; in Portugal, 200 per cent for overtime during the day, 250 per cent at night; in the United Kingdom, 150 per cent from Monday to Saturday, 200 per cent on Sundays and public holidays).

In some countries, such as the Federal Republic of Germany, the Netherlands and the United Kingdom, compensatory time off is given, which has the advantage of limiting the time actually spent at work and so of mitigating the possible repercussions of the strain due to excessive working time on the health of staff and the treatment of patients. In France, Hungary and Sweden, overtime hours are compensated either by time off or by extra pay.

The duration of overtime is subject to limits that vary greatly from country to country and from one establishment to another. However, because the health services have to function on a continuous basis and meet the needs of the public, the measures that limit or govern overtime in other sectors cannot always be applied. In Austria, for example, the general limits governing overtime work may, by collective agreement or with the permission of the inspectorate of labour, be raised to 20 hours per week with a maximum of 13 hours' work per day and 60 hours per week for the medical, nursing and technical personnel of hospitals and other health care establishments.

On-call duty

On-call duty is standard practice in hospital establishments, but may also involve other health services, particularly in small localities and in rural regions or in areas remote from the major health care centres. In developing countries, many of which suffer from an acute shortage of staff, the person on the spot may have to remain available for long spells or even round the clock. On-call duty affects all staff directly involved in caring for patients, but most particularly doctors working in hospitals (see box 3.6). Being on call or on stand-by duty is a severe strain for the staff affected; their freedom of movement is impaired, their working time is consequentially increased, and opportunities for enjoying rest and leisure are curtailed.

Compensation for stand-by duty, the limits of such duty periods or the extent to which the time on stand-by duty is to be taken into account in the calculation of working time vary. In the Federal Republic of Germany, for example, the maximum number of stand-by duties per month, for doctors and dentists in public hospitals, varies from six to 12. In Sweden, doctors on emergency duty or on call are entitled to a compensatory rest period plus an allowance for being on call for more than a certain number of hours (50 and 150 hours per month for being on call and emergency duty, respectively). Provision for compensatory time-off in such cases is also made in Argentina, Benin, Mali, the Netherlands, Niger and the United States. In other countries, for example Australia and Bahrain, the compensation for time spent on call takes the form of a cash allowance.

Night and shift work

The need for hospital patients to receive care 24 hours a day means that shift and night work are particularly common in hospital services. National regulations banning night work for women or other similar restrictions do not apply to the health service professions, and the nursing staff (largely female) have for many years performed night duty, in rotation where shift work is standard practice. In some cases nurses are exclusively on night duty.

Shift and night work create a number of problems for the workers concerned. Apart from the harmful effects on health, such as sleep disorders and the effects of changes in eating habits, continuous or frequent night work and shift work have a disturbing impact on family and social life. These problems can weigh particularly heavily on hospital workers since they are often associated with the other difficulties referred to above: long working days and weeks, frequent overtime and on-call duty, irregular hours, last-minute changes and calls to cope with emergencies. All these problems may affect job satisfaction and motivation, which are particularly important in health services, and may induce workers to change jobs or to leave the service altogether. This contributes to the staff shortages experienced in such areas as nursing.

From studies carried out in a number of countries, it appears that a high percentage of the health service staff work not only at night but also on public holidays and traditional days of rest, work irregular hours or according to special timetables. According to a survey conducted in the hospitals of the public assistance service in Paris, for example, 38 per cent of the (female) nurses start work at 7.30 a.m., where-

3.6 The special problems of doctors in hospitals

The position of doctors, interns, assistant doctors and doctors in training in hospitals is characterised by some special features. In common with workers who carry on an occupation or profession needing high or specialised qualifications and who perform responsible functions, their normal working time may not be fixed precisely or even specified at all. In France, for instance, the normal working week for full-time hospital doctors is fixed in terms of half-days (ten for doctors, 11 for interns).

Interns, assistant doctors, doctors in training and, in general, young doctors in hospitals frequently work very long hours because they have to perform on-call or stand-by duties. In the United States (New York State), for example, doctors, interns and house doctors often work for 100 hours a week and have to stay at their duty station for 36 hours on end; in New York State, action has been taken recently to restrict their working time to 80 hours and the time during which they have to remain at the duty station to 24 hours; these new limits are to come into effect in July 1989. In the United Kingdom, young hospital doctors regularly work 83 hours a week, and longer if they have to replace absent colleagues; legislation is now proposed to limit their working time to 72 hours a week. In Switzerland, according to a survey carried out recently in the Geneva hospitals, the average working time of assistant doctors is 70 hours a week (with six spells of on-call or stand-by duty per month). But they may have to work for 100 hours a week when they have to replace a colleague; almost half of the doctors covered by the survey work 55 to 65 hours a week, more than a third work 65 hours to 75 hours, and almost 10 per cent work 75 to 85 hours a week; those working less than 55 hours account for a mere 8 per cent (see figure 3.6.1).

Figure 3.6.1. Distribution of working time of assistant doctors in Geneva hospitals, 1988 (in percentages)

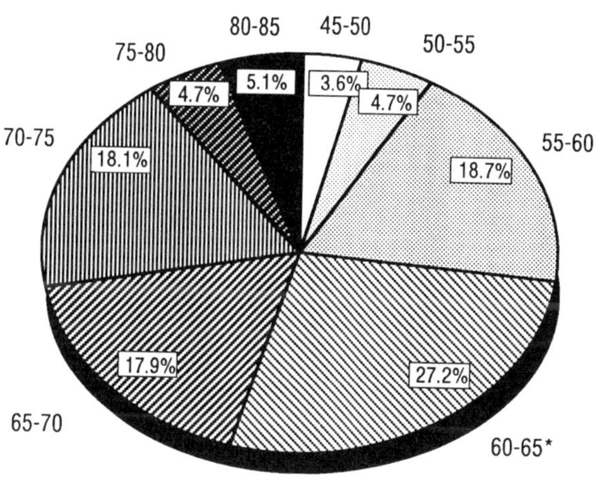

*Working time – hours per week

Source: *La Suisse* (10 Oct. 1988).

as only 12 per cent of all female workers do so; 20 per cent of the nurses do not start work before the afternoon – some at noon, others at 6 p.m. – and hence finish work at a late hour (only 7 per cent of all female wage earners have a comparable work schedule); for almost half the female nurses, the number of working days per week varies from one week to the next (compared with only 11 per cent of all women workers), and 38 per cent of the nurses are on duty for seven or eight days consecutively.

In some cases, "split" shifts are used whereby staff work two shifts several hours apart during the same day, in order to cope with peak workloads at certain hours; the consequence is that the volume of the day's work is greatly increased.

In the relevant regulations and collective agreements in force in many countries, provision is made for the granting of special allowances or pay increases for health service workers (e.g. Argentina, Australia, Austria, Bahrain, Bulgaria, Colombia, Finland, France (where, under the agreement of 1988 referred to above, persons qualifying for the specific night work allowance are to receive a 10 per cent pay increase), the German Democratic Republic, Hungary, the Netherlands, New Zealand, the Philippines, the United Kingdom, the United States, Uruguay, Zimbabwe).

In some countries, staff employed by the health service who are on night work or shift work are compensated in the form either of a reduction of normal working time (e.g. Argentina, Czechoslovakia, German Democratic Republic, Hungary, Norway, Sweden) or of extra annual leave (e.g. Australia and Romania), as is the case for shiftworkers in other sectors as well. In the Federal Republic of Germany, hospital doctors and dentists are entitled to extra leave for shift and night work varying from one to four days. In New Zealand, shiftworkers likewise qualify for extra leave days (generally one week's leave).

These compensations may be supplemented by other measures for mitigating the adverse effects of night work and shift work: provisions limiting the number of hours of night duty or the period during which a person may be placed on night duty (not more than four consecutive weeks or one-fourth of the year in private hospitals in the Federal Republic of Germany); provisions for avoiding last-minute changes (advance notice of timetables and duty rosters); consultations with the persons concerned; replacement of absentees; fair distribution of inconvenient duty hours; provision of certain facilities such as canteens; exemption of certain categories of workers; or, as noted earlier, provisions guaranteeing a weekly rest, ensuring that a certain number of weekly rest periods coincide with Saturday and that an uninterrupted period of rest and holiday can be taken. In Sweden shiftworkers who are on duty on Sundays, weekends or public holidays are entitled to nine days of rest per four-week period; these rest days are usually granted in such a way that they can be off duty for one weekend in two. In France, in the public hospitals, staff are entitled to four days of rest (at least two of which must be consecutive) in respect of a two-week tour of duty.

4. Concluding remarks

The main personnel management problems in the public service of many countries relate to political interference, recruitment and promotion procedures which are either outdated or not properly observed, and a lack of training and mobility.

While political leaders have a right to demand implementation of government policies and programmes, some opposition or dualism between political will and civil service expertise should be permitted. Civil servants should feel free to contribute advice and use their professional judgement without running the risk of having their loyalty questioned. Thus, a measure of autonomy, consistent with the needs of rational organisation and staff efficiency, is desirable. Personnel policies should not be based on personal connections with staff superiors or political leaders. To protect and develop the core of highly trained, experienced and motivated civil service professionals, to improve their efficiency, motivation and morale, it is important to preserve a certain distance and degree of freedom between the civil service and the political arena.

Personnel management in the public service can be constrained by sometimes unnecessary rules and regulations, old-fashioned selection procedures and outdated job designs and classifications. These limit managers' authority to recruit and select suitable and qualified staff, make necessary staff assignments and transfers as well as grant deserved promotions or other rewards. In fact, promotion is often based on seniority and personal connections. In some countries, managers move too rapidly from one post to another to have sufficient time to apply whatever skills they have acquired. In others, training for personnel managers has low priority and is therefore not sufficiently widespread. This partly explains why it is hard to improve performance: management teams are often too new and too soon broken up, with managers themselves frequently unable to cope with new methods or technology.

Personnel policies in the public service which actively promote the integration of under-represented groups, such as women and minorities, have contributed to a more equitable or less conflictual society. In the developed countries, the many programmes for equal opportunities have led to a better representation of women in the public service, sometimes at higher levels, but much more still needs to be done. In the developing countries, such programmes started more recently: some of them have been successful, but many have so far had little impact.

Public service employees are usually not very mobile. For workers with certain specific skills, as in education and health, this may sometimes be unavoidable. But it can lead to demotivation and inefficiency. An increasing number of countries are now trying to encourage mobility within the public service and between the public and private sectors. Barriers to public-private sector mobility exist in countries where pension rights are not portable between various schemes within the public service and between the public and private sectors. Moreover, geographical mobility is often hampered by circumstances such as the disruption of the spouse's career, variations in housing costs and the availability of good quality schools. Last but not least, mobility is too often not conceived within a broader strategy of staff development and may therefore clash with individual career development objectives.

Chapter 4

The remuneration package

People working in the public service have chosen to do so for various reasons. They may be attracted by interesting and more independent work or by the hope that work will be less stressful than in the private sector. They may value employment security more than high levels of pay. Or they may put a high premium on social security benefits, such as pensions and health insurance. On the other hand, their employers, the governments, are primarily interested in recruiting and maintaining an efficient and motivated workforce that is able to provide a wide variety of services, such as public administration, education and health.

For a complete comparison between conditions of employment in the public service and in the private sector, it is necessary to take the whole remuneration package and all other employment terms into consideration. Thus, public-private wage comparisons should not be limited to wage rates and earnings, but should also include pensions and other fringe benefits such as free (or below cost) medical services. Moreover, the comparison should extend to working conditions and stability of employment.

That said, pay is undoubtedly the most important term of employment and most of this chapter is devoted to examining its level and structure in the public service. Section 1 examines trends in real pay in the public service, while section 2 compares them with developments in the private sector. This section also provides some information on the increasing incidence of multi-employment and moonlighting in the public service, particularly in developing countries. Section 3 begins by examining pay differentials within the public service such as those between various occupations and sectors and between men and women. Most of the section is devoted to an analysis of salary scales. In section 4 a public-private comparison is made of social security protection. Section 5 makes some concluding remarks.

1. Trends in public service pay

Pay in the public service of most developing countries (DCs) is adjusted at irregular, and often long, intervals. In periods of high inflation, this leads to a considerable erosion of purchasing power, a mechanism used by many governments as a means to reduce public sector deficits while maintaining as much employment as possible. In various DCs and some industrialised market economy countries (IMECs), governments have eliminated annual increments or fringe benefits or reduced basic pay. However, in the IMECs, annual or two-yearly pay increases through a process of collective bargaining or joint consultation are a well-established principle. And even though these processes were suspended in some IMECs at the beginning of the 1980s (see the next chapter), they have in general prevented large drops in real public service pay.

Africa

Even though there are generally few data on trends in public service pay in DCs, the ILO recently conducted an extensive survey on civil service pay in Africa. Some of the main results are shown in table 4.1, which gives the real salary index for the lowest and highest basic salaries in the civil service for a number of African countries in 1985, where 1975 equals 100. In some of the countries, the basic salary used for calculation of the index included specific allowances: a cost-of-living allowance in Mauritania and Somalia, a residence allowance in Morocco, a service allowance in Togo and supplementary allowances in Tunisia. The index shows the relative change in real terms for the minimum of the lowest salary scale and the minimum of the highest scale over the period 1975-85.

Among all the grades and countries in table 4.1, only the lowest grade in Zimbabwe experienced an

Table 4.1. Indices of basic salaries and basic salaries plus increments in the civil service of selected African countries, 1985 (1975 = 100)

Country	Grade [1]	Real basic salary (1)	Real basic salary plus increments (2)
Benin	L	43.2	54.8
	H	43.2	63.0
Central African Republic	L	48.9	66.0
	H	36.9	54.0
Ethiopia	L	62.6	81.4
	H	31.3	31.3
Gambia	L	39.5	50.1
	H	36.3	43.6
Kenya	L	58.2	87.6
	H	42.2	50.3
Mauritania	L	60.6	...
	H	43.8	...
Morocco	L	66.3	73.8
	H	53.1	75.0
Niger	L	46.2	...
	H	46.2	...
Nigeria	L	42.2	46.4
	H	25.3	27.7
Sierra Leone	L	23.4	23.8
	H	16.0	18.0
Somalia	L	5.2	5.2
	H	4.0	4.0
Sudan [2]	L	74.1	83.0
	H	58.1	58.1
United Republic of Tanzania	L	22.9	23.8
	H	18.8	18.8
Togo	L	58.1	84.0
	H	58.1	78.2
Zimbabwe	L	150.6	161.5
	H	58.1	58.1

... = not available.

[1] L = lowest grade, lowest step; H = highest grade, lowest step. [2] The data refer to basic salary plus standard allowances.

Source: Preliminary data from D. Robinson: *Civil service pay in Africa* (Geneva, ILO, forthcoming).

increase in real basic salary between 1975 and 1985. There were deep cuts in real basic salaries in other countries, particularly for the highest grades. In Somalia, the real basic salary for the lowest grade in 1985 was only 5.2 per cent of its 1975 value, and that for the highest grade a mere 4.0 per cent. In Sierra Leone and the United Republic of Tanzania, the real purchasing power of basic salaries dropped by roughly four-fifths. Appreciable falls also occurred in Gambia, Nigeria and the Sudan. In Ethiopia, Morocco, Kenya and Togo the lowest grades suffered reductions of roughly 35-40 per cent. And in many countries, the fall in the real basic starting salary for government employees was steeper than the decline in real per capita GDP, suggesting that public servants bore a large share of the burden of structural adjustment of the economy.

The large reductions in basic real pay, shown in column 1 of table 4.1, do not necessarily apply to the individual salaries of civil servants. Somebody who started at the minimum level of a particular wage scale in 1975 will have received a number of increments between 1975 and 1985. Theoretically, it would be possible for the purchasing power of individual salaries to go up while that of starting salaries went down. Thus, column 2 of table 4.1 shows how the "basic salary plus increments" (BSI) of the grade in 1985, expressed in real terms, compares with the starting salary level for that grade in 1975. In calculating the BSI, it was assumed that civil servants received all increments for which they would be eligible under normal circumstances, that is, that none were withheld for disciplinary reasons and that they were received at an average rate.

The comparison of columns 1 and 2 shows that the real value of the lowest basic salary in Ethiopia fell from 100 in 1975 to 62.6 in 1985, but that the real basic pay of an individual hired at the lowest step of the lowest grade in 1975 would have fallen only to 81.4 in 1985 due to increments. In some cases, such as Kenya and Togo for the lowest grades, there was a sizeable difference between the two measures, and the fall in real pay calculated on the BSI basis was significantly less than for the salary scale minimum. In other cases, such as Sierra Leone and the United Republic of Tanzania, the difference was almost the same, indicating that increments are very small. In some cases, such as the highest grade in Ethiopia and the United Republic of Tanzania and both grades in Somalia, there was no difference between the two measures, in the United Republic of Tanzania because the grade concerned had only a single salary level, and in the other two examples because increments were not paid as a result of policy decisions.

In seven (Ethiopia, Gambia, Kenya, Nigeria, Sierra Leone, Somalia and the United Republic of Tanzania) of the 13 countries in table 4.1, the real basic salary plus increments for one or both grades fell by 50 per cent or more between 1975 and 1985; in Sierra Leone, Somalia and the United Republic of Tanzania, the drop was more than 75 per cent. It is noteworthy that, except for Benin and Morocco, real BSI for the highest grade declined by a larger percentage than for the lowest grade.

It is of course possible for falling real basic salaries to be partly or totally offset by increasing cash allowances or payments in kind (e.g. housing provided by the government). Reliable data on the type, worth and incidence of allowances to government employees are notoriously difficult to obtain. However, from the fragmented data available, it would appear that, while such allowances have indeed provided some compensation, particularly for certain higher-level grades, the impact on falling real incomes has been quite limited.

Latin America and Asia

As noted in Chapter 1, the recession during the 1980s depressed real wages in all sectors of the Latin American economies. In most of them, public sector wages suffered more than those in the private sector (see table 4.2), though not as dramatically as in Africa. In some countries, particularly Argentina, Chile and Uruguay, the slide in wages had already started during the 1970s. In others, public sector wages continued to rise at the beginning of the 1980s but declined afterwards. In Colombia and Venezuela, for example, real public sector wages went up by more than 10 per cent during the early 1980s, but then fell steeply. In Brazil, real government pay remained constant between 1980 and 1982 and declined by only 5 per cent between 1982 and 1986. But since 1986 it has slumped, because salaries have been only partially compensated for the very high inflation rate which reached almost 1,000 per cent in 1988. In Costa Rica, the opposite occurred: real central government wages dropped by more than 30 per cent between 1980 and 1982, but recovered somewhat afterwards to 15 per cent below the 1980 level in 1986. In the private sector, real wages returned to 1980 levels in 1986.

The fragmented information available shows that the same process of decline occurred in Asia. In Bangladesh, the real basic starting salary of senior civil servants in 1983 was less than 15 per cent of its value in 1970. In India, all central government pay scales except the lowest fell dramatically in real terms in the 20 years 1960-80. In Thailand, real salary scales of civil servants in 1983 were around 80 per cent of their 1974 levels. Generally, increments and promotions softened, but did not prevent, cuts in real basic

Table 4.2. Real wage indices for public and private sectors, Latin America, 1970s and 1980s

	Sector	Wage group	Year 1	Index	Year 2	Index	Year 3	Index	Year 4	Index
Argentina	cgov	cat 1	1970	100.0	...	...	1985	70	...	...
	cgov	cat 24	1970	100.0	...	...	1985	32	...	...
Brazil	tgov	all	...	...	1980	100.0	1982	100.5	1986	94.7
	prfr	all	...	...	1980	100.0	1982	104.7	1986	85.8
Chile	publ	all	...	...	1981	100.0	1984	76.5	1987	74.6
	all	all	...	...	1981	100.0	1984	80.5	1987	84.0
Costa Rica	cgov	all	...	...	1980	100.0	1982	67.7	1986	85.6
	priv	all	...	...	1980	100.0	1982	62.9	1986	99.8
Colombia	cgov	all	...	...	1980	100.0	1984	113.3	1986	102.7
Venezuela	publ	mod	...	...	1978	100.0	1985	112.6	1987	92.6
	priv	mod	...	...	1978	100.0	1985	85.6	1987	78.6
Uruguay	publ	all	1968	100.0	1975	82.5	1980	67.3	1985	56.2
	priv	all	1968	100.0	1975	87.7	1980	57.9	1985	54.4

... = not available.

Note: cgov = central government; tgov = total government; prfr = private formal; publ = public sector; priv = private sector; mod = modern sector.
Source: A. Marshall (ed): *El empleo en el Estado en América Latina* (Geneva, International Institute for Labour Studies, forthcoming).

salaries received. Salary erosion was greater for the upper than for the lower grades.

There were, however, exceptions in Asia to the more common pattern of falling real wages for civil servants. In Malaysia, civil servants received a wage increase of 40 per cent in 1980 when government revenue soared. But during the subsequent economic recession and deterioration in public finances, real salary levels fell back again. In Singapore, a deliberate government policy of raising salaries in the public sector was introduced in 1982 to minimise the brain drain to the private sector and to raise professional standards in the public sector.

Industrialised market economies

In the IMECs, real government pay has risen in some countries and fallen in some others since the beginning of the 1980s. However, the same pattern as in other parts of the world is found with respect to the private sector. Private sector pay has increased more rapidly than government pay, not only in the 1980s but for most IMECs also in the 1970s. Table 4.3 is based on National Accounts data on compensation, which include not only wages but also contributions of both employers and employees to social security. Over the past 20 years, social security contributions have grown faster than wages, so that the trends in real compensation shown in table 4.3 overestimate those in wages. Another disadvantage of these data is that they refer to employees whose average working time has decreased over the past 20 years (through reduction of normal working time or increased part-time work). For some countries, there is information on compensation per working hour; this does affect trends in the 1970s but not significantly those in the 1980s. On the other hand, the advantage of these data is that they come from the same data source, so that they are more comparable between countries. Finally, it should be remembered that there can be considerable differences in compensation trends within the public service. Compensation trends in public administration and education usually run parallel, but are often different from those in the health sector. In addition, trends may vary according to level of government. In the United States, for example, real wages at the federal level have not kept up with private sector wages, while the opposite has happened in many states and municipalities.

In most countries for which data are available, real compensation per public service employee (PSE) went up between 1971 and 1980 with percentages ranging from 6 to 40 per cent, while in two countries there were slight decreases. Between 1980 and 1986, real compensation per PSE went down in five countries with percentages ranging from 1 to 16 per cent and up in seven countries with percentages ranging from 3 to 17 per cent. Between 1971 and 1980, real compensation per employee in the private sector rose faster than that for PSEs in most countries and the same pattern continued between 1980 and 1986.

Table 4.3. Real compensation per employee in government and the private sector: IMECs, 1971-80 and 1980-86 (percentage change)

	Government		Private sector	
	1971-80	1980-86	1971-80	1980-86
Australia	...	–13.2	...	1.1
Denmark	–4.9	–1.2	14.4	2.1
Finland	6.3	17.1	33.5	12.5
France	...	2.8 [1]	...	4.8 [1]
Germany, Fed. Rep. of	17.2	–2.2	32.1	6.1
Italy	...	13.0	...	7.8
Japan	38.9	14.5	28.9	10.4
Netherlands [2]	...	–15.8	...	–2.4
Norway [2]	16.1	3.4	24.4	5.7
Sweden	11.2	–7.1	20.8	2.3
United Kingdom	...	11.5	...	9.6
United States	–2.4	10.5	–0.4	3.6

... = not available.
[1] 1984. [2] Work-year.
Calculated from: OECD National Accounts.

2. Public-private pay comparisons

Most public-private pay comparisons are based on the notion that – for a particular occupation – employees in the public and the private sectors should receive the same pay. There are various techniques to make such comparisons, the results of which are shown in this section for both low and high-level occupations in the public service.

The principle of wage parity

Many governments accept the view that, in principle, pay levels in the private sector, and sometimes those in public enterprises too, should be used as a reference for public service pay levels. But for various reasons, this principle of wage parity has played a decreasingly important role in public service pay determination in recent years. The most important factor has been the deteriorating state of government finances (documented in Chapter 2) which has prompted governments to use public service pay as a major means of adjustment. In some cases, it has been argued that public-private pay inequalities are compensated by differences in other employment conditions, such as better social security provisions and greater stability of employment.

The erosion of the wage parity principle also stems from the relative size of the government as an employer on the labour market and from the procedures and institutions through which public service pay levels are adjusted. In sub-Saharan countries and many Asian countries, the public sector is the dominant employer in the formal sector. Even if public sector wages are lower than those in the private sector, public sector pay increases can generate imitative behaviour by the private sector, particularly for categories of workers in short supply in the economy. In Nigeria, for example, the restructuring of public sector pay in 1975 by the Udoji Commission brought about virtual parity with the private sector. The latter, however, swiftly restored its competitive pull for skills in short supply. In other cases, efforts made by governments to reach parity for PSEs were quickly eroded when, during a subsequent inflationary period, wages in the private sector adjusted more quickly to price rises.

In many African and Asian countries, salaries of civil servants are only infrequently adjusted by the government, sometimes on the recommendation of civil service salary review commissions. In an increasing number of Latin American countries, public service pay is determined through a process of joint consultation or collective bargaining while in the IMECs collective bargaining has become predominant. Collective bargaining and joint consultation give some guarantee that the wage parity principle will be taken into account but, as noted earlier, the precarious state of government finances has had a dominant impact on public service pay determination in the 1980s. In IPECs, the wage parity principle is built into the national job evaluation system, but there can be considerable gaps between pay in the so-called "material" and "non-material" sectors (see below).

Overall comparisons

Some governments in IMECs, for example, Japan and the United States, carry out regular surveys to compare public service and private sector pay, even though – as will be noted in the next chapter – the outcomes of these surveys are not always followed up. The results of the US survey in 1986 showed that, at the two lowest grades, federal government salaries were 10-17 per cent below those in the private sector, while at the highest grades they were 25-30 per cent below. A specially commissioned study for the Netherlands showed that, in 1984-85, net disposable incomes in the public service were only 4 per cent less than in the private sector at lower grades, but at higher grades the difference was more than 30 per cent.

The crucial problem for any wage comparison is to find similar occupations or tasks in the public and private sectors. For many jobs in the public sector, there may not even be roughly similar jobs in the private sector, particularly where, as in many developing countries, the formal sector may be limited in size and public sector employment dominant. Moreover, the same occupational title in different enterprises can hide considerable differences in levels of duty, responsibility and skills. Thus, subjective decisions must be made as to how a job should be classified. As a result, instead of focusing on the earnings of workers with comparable job characteristics, some researchers have focused on the earnings of workers with comparable personal characteristics, such as age, sex, level of education and length of service. Employing this methodology, studies have found that in the United States federal/private differentials are larger for women than for men and for non-White males than for White males (see also box 3.1). Moreover, moving down from the federal, to the state, to the local government, level, the size of the government/private earnings differential diminishes.

For the industrialised planned economy countries (IPECs), some comparisons can be made for two subsectors in the so-called "non-material" sector: education and culture; and health, social security, sports and tourism. As noted in Volume 3 of the *World labour report*, average wages in these sectors in all IPECs are lower than in the economy as a whole and in most the gap has widened during the 1980s, particularly in Hungary (see figure 4.1). In Bulgaria and Czechoslovakia, the differential is about 10 per cent, while in Hungary, Poland and the USSR it is between 15 and 30 per cent.

Traditionally, IPECs have given high priority to the industrial sectors which were considered the engine of economic growth; production in the "non-

Figure 4.1. Wage differentials in the socialised sector: Planned economies, 1980 and 1987 (average wage in the total economy = 100)

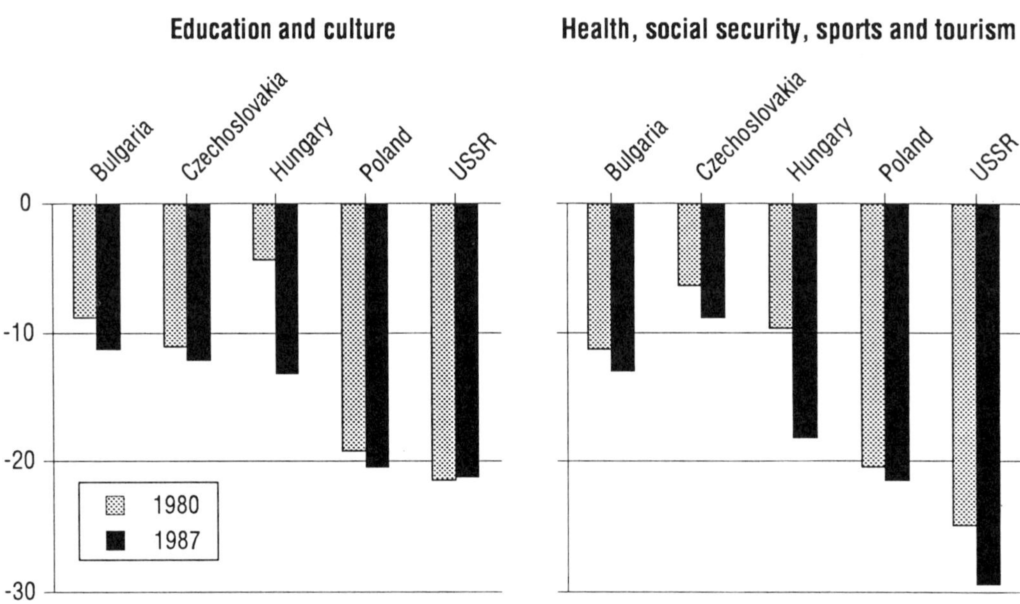

Calculated from CMEA: *Statistical year book 1987* (Moscow, 1988).

material" sector was deemed less important. As in most other countries, employees in social and cultural services have higher qualifications than those in the "productive" sectors of the economy. And, as also noted in Volume 3 of the *World labour report*, women represent 60 to 70 per cent of employees in "non-material" sectors.

Low and medium-level occupations

With real wages of PSEs falling over the past decade and a half in many DCs and some IMECs, a public service pay advantage for low-level occupations has become less evident. Recent analysis based on the ILO's October Inquiry and covering a few low and medium-level occupations finds that typists, office clerks, computer programmers and data entry typists earn less than their colleagues in banking and light and power (private or public enterprises). On the other hand, professional nurses in the health sector and refuse collectors in the public service earn more than a safety and health nurse in the iron and steel sector and unskilled construction labourers, respectively. The disadvantage for public service typists and office clerks in IMECs, and particularly in IPECs, is usually smaller than in DCs. The disadvantage is highest in sub-Saharan Africa and Latin America, where earnings or wage rates for these occupations in the public service can be 40-60 per cent lower than in the private sector. Since 1983, wage rate differentials for typists and office clerks have been more stable in DCs than in IMECs where they have deteriorated. However, for middle-level and newer occupations, such as computer programmers and data entry typists, pay differentials in IMECs have shrunk. This seems to indicate a more general trend towards greater pay flexibility in IMECs.

Other studies on public-private wage differentials for low-level occupations provide mixed evidence. The ILO study on civil service pay in Africa found that messengers and unskilled labourers were paid less by the government than by private enterprises in Ethiopia, Kenya, Nigeria, the Sudan and Zimbabwe in recent years. Other studies confirm that the public service usually offers lower wages than public enterprises, where pay determination is more akin to that in the private sector. For example, a survey in Mali revealed that civil servants were generally paid less than their counterparts in state companies. An independent study of the United Republic of Tanzania found that employees of public enterprises in both 1971 and 1980 earned significantly higher wages than civil servants, after standardising for educational level, job experience and other worker characteristics. In Thailand, public enterprises paid more than the civil service throughout the 1970s and 1980s for all categories of workers. In Zambia, a premium favourable to public enterprises existed for comparable jobs, ranging from 13 to 48 per cent for unskilled workers. Even when uniform or related pay scales in the entire public sector have been formulated in a particular country, public enterprises usually end up paying more than the public service.

However, it seems that wages for unskilled labourers in a number of Asian developing countries still remain higher in the public as compared to the private sector. This unskilled wage differential in favour of the public sector (which includes public enterprises) appears to be greater in Bangladesh and India than in South-East Asia and has been attributed to stronger labour market segmentation in South Asia than in Indonesia, Malaysia or the Philippines, and to the influence of trade unionism. In Africa a few country studies on civil service pay undertaken for the World Bank suggest that the governments concerned still pay higher wages for unskilled workers than the private sector. The authors emphasise, however, that the data base for making a careful analysis of wage differentials between the private and public sectors is extremely weak.

High-level occupations

There is greater consensus that the private sector pays more than the government for higher-level occupations and that, in many countries, this wage differential has widened during the 1980s. In Kenya, Nigeria, Uganda, Zambia and Zimbabwe, salaries for higher-level staff have been reported to be greater in private enterprises than in government service during the early 1980s. In Asian developing countries, the differential for graduates of tertiary institutions is typically in favour of the private sector. Practically all categories of professionals earn higher incomes in the private sector than in government employment. Singapore is an exception to this common pattern. With the government raising civil service pay as a deliberate policy, the entry-level salary for university graduates was higher in government employment than in private enterprises during 1983-85. In Malaysia, the entry-level salary for graduates is roughly comparable between the civil service and private companies, although experienced professionals normally earn more in the private sector.

The same pattern can be found in Latin America (for a detailed account for Venezuela, see box 4.1) and the IMECs. As noted earlier, high-level civil servants in the Netherlands and the United States earn about 30 per cent less than their colleagues in the private sector, which results in serious recruitment problems, demotivation and an exodus to the private sector.

4.1 Senior civil servants' pay in the 1980s: The case of Venezuela

Compared with other occupation levels, civil service managerial or directorial posts have incurred the greatest relative disadvantage. This is the result of (1) stricter salary legislation which excludes these officials from rights to severance pay and increments given to other career officials for length of service, efficiency and training, as well as overtime and holiday pay; (2) the fiscal policy of the Government which bears directly on wages. In effect, the wages of senior civil servants remained unchanged from 1982 until 1986. In this period, they were adversely affected by the elimination of some budget items which provided extra allowances (vehicles, expense accounts, etc.).

In addition to the exclusion from general pay rises decreed in this period, a ceiling was set on salaries in 1984 as part of austerity measures, and a salary reduction of 10 per cent was decreed for officials earning over Bs16,000, all of whom were managers. Although in 1986 this 10 per cent was reinstated upon the implementation of a new scale of wages and salaries, the average director's pay suffered a drop in real terms of more than 30 per cent.

In 1985, the average salary for these positions was Bs8,674. A study conducted in that year concluded that ministers (top civil servants) earned between 40 and 80 per cent less than general managers in private companies. If pay-related benefits were included, the salary of an average company manager would still be 1.6 to 2.5 times that of a minister. The same source reported that salaries for lower managerial positions in public administration are equivalent to those of line supervisors in large private enterprises.

Table 4.1.1. Managerial posts in national administration:[1] Salary components

Concept	Content
Basic salary	Between Bs7,700 and Bs15,400/month
Hierarchy premium	Between Bs800 and Bs2,000/month
Year-end bonus	22½ days' salary
Vacation bonus	3 to 15 days according to length of service

[1] Institutions under administrative career law.
Source: Oficina Central de Personal. Caracas internal records, 1988.

Table 4.4. Non-wage benefits for public and private sector employees: Côte d'Ivoire and Peru, 1985 and 1985-86 (percentages)

	Côte d'Ivoire (1985)		Peru (1985-86)	
	Public	Private	Public	Private
Contract	54.7	33.2	42.1	22.5
Paid holiday	92.5	53.2	91.7	59.3
Paid sick leave	90.1	48.5	91.6	57.3
Retirement pension	91.5	40.9	90.0	53.6
Social security	62.7	27.0	62.2	59.2

Source: J. van der Gaag, M. Stelcner and W. Vijverberg: *Public-private sector wage comparisons and moonlighting in developing countries: Côte d'Ivoire and Peru.* Living Standards Measurement Study Working Paper No. 52 (Washington, DC, World Bank, 1989).

Pay and motivation in the public service

While difficult to measure with precision, there is a positive association between sizeable cuts in pay and work efficiency. Many observers have linked the reduced morale and productivity of serving officials with the pay cuts they have suffered. Poor work and irregular attendance can become the norm for many who see little reason for working as hard as before when their real salaries have dropped by half or more. Their supervisors, themselves demoralised, find it difficult to enforce reasonable standards of performance. Under pressure to offset real income declines, subnormal effort may be rewarded by receipt of increments, irrespective of provisions specifying satisfactory performance, or even promotion. Supervisors are loathe to withhold increments from their staff who already have difficulties in making financial ends meet. Good work and devotion to duty become devalued and discourage even further application and effort. Falling living standards may encourage, if not compel, employees to seek supplementary, *sub rosa* forms of income.

A recent World Bank study on Peru and Côte d'Ivoire found that the public-private wage gap is partly responsible for the moonlighting activities of government workers. In Lima (Peru), more than a quarter of public sector employees have a secondary job, against less than 15 per cent in the private sector. In Côte d'Ivoire, where the phenomenon seems less prevalent, these percentages are 10 and 5 respectively. Most second jobs are in self-employment. The study also shows that other benefits, such as pensions and holidays, are much more prevalent in the public than in the private sector (table 4.4). In Côte d'Ivoire, about 55 per cent of public sector workers have a signed contract, compared with 33 per cent of private sector employees. Having a contract may be a proxy for job security and it is, therefore, likely that public sector workers are willing to forego some salary to obtain job security or tenure. Thus, the higher incidence of secondary jobs in the public sector may be explained by two factors: first, public sector wages are lower than those in the private sector; and second, employment security and lower work discipline in the public sector may make it easier for public sector workers to take on a second job.

In various sub-Saharan African countries, minimum wages and low wages in the public service have sunk to the point that a growing proportion of wage-earning households has been pushed below the poverty line. As a result, many PSEs supplement their wages by growing food. (See box 4.2 for the situation in the Ugandan civil service.)

3. The structure of public service pay

One consequence of the decline in the relative pay position of the public service has been the erosion of

4.2 Income and hours of work of civil servants in Uganda

Many African governments have recently undertaken a census of civil servants as a first step to civil service reform. The 1987 Census in Uganda, which was carried out with the ILO's help, shows a breakdown of normal working relations. The following is a quotation from the report's conclusions on income and hours of work.

"Almost all civil servants reported the inadequacy of salaries/wages to meet their basic needs. Nearly two-thirds (67 per cent) earned between UShs150-UShs199 for the month of May 1987. Therefore, civil servants have to spend some of the office time in parallel income-generating activities as a matter of survival. This reduces commitment to work, hence late coming, absenteeism, inefficiency, corruption – all of which lead to low work output. A similarly high percentage is reported to be engaged in agricultural related activities to make ends meet. Although the authenticity of some of those answers can be questioned, it has great bearing on the actual number of hours civil servants spend on productive office work. Also, it implies that the standing regulation regarding office hours (8.00 a.m.-12.45 p.m. and 2.00 p.m.-5.00 p.m.) has lost its effectiveness. It may be argued that, to some extent, transport difficulties have been a contributory factor to late coming and early departure from work, hence low work output. The provision of government transport to and from places of work to civil servants if properly co-ordinated and implemented will make some contribution to the global solution to the problem."

Figure 4.2. Pay differentials in the public service (office clerk = 100); mid-1980s (median value of index per group of countries)

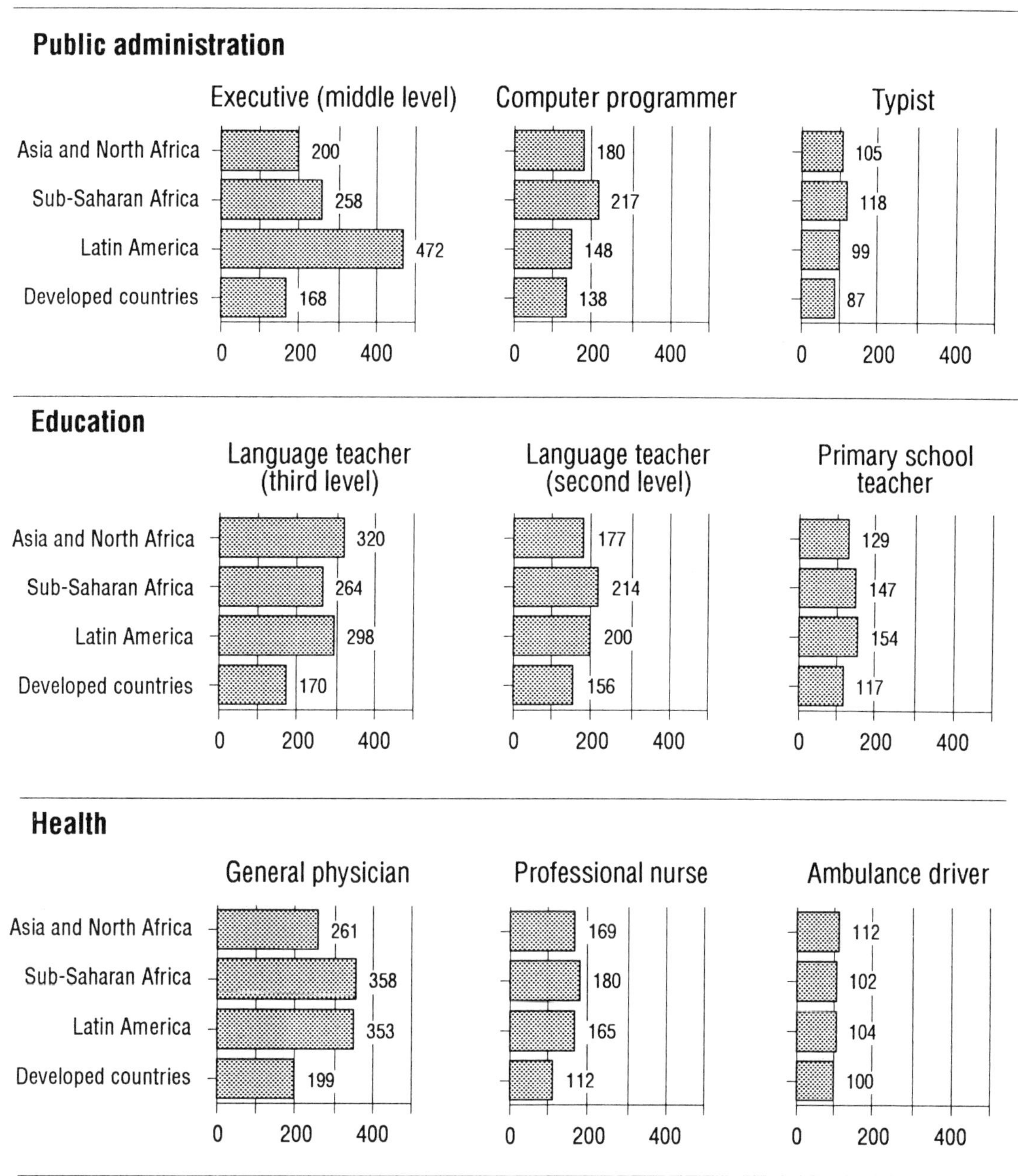

Source: Calculated from the ILO October Inquiry.

pay systems and related personnel practices. With basic pay increases restricted, attempts have been made to protect public service pay in other ways, such as the granting of additional increments, easy promotions, further allowances and bonuses and more extensive payments in kind and other fringe benefits (such as housing). These various manipulations have often undermined the overall logic of the

Table 4.5. Women's pay in government occupations: 1985 (men's pay = 100)

Country	Public administration					Health			Education	
	Pay concept	Middle-level manager (central government)	Pro-grammer	Typist	Office clerk	Physician	Nurse	Physio-therapist	Language teacher (3rd level)	Primary-school teacher
Developing countries										
Cyprus	ea	63	91	...	87	94	90	...	104	96
Jordan	wr	100	82	98	76	87	83	80	68	92
Kenya	wr	...	91	97	68	95	73	...	113	81
Korea, Republic of	ea	...	...	...	...	94	106	72	86	80
Nigeria (Lagos)	ea	...	...	...	...	99 [2]	88 [2]	...	...	...
Mauritius	ea	...	...	...	...	...	...	...	102	...
Peru (Lima)	ea	...	85 [1]	...	88 [1]	75 [1]	95 [1]	85 [1]	...	90 [1]
Singapore	wr	94	87	80	81	81	79	105 [3]	84	119
Thailand	ea	...	...	...	...	...	100	86	97	99
Developed countries										
Canada	wr	...	94	93	97	...	...	...	...	...
Czechoslovakia	ea	97	...	...	...	...	...	...	...	...
Finland	ea	81	107	117	105	85	100	109	82	95
Norway	ea	97	...	...	...	...	101	103	...	97
Sweden	ea	...	...	...	...	94	100	103	97 [1]	98 [1]
United Kingdom	ea	...	...	...	...	...	86 [1]	...	...	...
United States	ea	...	85 [3]	...	...	...	...	...	75 [1]	...

... = not available.
Note: ea = earnings; wr = wage rate.
[1] 1987. [2] 1983. [3] 1986.
Source: ILO October Inquiry.

public service pay system, in terms of both effectiveness and equity. But before examining the questions of basic pay and allowances, we give a brief impression of pay differentials within the public service – between subsectors and some occupations, and between the sexes.

Pay differentials within the public service

The ILO October Inquiry publishes statistics on pay for 21 occupations in the three main subsectors of the public service: public administration, education and health. For most occupations, it reports earnings or wage rates per month. Earnings and wage rate differentials between occupations in the public service do not differ much because few government employees receive overtime payments.

Differentials between occupations

Out of the 21 occupations for which data are available, ten were chosen as most characteristic of pay differentials in the public service. Then a differentials index was calculated for all ten occupations on the basis of an office clerk's pay. For each regional grouping shown in figure 4.2, the median value of the index was calculated for about ten countries.

Differentials are highest in Latin America where the pay of a medium-level executive in public administration is five times that of an office clerk while a university teacher's pay and that of a general physician is three and three-and-a-half times as high respectively. In sub-Saharan Africa, pay differentials in health – though not in education and public administration – are greater than in Latin America. However, it is noteworthy that the relative pay of middle-level occupations, such as computer programmers, second-level language teachers, nurses and X-ray technicians, is higher in sub-Saharan Africa than elsewhere. This is probably due to the shortage of this type of personnel. Pay differentials are again smaller in Asia and North Africa, particularly in health and public administration. By far the lowest differentials are found in the developed countries where pay for high-skilled occupations is on average not more than twice that of office clerks.

Pay differentials can also be examined from other angles. For example, in planned economy countries pay differentials are considerably lower than in market economy countries. And in French-speaking African countries, pay levels in education are high in comparison with other sectors of the public service.

Differentials between men and women

In two previous *World labour reports* (Volumes 2 and 3), pay differentials between men and women were examined for the manufacturing sector. Based on data from the ILO *Year book of labour statistics*, fairly large differentials were found, ranging from 10 to 55 per cent. A substantial part of this wage gap is due to occupational segregation – the fact that men tend to work in high-paid and women in low-paid occupations. This segregation is explained by many factors, such as education, culture and attitudes, all of which can have an indirectly discriminating effect. An idea of the directly discriminating effect can be obtained by comparing pay differentials between men and women for the same occupation. Yet not all the wage gap can be explained by direct discrimination or, in other words, by the violation of the equal pay for equal work principle. Men often have higher pay because they stay longer in the job than women and therefore have accumulated longer service.

In most countries, pay differentials between men and women are smaller in the public service than in the private sector. Governments often wish to be model employers and are therefore more sensitive to criticism of discrimination. But there are also some economic and practical reasons why pay differentials are smaller in the public service. As noted in Chapter 2, women represent a much higher proportion of government employment than of private sector employment. Moreover, women often pursue a career in the education and health sectors. At the same time, some occupational segregation exists in these sectors, because relatively higher proportions of women work in lower-paid occupations, such as kindergarten and primary-school teachers or as auxiliary and professional nurses.

Thus, it is understandable that wage differentials are smallest in lower-paid occupations, where women are strongly represented (table 4.5). In typically female occupations such as typing, nursing and primary school teaching, the wage gap can vary between –20 and +20 per cent, while in higher-paid occupations such as middle-level managers (in central government) and physicians, the wage gap is consistently unfavourable to women, ranging between –25 and 0 per cent.

Basic salary: Scales and steps

Government is usually the largest employer of highly qualified personnel and in most developing countries, particularly in sub-Saharan Africa, it is a dominant employer in the formal labour market as well. In setting salary scales for its employees, the government has to take into account various considerations, such as its programmes, its ability to pay and the wages of alternative jobs in the private sector. Once salary scales have been set, they are often not reviewed regularly, with the result that they can get out of line with salaries paid elsewhere in the economy. Another tricky issue is deciding the number of steps within each salary scale and the criteria for which these increments are given. In most countries, public service employees receive increments either for years of service and/or as a reward for merit.

This section deals specifically with the issue of wage compression, which was touched on earlier in this chapter, and the length of salary scales. Finally, it provides an overview of how performance pay is applied in the public service of industrialised market economies.

Wage compression

Since the 1970s, the salary scales for public service employees have become more compressed in most countries. In figures 4.3 and 4.4 this is measured by the ratio between the minima of the top and the bottom scale, except for French-speaking African countries where available data only allow a comparison between the maximum of the top scale and the minimum of the bottom scale. In all African countries with a British-type personnel system except Kenya, the ratio fell between 1975 and 1985. The fall was most dramatic for Zimbabwe, where the ratio dropped by 61 per cent, and Ethiopia, where it was halved. Secondly, the ratio continued to differ noticeably among countries in 1985, although not as much as in 1975. For African countries with French-type personnel systems, the experience was different in two important ways. First, the ratio did not decline in four French-speaking countries (Benin, Chad, Niger and Togo), although it did decline in the other five. Secondly, the ratio tended to be lower under French-type structures than British-type ones. All three countries with the lowest ratios in 1985 had French-type systems (Mauritania, Morocco and Tunisia).

A trend towards basic salary compression was also found in other non-African countries for which the ratios are available. It was very strong in Pakistan where the ratio declined from 30 to less than 10 between 1972 and 1987. The same trend is found for some IMECs, though the ratio is usually lower than in the developing countries.

The concern of governments to protect the living standards of low-paid public servants against the ravages of prolonged inflation at a time of severe constraints on government expenditure helps explain the narrowing of occupational differentials in the civil service in many countries. Flat-rate, across-the-board salary increases or increases which favoured the lower paid were common during the 1970s and 1980s and naturally compressed top-bottom differentials. Concern with egalitarian ideals may also have prompted a few governments to narrow the spreads. The expanded output of tertiary educational institutions in many developing countries raised the supply of graduates in the labour market and could also have contributed to reducing occupational differentials.

Length of salary scale

In most countries, public service employees are paid according to salary scales. The number of steps within each scale is often dependent on the grade, with low and middle grades having more steps than high grades. The number of steps for the typical government employee varies between 8 and 20. However, there may be only one step in the salary scale of top civil servants, as in many countries with a British-type personnel system. It is generally accepted that public service employees with a lifelong career should be paid more with rising age and family responsibilities, irrespective of any change in the nature of duties. It is also felt that efficiency considerations are served by the periodic granting of increments that strengthen the employee's attachment to his employer and permit a reward for experience. Efficiency may be even better served if increments are paid on condition of satisfactory performance of work. This motivation disappears when increments are automatically received although the stronger attachment to the employer remains.

Scales with many increments have their critics and their defenders. Critics claim that lengthy scales are inefficient and uneconomic. They argue that, with the passage of time, increments tend to be given almost automatically, except for flagrantly shoddy work. Employees who are less than efficient, unless outstandingly so, will still receive their increments. Long scales are uneconomic as these employees will continue to receive increments until they reach the maximum of their scale, which can be considerably higher than the scale minimum. In Ethiopia, there is one scale with a maximum salary of nearly three times the minimum. In Zimbabwe, the maximum of one scale offers slightly more than twice the scale minimum. In Pakistan, for seven scales, the ratio of the maximum to the minimum salary ranges from 2.0 to 2.2. However, in most countries and for most grades, the maximum of a scale is usually not more than 50 per cent above its minimum.

Defenders of long scales argue that the economy of short scales is illusory. With short scales, many employees soon hit the ceiling. The ensuing stagnation of basic salaries is not consistent with offering lifelong, career employment, and the pressures to promote employees at the scale maximum out of their grade will prove irresistible in practice. Once promoted, they naturally receive more than the maximum salary of their previous grade. Thus, the economy of short scales is more apparent than real. Moreover, efficiency is not served when employees are promoted who would not have been promoted had they been on longer salary scales.

The optimal length of a salary scale is related to the rules and practices governing promotion. There can be no rigid or doctrinaire approach. Where there are sufficient promotion possibilities for certain grades, scales may be short. But longer scales may be appropriate in the following circumstances: where there are few promotion opportunities to other grades, as in education and health; where vacancies for the next grades up are filled by recruitment from outside; or where the organisation of work results in relatively few posts in the grades just above.

In many OECD countries, governments have been looking for new ways to motivate their staff. Their search has been prompted by a more economic approach to government service management, at a time when government budgets are being cut and public scrutiny of its efficiency and effectiveness has increased. Moreover, traditional incentives, such as promotion prospects, have been reduced in recent years by cut-backs in staffing levels. In addition,

Figure 4.3. Ratio of top to bottom pay in the civil service: African countries, 1975 and 1985

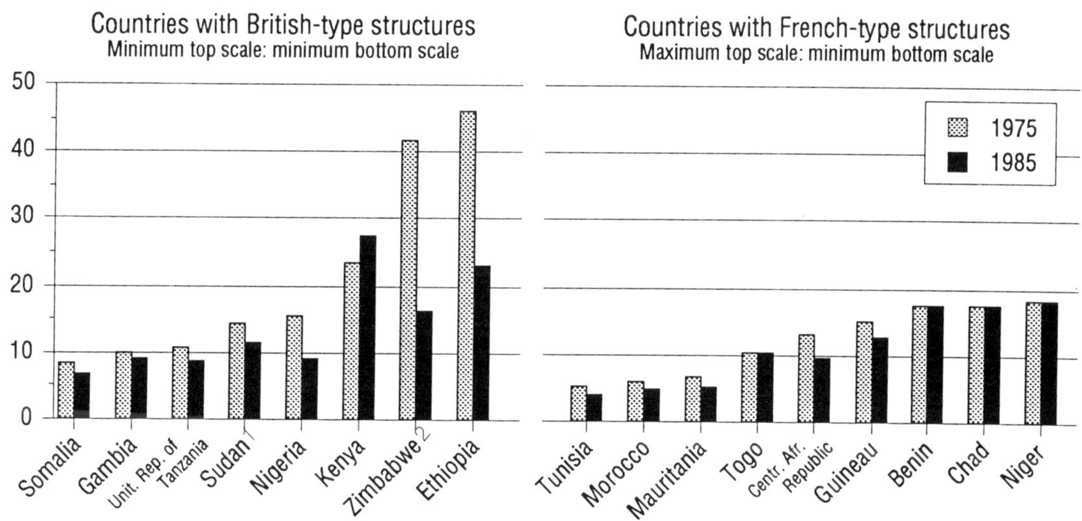

[1] The second ratio refers to 1986 rather than 1985. [2] The first ratio refers to 1976 and the second to 1986.
Source: Preliminary data from D. Robinson: *Civil service pay in Africa* (Geneva, ILO, forthcoming).

pride in performing a service for the public and intrinsic job satisfaction have lost some of their shine, even though they are still important sources of motivation for senior civil servants. Box 4.3 reports on recent experience with performance pay.

Expansion of allowances

Falling real basic salaries of public servants and the compression of the salary distribution have contributed, almost inevitably, to an expansion of cash and non-cash allowances, particularly in the developing countries. The list of allowances is long, though not all will be found in any one country, and includes cost-of-living allowance, government-provided housing at nominal rent or housing allowance, transportation allowance, nature-of-work allowance, representation allowance, family allowance, leave travel allowance and qualification allowance for higher qualifications. Increasing the rates of allowances and introducing new ones have helped to slow the erosion in earnings but generally have not been sufficient to prevent real pay from shrinking. Allowances now constitute a significant portion of the total pay of civil servants in many developing countries. The ILO study on civil service pay in Africa estimates that the share of allowances in total pay was 27 per cent in Ethiopia in 1983, 45 per cent in Morocco in 1984 and 29 per cent in the Sudan in 1985.

With a few exceptions, notably the cost-of-living allowance, allowances are more likely to be received by higher-level officials (e.g. government housing or a representation allowance). Of particular importance in this connection is government-provided housing at nominal rent to senior civil servants. However, new problems of equity arise when there is insufficient government accommodation for all the officials eligible for this benefit. The unsuccessful official in effect suffers a significant pay reduction relative to his colleagues in the same grade provided with government housing. Disappointment can be transformed into resentment. Furthermore, the system of allocating housing to applicants can become a source of patronage, while applicants expend office time and effort trying to improve their chance of success.

It appears that in many countries allowances are more generous in private corporations and public enterprises than in the civil service. Where basic salaries are already lower for civil servants, the pay comparison becomes even more invidious, with obvious implications for resignations from the public service. Private and parastatal companies may sometimes have used better allowances to circumvent government-imposed wage restraint measures and wage guide-lines.

The expansion of allowances has made the task of monitoring government expenditure on civil servants more difficult. Some cash allowances are not considered part of the wage bill. Non-cash allowances like government-supplied houses or cars may

Figure 4.4. Ratio of top to bottom pay in the civil service (minimum top scale; minimum bottom scale): Selected countries in Asia, Latin America and IMECs, 1970s and 1980s

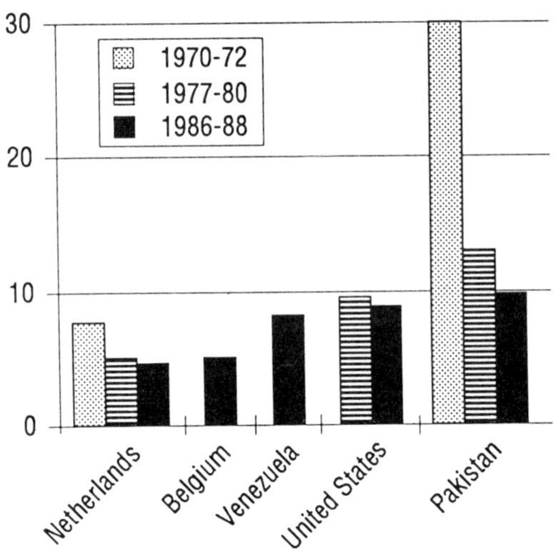

Source: ILO Secretariat.

be omitted completely from government current expenditure.

Allowances are more likely to be abused than revisions of basic salaries, not least because they are less transparent. In one country, the foreign travel allowance was so generous that a number of senior civil servants spent at least one-third of each year abroad. In another country, a meeting allowance was given to officials for attending meetings during which the normal business of government would be discussed. The number of meetings rose dramatically and, as a result, some officials were rarely to be found in their offices. In a third country, an overnight allowance was provided to agricultural extension workers when they had to travel to locations more than 25 kilometres from their duty station. Farmers living within the 25 kilometre radius were rarely visited.

Problems such as these have caused some countries to have second thoughts on the growing importance of allowances, and to consider whether it would be better to reform or abolish some allowances by incorporating them into basic salary.

4. Public-private comparison of social security protection

Public service employees may be covered by a wide variety of social security schemes. There are often special schemes for the army and the police. In some countries, particularly English- and Spanish-speaking, teaching personnel have their own scheme. Other special schemes exist in a number of countries for particular public services (such as the judiciary). In countries where central government staff are covered by an unfunded scheme – that is, directly financed by the state budget – local government staff are usually covered by a funded pension scheme.

Some studies carried out in Latin America in the 1970s ranked social security schemes according to their benefits; members of the armed forces, followed (or in some countries preceded) by civilian civil servants, topped the list, workers in certain public services or undertakings came next in some countries, and salaried employees and manual workers in the private sector came third. Policies for harmonising and unifying social security, which countries are pursuing with varying degrees of determination and success, are no doubt contributing to mitigating such differences.

In a decreasing number of developing countries, civil servants are practically the only category of workers that benefit from social security protection. This is the case, for example, as regards invalidity, old-age and survivors' benefits in Afghanistan, Botswana, Burma, Ethiopia, Malawi, Sierra Leone, Somalia and Thailand. In some African and Asian countries, where public service employees are covered by a pension scheme, private sector workers are covered only by a provident fund (i.e. a compulsory savings scheme).

Thus, for a number of countries and certain categories of PSEs, it is not possible to make a comparison with the private sector. Moreover, in some countries, there is an important distinction between civil servants and other PSEs employed under contract. Civil servants who hold a permanent post and enjoy stability of employment are generally covered by their own social security scheme in these countries, while those employed under contract are usually covered by the statutory scheme for private sector workers. In developing countries, a much higher proportion of workers in the public service – civil servants and employees under contract – than in the private sector is normally covered by a social security scheme. Finally, there are a number of countries where civil service social security schemes are integrated into a general scheme, at least for some contingencies, with the result that public-private sector differentials are small or non-existent. This section

4.3 Performance pay in the civil service (OECD countries)

The main types of performance-related pay used in the public service of OECD countries include:

- lump-sum bonuses;
- variable progression on fixed incremental scales;
- increments of variable size;
- additional increments on top of the normal pay scale.

Lump-sum bonuses are widely used. In Canada, under the scheme covering senior civil servants, bonuses are given to high performers who have reached the top of their salary range. Those rated "outstanding" receive a bonus of up to 10 per cent of their basic annual salary; those rated "superior" a bonus of up to 7 per cent. In Japan, almost all employees can receive a "diligence allowance" twice a year. In June, the allowance can vary between 35 and 75 per cent of the June reference salary; and in December between 40 and 90 per cent. In the Netherlands, high performers at the top of their salary scales can receive one-off bonuses of up to 15 per cent of the annual reference salary for most senior grades, and up to 3 per cent for the most junior ones. In the United States, lump-sum performance bonuses are awarded to members of the Senior Executive Service (between $10,000 and $20,000) and to staff covered by the Performance Management and Recognition System (between 2 and 10 per cent of annual salary, depending on the appraisal rating). In most remaining countries, the award of performance bonuses is not explicitly linked to appraisal ratings, and this often creates confusion and envy.

Under the system of variable progression along fixed incremental scales, not only seniority or length of service but also performance are taken into account to determine the rate of progression. This system is quite widely used in the United States and is also found in Japan and the United Kingdom. In the United States, pay can be increased to any (of the six) pay levels for senior executives, or reduced one level. Salary progression for middle managers and supervisors consists of annual general pay adjustments and within-grade step increases (called merit increases). The general pay adjustment is fixed at a given percentage each year, but the amount of the increase actually received depends on performance ratings.

Under the system of increments of variable size, there is a salary range but no fixed rate of incremental salary progression. In Canada, senior civil servants are given annual salary increases ranging from 0 to 10 per cent of base salary, solely on merit.

Some systems provide additional performance-related increments for staff who have reached the top of their salary scale. These additional bonuses represent a permanent salary increase rather than a one-off lump sum. This system is practised in the United Kingdom for Grades 2 to 7. The discretionary, permanent increments are based on appraisal ratings and can range from £3,000 a year for a Deputy Secretary (Grade 2) to £850 for a Principal (Grade 7).

A crucial issue for all performance-related systems is whether and how to control the proportion of staff qualifying for performance awards. This has important implications, not only for the cost of the system, but also for the impact on staff motivation. One approach is to establish a quota for the proportion of staff who may receive awards. This was done for an experimental performance bonus scheme in the United Kingdom. But the system was abandoned in 1987 because, in the case of Grades 2 and 3 and scientific and technical staff, control of the numbers receiving awards is exercised via performance rating distributions. In the Canadian system, only 5 per cent of an agency's staff can be rated "outstanding", and up to 25 per cent "superior". These proportions are taken into account when drawing up the performance-pay budget. In the United States, the allocation of awards is controlled by a budget limitation, ranging from about 3 per cent of the aggregate payroll for executive personnel to about 1 per cent for middle managers and supervisors.

There has been very little systematic analysis of whether these schemes have in fact improved performance. The available evidence shows rather mixed results. In general, pay-performance schemes that are not linked with a clearly defined appraisal system give rise to much negative reaction from employees. This happened, for example, with the performance bonus scheme for senior executive personnel in the United States. In 1987, the General Accounting Office noted that a disproportionate number of bonuses had gone to high-level executives. The size of the bonus can also be a bone of contention. Where marginal tax rates are high, most of the awarded lump sums may flow back to the Treasury. Such problems are less likely in the case of salary increments which are usually permanent. Inadequate funding and salary compression also pose problems. In both Canada and the United States, the potential impact of performance-related pay systems on motivation of senior managers has been undermined by problems in the overall salary structure for these groups.

first establishes to what extent civil service social security schemes are integrated into a general scheme (covering either all residents or all employees) and then concentrates on comparing the statutory schemes applicable to civil servants and private sector workers separately.

Coverage of general social security systems

Civil servants and members of the armed forces were among the first occupational groups to receive the benefit of social protection, more specifically of pensions. Such a benefit was originally granted as a favour by the sovereign before the right thereto was recognised in return for past service. This explains why for a long time the prospect of a pension, like security of employment, was one of the attractions of public service, compensating to some extent for the restrictions inherent in the service.

In the industrialised countries, the special schemes for civil servants remained in effect when the earliest schemes of protection were established for other categories of workers. However, in the light of social security policies based on the principles of unity and universality, which characterised the changes in social protection that occurred after the Second World War, doubts began to be voiced about the separate status of schemes that covered only limited social or occupational categories, including the special schemes for civil servants or public service employees. In most developing countries these schemes generally originated with the colonial administration and, with the exception of Latin America, they were established relatively recently. As a result, they were generally set up from the beginning on a unitary basis, for reasons of efficiency, equity and economy of resources.

In a number of IMECs, civil servants participate in schemes established for all residents, in particular a pension scheme. In Finland, New Zealand and Sweden, the general system provides a flat-rate benefit or one containing a flat-rate component. In Canada, Denmark, Japan, the Netherlands and the United Kingdom, the general system provides all or part of the total benefits according to the length of residence or the period of insurance. In Switzerland, these benefits vary according to the past earnings of the beneficiaries or of their bread-winner, but are subject to an upper limit. In Australia, a large number of retired civil servants benefit from a means-tested social assistance scheme, because their pensions are too low. The integration of civil servants in a general social security scheme may furthermore be accomplished at a second level if the universal basic scheme is coupled with a supplementary scheme covering private and public employees alike (as in Canada, Japan, Norway and Sweden). The impact of integration on civil servants' pension schemes is discussed in box 4.4.

As regards medical care, in the countries where there is a national health service covering the entire population, as in Australia, Denmark, Greece, Italy, New Zealand, Portugal and the United Kingdom, the benefit of this service is available to civil servants as well. The same is true of the national insurance schemes, like those in force in Norway and Sweden, and of the similar provincial schemes in Canada.

In the USSR and the other planned economy countries, where the State is involved in all sectors of the economy, the mere fact that they are in the service of a public authority does not as a rule give civil servants a special status vis-à-vis other workers; they are in principle subject to the same social security system.

The integration of civil servants in a single social security scheme covering everyone in employment or carrying on an occupation has been achieved in several countries of Latin America, for example, Bolivia (since 1949), Costa Rica (1947), Ecuador (1963), Panama (1941), Peru (since 1947 part of the pension scheme for salaried employees, which was itself amalgamated in 1973 with the scheme for manual workers) and Nicaragua; in the English-speaking countries of the Caribbean, notably Jamaica (since 1965), Barbados (1966), Guyana (1969) and Trinidad and Tobago (1971); as well as, among African countries, Algeria (since 1 January 1985), the Libyan Arab Jamahiriya (since 1 June 1981), and Rwanda (since 1962); and, among countries in Asia, Fiji (since 1971), Kuwait (1976) and Singapore (as regards certain categories of civil servants). Most commonly, the integration of civil servants in these schemes is part of a policy for unifying the social security system; in some cases, for example, in Peru, this integration was an important stage in the unifying process; in others, such as Algeria, it was the culmination of the process. In the United States, on the other hand, "social security" (that is, the federal pension scheme) was established as a unified scheme in 1935. The integration of civil servants from 1987 was both a means of broadening the financial base of the scheme – in order to cope with future liabilities resulting from the ageing of the population – and of bringing the social protection of civil servants – for whom a new supplementary pension scheme has been instituted – into line with that of workers in the private sector.

Financing

In some countries, benefits in the event of temporary incapacity for work (owing to sickness, maternity or accident), or pension benefits in case of a long-term contingency, are financed directly by the state budget and not by employer and employee contributions. The soundness of this solution, a salient feature of which is that the civil service scheme is not financially independent of the state budget, has recently been questioned in several developing countries. It presupposes that current outgoings for pensions are financed by current receipts, according to what is known as the pay-as-you-go or assessment technique. No capital is accumulated to meet future expenditure, the amount of which may vary over time. This contrasts with schemes that are financially autonomous and have their own resources (see box 4.5). On the other hand, in the great majority of countries, the protection of wage earners in the private sector is financed, at least in part, through con-

4.4 Integration of civil servants into general pension schemes: Problems and issues

The integration of civil servants into a generalised social security pension scheme gives rise to a number of questions for which there is no general answer. Should a special pension scheme for civil servants be allowed to continue? Should such a scheme remain in effect even if the general social security scheme provides benefits proportional to earnings? Should the civil servants' special scheme be co-ordinated with the basic scheme or schemes? Should the entire special scheme remain in effect as a transitional measure? The answers to these questions depend on a comparison of the levels of protection offered by the two schemes. Much depends, in particular, on the ceilings for benefits; the guaranteed replacement rate (benefits as a proportion of earnings) and the basis for the calculation of pensions; whether there are supplementary schemes in the private sector and their coverage and level; and, more generally, the ability to finance a possible supplementary scheme for civil servants.

Integration could well fall short of its objective – to ensure greater solidarity while at the same time improving where necessary the protection of those concerned – if the civil service pension scheme remains intact. This could result in the State and the employing authority incurring a double liability, and the provision of unjustifiably high protection for the beneficiaries, with both schemes together producing an excessively generous replacement rate.

Such considerations prompted the United Kingdom, when national insurance was introduced and extended to cover civil servants in 1948, to deduct a certain amount per year of service from civil service pensions. Deductions based on different calculations are also made in the Bahamas, Barbados, Canada, Cyprus, Norway, Panama, Sweden and Switzerland. The net effect is to limit the role of the civil service pension scheme to provision of a supplementary guarantee to that provided by the generalised social security scheme.

In several developing countries, for example, Algeria, Ecuador, Libyan Arab Jamahiriya and Peru, a simpler and much more radical solution has been applied, as in the USSR and other planned economy countries: the integration of civil servants into a unified social security scheme without the maintenance, even as a supplement, of a special scheme for civil servants. This was also the route taken for the integration into the general scheme of protection of civil servants in Fiji, and of some categories of civil servants in Singapore, though in Singapore they were integrated into a National Provident Fund.

Transitional measures may be needed to protect the acquired rights of civil servants who were already in the service when the integrated scheme came into force. Thus, in some instances, it was decided – as in Fiji, Peru, Singapore and the United States – that the previous scheme would remain as a transitional measure and would continue to be applicable to civil servants already in the service, at least to those who opted for this solution. By no means all the countries referred to earlier have adopted such transitional measures, because several of them concluded that – all things considered – the unification did not materially affect the rights of civil servants.

Today the trend towards schemes covering all workers is visible in countries of diverse political, economic and social backgrounds. But it is by no means general. In addition, it should be remembered that the integration of public employees in a general scheme does not always imply the disappearance of special schemes, which sometimes remain in force as supplementary schemes. Finally, integration often leaves untouched certain categories of public employees who, for various reasons, continue to qualify only for benefits of already established special schemes: they may enjoy special conditions of employment; very often they hold a privileged position in public life; and/or they are able to defend their corporate interests. This is the situation *a fortiori* in countries and sectors where state employees have not been integrated in the general social security schemes and separate provision is made for them.

tributions (which does not necessarily involve use of the technique of funding). The consequential advantage for civil servants should be judged on a comprehensive evaluation of their position compared with that of workers in the private sector, including salaries and wages after deduction of contributions. It should be stressed that the financing of civil servants' pensions through the budget in no way excludes the possibility, if not of charging contributions, of at least making deductions from their salaries for pension purposes (as happens e.g. in Austria, France, Italy, Norway, Portugal, Spain, Togo and the United Kingdom), even though the proceeds are merged into the state budget and are not specifically allocated to the financing of pensions.

Pension benefit levels

The level of pensions depends on a combination of several factors: the remuneration on which benefits are calculated, the method of computation, and the mechanism for adjusting the level of benefit once in payment. On all three counts, pension benefits of civil servants are better than those of private sector workers. The remuneration on which the calculation of civil service pensions is based is generally either the final salary, which is normally a career peak, or the average salary received during a relatively short period before retirement. For private sector workers, the reference period is generally longer (and not necessarily the most recent, in order to allow for possible fluctuations of earnings) or corresponds to the entire duration of the person's working life. Moreover, under most statutory private sector schemes, the earnings taken into account are subject to a ceiling, while this is rarely applied to civil servants' salaries. Finally, the formula for calculating pensions is generally more favourable for civil servants. Thus the replacement rate (the ratio between

4.5 The financing of public employee pension schemes

Information gathered through the ILO inquiry on the cost of social security indicates that the majority of public service pension schemes are unfunded, although there are instances of funded schemes. This applies in both the industrialised and the developing countries. Furthermore, unfunded schemes generally appear to be financed uniquely by the public authorities, while there is usually employee participation in the financing of funded schemes.

In funded schemes, governments still carry the largest part of expenditure and their participation is often more than double that of employees (box table 4.5). But as the scheme reaches maturity, a larger part of its revenues originates from investment income. It is understandable that benefit payments make up the bulk of total expenditure, but it is noteworthy that surpluses in 1983 were high, often more than 50 per cent of total receipts.

The intrinsic financial characteristics of public service pension schemes are similar to those of occupational pension schemes in the private sector or a statutory national pension scheme. The considerations relating to funding of public employee pension schemes are, however, different from those concerning the funding of occupational pension schemes in the private sector.

The perpetuity of government and its taxing power, in themselves, ensure the security of public employee pensions. Moreover, funding will not reduce the future tax burden if the assets of the public employee scheme are held in the government's own securities, because the interest payments on these securities will in any case have to be found through taxation. On the other hand, funding constitutes an acknowledgement by the government of its responsibility for the accrued pensions of its employees and awareness of the size of the liabilities will discourage undue generosity.

The growth of pension costs, a feature of maturing pension schemes, is particularly acute in developing countries and has given rise to budgetary difficulties in certain countries. In the circumstances, scheme modifications have been considered such as introducing employee contributions, reducing the level of benefits or changing the nature of the benefits. However, the protection of civil service pensions which is enshrined in certain constitutions has presented an obstacle to such action.

Table 4.5.1. Financial structure of funded pension schemes for civil servants, 1983 (percentage of receipts)

Country	Receipts				Expenditure		Surplus for the year
	Employee contributions %	Government participation %	Investment income %	Total receipts [1] %	Benefits %	Total expenditure [2] %	%
Australia [3]	16	40	27	100	48	53	47
Canada	25	24	40	100	18	19	81
Colombia [4]	20	77	3	100	86	91	9
Japan [4, 5]	24	56	20	100	77	77	23
Netherlands	17	30	53	100	37	38	62
Philippines	35	40	20	100	39	52	48
Switzerland	19	54	26	100	49	51	49
United States	12	55	33	100	50	52	48

[1] Including, in certain cases, miscellaneous income. [2] Including, in certain cases, administration or miscellaneous expenditure. [3] Federal employees. [4] Including medical benefit. [5] National Public Service Mutual Aid Assocation.

Source: ILO: *The cost of social security, 1981-83* (Geneva, 1988).

pensions and earnings) is higher for civil servants than for members of statutory private sector schemes, even in countries where civil service pensions replace rather than supplement the pensions guaranteed by general schemes. These advantages – absence of a salary ceiling and preferential rates of benefit – are also applicable to other cash benefits, such as sickness and maternity benefits.

However, in comparing pension benefits for civil servants and private sector workers, two additional considerations have to be taken into account. First, the comparison has so far been based solely on statutory social security schemes. While some groups of civil servants are covered by supplementary occupational schemes, coverage is widespread in the private sector, at least in the industrialised countries. In some countries, for example, Belgium, Bolivia, France, the Netherlands and Switzerland, this protection extends to all or nearly all workers in the private sector. In several countries, such as France, the Federal Republic of Germany and Morocco, there are also supplementary pension schemes for public service employees other than state civil servants, whose basic protection is provided by the general social security schemes. In addition, certain rules applicable to private sector schemes have been introduced into public service schemes, so as to achieve greater comparability. Such modifications may reduce the pension levels of civil servants. In the United States, for example, under the pension scheme for federal civil servants in force since 1984, the retirement pension of each member of a married couple of civil servants is reduced by 10 per cent, unless both spouses waive the right to a survivor's pension. In Australia, the option of converting pensions into the payment of a capital sum has been liberalised, which if exercised saves the cost of adjusting pensions to the movement of salaries or prices. In addition, there are some countries where the actual replacement rate of civil servants' pensions is very low. Pensions may be calculated on a lump-sum basis unrelated to salaries – a state of affairs which in Spain was partially rectified by the introduction of a supplementary contributory scheme. Or various allowances which may constitute a large part of aggregate pay are not taken into account in calculating pension benefits (see section 3). This is particularly so for those holding responsible posts, in such countries as Côte d'Ivoire, France, Gabon and Morocco.

Another aspect of the public-private comparison is the procedure for adjusting pension benefit levels to changing economic conditions. In the private sector, the adjustment of pensions generally takes into account the movement of wages and prices. In the case of civil servants, there are two main procedures. Under the first, the adjustment reflects the movement of the salaries of serving personnel, as in Austria, France, the Federal Republic of Germany, Ireland, Mali, Morocco, the Netherlands and the Philippines. The salaries themselves are adjusted in the light of trends in the cost of living and wages. Under the second procedure, the adjustment reflects directly changes in the cost of living, as in Canada, Japan, the United Kingdom and the United States, though there are also some mixed systems, for example, in Belgium and Cyprus. In some other industrialised countries, and in many developing countries, there is no regular adjustment procedure. Thus in Portugal, for example, civil servants do not generally retire before reaching the upper age limit of 70 years, unless they have other sources of income or have an opportunity of finding employment in the private sector.

Table 4.6. Pensionable age [1] for civil servants and wage earners in the private sector

	Civil servants	Wage earners in the private sector
Belgium	65	65/60
Burundi	60/55	55
Canada	60	65 [2]
Colombia	55/50	60/55
Finland	63	65 [2]
France	60	60
Germany, Fed. Rep. of	65	65
Greece	65	65/60
Italy	65	60/55
Mexico	55	65
Nigeria	60	55
Pakistan	60	55/50
Philippines	60	60
Senegal	55	55
Sri Lanka	55	55/50
Switzerland	62/60	65/62 [2]
Turkey	65	55/50
United States	62	65 [2]
Venezuela	60	60/55

Note: In the following countries where the same rules apply to civil servants and to all wage earners in the private sector and where there is no special supplementary scheme for civil servants, pensionable age is normally as follows: Algeria: 60/55; German Democratic Republic: 65/60; Libyan Arab Jamahiriya: 65/60; Peru: 60/55; Rwanda: 55; USSR: 60/55; Yugoslavia: 60/55.

[1] Where two ages are shown separated by a stroke, the first relates to men and the second to women. [2] Rules applicable also to civil servants.

Source: ILO: *The cost of social security, 1981-83* (Geneva, 1988).

Eligibility for pensions

Civil service and private sector pension schemes usually differ on the age at which a person becomes eligible for a pension (see table 4.6). While in some countries pensionable age – in the case of civil servants often also the mandatory retirement age – is the same as for workers in the private sector, in other countries the pensionable age is higher for civil servants, who are thus at a disadvantage. This difference exists because the pensionable age for women is lower than that for men under the general social security schemes applying to the private sector. Since a distinction based on sex is nowadays often challenged, the difference could either be gradually reduced by making the rules governing pensionable age more flexible or be eliminated by raising the pensionable age under the general schemes.

In several countries, the mandatory retirement age is fixed above the minimum retirement age for certain categories of civil servants such as members of the judiciary and university professors, as in Belgium, Côte d'Ivoire, France (some categories and grades), Italy, Morocco and Tunisia. More generally, the mandatory retirement age is fixed above the minimum retirement age for all civil servants who wish to carry on working in Argentina (65 years), Finland (67), Norway (70) and Portugal (70). In the United States, the age limit was totally abolished in the public service in 1978, a liberalising measure which has since been extended to the private sector.

Conversely, a lower-than-normal retirement age is fixed for certain categories in the public service either because of the hardships peculiar to their functions, such as members of the armed services or police force, or by reason of the arduous or unhealthy nature of their work. In addition, the option of early retirement is available to all civil servants who satisfy certain conditions concerning length of service: for example, 30 years' service by the age of 55 in Canada, 20 years' service by the age of 60 in the United States, 15 years' service by the age of 45 in Madagascar, or without any condition as to age, after 15 years' service in Côte d'Ivoire, 21 in Morocco, 25 in Madagascar, 30 in Burundi, 30 in Portugal and 40 in Italy. In Norway a civil servant can choose to retire when the sum of the years of service plus age is equal to not less than 85 years. While early retirement is also an option for private sector workers, it is more widely available to civil servants and members of the armed services.

A relative disadvantage for civil servants is that they must have served for longer periods than private sector workers before becoming eligible for pension benefits; in other words, private sector workers can be entitled to a proportional pension based on a shorter period of service. For example, the minimum qualifying period in the public and in the private sector, respectively, is 15 years and 60 months in Benin, 20 years and 50 weeks in Colombia, 15 years and 500 weeks in Mexico, 180 and 120 months in the Philippines, and 15 years and 1,800 days in Turkey, while the private sector schemes in Belgium, France and Senegal do not, or no longer, prescribe any qualifying period. These differences exist because civil servants normally enjoy stability of employment, since they are expected to make their career in the public service. But the reality by no means always corresponds to this traditional image, so that, as noted in Chapter 3, co-ordination with the various statutory and occupational private sector schemes remains an important requirement.

Other cash benefits

So far as *invalidity* is concerned, some special schemes for civil servants make no allowance for partial invalidity, but limit the definition of invalidity to permanent and total incapacity to perform the particular function. The reason seems to be that in the event of partial incapacity a civil servant is kept on in the service; otherwise his service has to be terminated. The result is a certain rigidity, which could be overcome by such means as developing part-time work in the public service. Benefits and medical services provided to civil servants in the event of maternity, work accidents or occupational diseases do not always take into account all aspects of these contingencies, such as loss of income and need for medical care. As a result, these benefits and services are sometimes less generous for civil servants than for private sector workers.

In many countries, civil servants are not covered by *unemployment* insurance, because they enjoy security of employment. There are, however, some countries – for example, Canada, Cyprus, Denmark, Malta, Norway, Spain, Sweden, Switzerland, the United Kingdom, the United States and Yugoslavia – where they are nowadays covered by the unemployment benefit schemes that are mandatory or optional for wage earners. In some countries, such as Denmark, Norway and Sweden, coverage against unemployment is the counterpart of the absence of special employment security for civil servants who, by reason of their status, enjoy additional financial safeguards in the event of dismissal. In other countries, the participation of civil servants is attributable rather to the need to broaden the financial base of the unemployment insurance schemes by appealing to their solidarity, even though their chance of becoming unemployed is much lower than that of private sector workers. The idea of solidarity is the sole – and explicit – reason why in a few countries workers not covered by unemployment insurance schemes are now required to pay contributions to them. This is the case for civil servants in Belgium and France, and for income tax payers in Luxembourg. By contrast, in several developing countries where governments are cutting the size of the labour force in the public service, the social security system is, as a general rule, unable to cover the risk of unemployment.

Health protection

In most of the industrialised countries, civil servants are covered by health schemes applicable to all residents or wage earners. In some countries, such as Switzerland and the United States, the coverage is voluntary. None the less, public authorities in the

United States usually pay a contribution into a private health insurance scheme. In Switzerland, the federal Government does not contribute to any statutory insurance scheme, but the federal sickness insurance legislation empowers the cantons and communes to make this coverage mandatory, if they so wish. In other countries, where all private sector workers are covered by a health insurance scheme, civil servants belong to special schemes. In the Federal Republic of Germany, for example, part of the medical expenses incurred by civil servants is reimbursable out of the state budget, the reimbursable portion varying from 50 to 80 per cent, according to family size; moreover, they may take out an additional private insurance policy, a system which on balance seems to be costlier than the social insurance for private sector workers, particularly for civil servants with large families. In Japan there are statutory mutual schemes for state civil servants and for those in local authority service which provide coverage similar to that of sickness insurance for workers in the private sector.

The situation is much more varied in the developing countries. Rare are the countries where, as in Bahrain and Kuwait, civil servants enjoy the benefit of a national health service covering the entire population or where, as in Bolivia, Costa Rica, Ecuador, Egypt, Panama, Peru and the Philippines, they are affiliated to the same health insurance scheme or, as in Singapore, to the same Provident Fund (MEDISAVE) as private sector employees. In Argentina, Colombia, India, Mexico, Pakistan, Tunisia and Venezuela, there are special health insurance schemes for civil servants, in most cases with their own hospitals and medical services. In most other developing countries, there are public health facilities, often of limited capacity, where patients other than the poor generally have to pay a fee. Thus, in some of these countries, private sector workers have been given access to additional medical care in various ways. Employers may be obliged, by law or by agreement, to provide medical services within the enterprise; social security contributions may be used to support the public health services in return for which workers receive treatment free of charge; or the private sector social security scheme may itself provide facilities for out-patient or hospital treatment. So far as civil servants are concerned, in some countries their expenses for medical care and medicaments are paid for by the State if the treatment is provided in a public hospital. In Cyprus, the State pays 100 per cent; in Central and West African French-speaking countries, it pays 50 per cent, the share payable by the person concerned normally being withheld from the salary if the treatment was provided in a public health institution. But since the state budget is the sole source of funds for these purposes, the scope of protection is limited. This explains why some countries have set up a fund described as a "mutual" fund for civil servants, even though membership is mandatory. Such a fund provides a more solid financial base through contributions either from civil servants only, as in Côte d'Ivoire, or from civil servants and the State jointly, as in Burundi and Morocco. The net effect of the latter comes close to the special social insurance scheme which exists in Suriname. In some countries, civil servants and/or private sector workers have set up their own networks for the provision of health care.

5. Concluding remarks

Public service basic pay has fallen throughout the world since the mid-1970s. The difference between regions lies only in the steepness of the decline. The drop has been particularly marked in sub-Saharan Africa, followed by Latin America and some Asian countries. Within individual countries, senior public servants have suffered deeper pay cuts than lower grades. Pay differentials within the public service have been compressed in many countries.

Almost universally, public service salaries have fared worse than those in the private sector. The public-private salary differential has moved against the public service. Where the differential was already adverse, as with high-level occupations, it has widened. Where the differential was in favour of the public service in an earlier period, as was claimed to be the case for unskilled workers in many developing countries, it has been narrowed or reversed.

Falling basic salaries in the public service have prompted the expansion of allowances in cash and in kind, especially in developing countries. However, while helping to slow the erosion in pay, allowances have not been able to prevent real earnings from declining. Moreover, in many countries, allowances are more generous in the private sector and in public enterprises than in the civil service. The public-private differential is thus further accentuated.

Falling pay of public servants aggravated by better prospects elsewhere has induced malaise within the public service in many countries. Civil servants with marketable skills have resigned for the private sector or public enterprises. Others have sought employment overseas. Shortages of certain skills in the public service, especially professional and technical skills, have been made worse by these departures. Civil servants have been pushed into taking second or third jobs. When at work on government duties, their efficiency has declined.

Where public service pay has fallen markedly, the effects on efficiency may outweigh the financial savings. Thus, apart from considerations of equity for public servants, it may be time to reverse the trend. The size and speed of salary increases will of course have to take into account the financial position of the government and the state of the economy. In some countries, the objective of a decent salary for public servants may have to be reached in stages over a period of years. The first corrective steps should, however, be taken soon. Another crucial policy issue is whether salary compression has been excessive for senior public officials, thereby demoralising policy-makers and other key technical and supervisory staff and endangering the performance not only of these key personnel but also of the individuals they supervise.

In many respects, pensions for civil servants are better than those for private sector workers. The level of pension benefits is generally based on the level of earnings over the final year – or the last few years before retirement. For private sector workers, the reference period can be much longer and the earnings used for calculating the pension benefit level may be subject to a ceiling. In addition, the formula for calculating benefit levels is usually more favourable for civil servants. As a result, the so-called replacement rate of civil servants' pensions (the ratio between pensions and earnings) is much higher than for private sector workers.

However, there are various ways in which this basic finding needs to be qualified, depending on the peculiarities of each country. Generally, there are more supplementary social security schemes in the private sector and, for some categories of high-level civil servants in the developing countries, various allowances are not taken into account in calculating benefit levels. Since public service wages have fallen further behind private sector pay during the 1980s, private sector pension benefits must have come closer to those in the public service. Conversely, civil servants have more opportunities to take early retirement than private sector workers.

In a number of industrialised countries, civil servants are covered by health schemes applicable to all residents or wage earners. But in many developing countries, civil servants typically depend on a public health service that has deteriorated during the 1980s and for which – increasingly – fees have to be paid. For private sector workers of various developing countries, additional provisions have been made, such as medical services within the enterprise, facilities for out-patient or hospital treatment or access to the public health services in return for the payment of social security contributions. As a result, civil servants in some developing countries have begun to set up mutual health funds financed by themselves and sometimes supplemented by state contributions. The advantage of such a system is that it provides more financial stability than dependence on the state budget.

In countries where a universal social security system does not yet exist, the trend seems to be towards creating a basic system covering both the public and the private sector. Such a system facilitates mobility between sectors and guarantees a minimum or basic level of protection.

Chapter 5

Collective labour relations

During the 1980s the public service has been in the forefront of labour relations in most IMECs and increasingly in DCs as well, particularly in Latin America. Public service labour relations have been marked by serious conflicts, particularly at the beginning of the 1980s when many governments took draconian measures to bring their budgets under control. This often meant (see Chapter 2) that labour relations were suspended, with employment conditions determined unilaterally by the government. Since the mid-1980s things have changed for the better. In the IMECs the economic situation has improved and in some DCs governments have been prepared to give public service unions a greater say in the determination of pay and other employment conditions.

In market economies public service labour relations are complicated by the dual role of governments in bringing about, and creating a favourable climate for, social and economic development and in acting as a leading employer. The government's role is further complicated in countries where parliament or local assemblies have the final authority to determine the employment conditions of public service employees (PSEs) (see section 1). In an increasing number of countries PSEs have gained the right to organise themselves. This has led to substantial unionisation with a wide variety of organisational patterns (section 2).

There is also considerable variety in the mechanisms used to determine employment conditions. In a dwindling number of countries governments still determine employment conditions unilaterally, but in most countries public service unions have a say in the process. This may take the form of joint consultations or, to a growing extent, even of collective bargaining (section 3).

The settlement of labour disputes has become an increasingly important issue as a result of the many serious conflicts during the 1980s. Section 4 reviews the experiences of various countries and tries to assess the value of different procedures. The chapter ends with a section on the main policy issues for the 1990s.

1. The government as employer

Employer representation is one of the more complex and difficult issues in public service labour relations. A basic problem concerns the role of elected representatives of the community (parliament or local assemblies). In a number of countries the fact that public servants' pay (like other government expenses) must be voted by parliament has been taken to imply that government executive organs (i.e. the immediate employers) do not have the authority to take decisions on pay and other employment conditions unless this authority is explicitly delegated by parliament. Where no such delegation has been made, there cannot be collective bargaining in the public service because the legislature cannot be party to a bargaining process. Increasingly, however, parliaments have to varying degrees explicitly or implicitly delegated their authority to the executive organs of government.

Within the executive, employer responsibilities tend to be much more diffused than in a private firm. The private employer is readily identified as an entity, and the line of management responsibility for bargaining is usually clear and direct. In the public service, on the other hand, several branches of administration are formally or informally involved in decision-making on managerial issues. The direct employing authorities are normally not financially autonomous, and are therefore unable to make commitments in their dealings with public employees without involving the administrative branches responsible for finance.

Central government

At the level of central government employer representation in collective bargaining or joint consultation is often entrusted to the Minister of Finance or the Treasury, as in Denmark, Finland and the United Kingdom. In some countries employer representation is mainly the responsibility of the Minister of the Interior or Home Affairs. In the Federal Republic of Germany the Interior Minister not only leads the bargaining committee but also prepares the salary laws for public servants with a statutory employment relationship *(Beamte)*. In the Netherlands the Minister for Home Affairs represents the Government in joint consultation machinery.

Other countries have established a body with general responsibility for the management of the public service, which represents the government in its dealings with staff organisations. In France, for example, the prime responsibility for negotiating with public service unions is given to the Minister in charge of the civil service and administrative reform. In Belgium, too, the joint negotiating committee for central Government is chaired by the Minister for Public Service. In Malaysia the Director-General of the Public Services Department chairs the National Joint Councils, although in recent negotiations on pay the Prime Minister and other senior ministers seem to have represented the employer side in practice. Public service boards or commissions represent central government employers in such countries as Australia (states), Fiji and Papua New Guinea. This was also the practice of the Australian Commonwealth (federal) Government; but since the reorganisation of the Australian public service in July 1987, the Public Service Board has been abolished and functions related to public service arbitration, pay and conditions have been transferred to the Department of Industrial Relations.

In a number of countries the government is represented jointly by representatives from several ministries or departments. In Argentina the employer side in the Participative Commission on the Legal and Pay Structure of the Central Administration *(La Comisión Participativa para el Régimen Jurídico y Salarial de la Administración Central)* is represented by the Secretary of the Public Administration and a representative of the Ministry of Economy. In Peru, in joint consultation on pay issues in the public service as a whole, the Government is represented by an ad hoc committee composed of two representatives from the National Institute for Public Administration *(Instituto Nacional de Administración Pública)*, two from the Ministry of Economy and Finance, and two from the Ministry of Labour. In Uruguay the Ministry of Labour, the Ministry of Economy and the Planning and Budget Office *(Oficina de Planeamiento y Presupuesto)* jointly represent the Government in pay negotiations in the public service. In Canada the Treasury Board, a senior cabinet committee with overall control of the Government's budget, is designated by law as the bargaining agent for the federal Government. In India the official side in the National Council for Joint Consultation in the central Government includes senior officials from the Cabinet Secretariat, Ministries of Home Affairs, Labour, Communications, Defence, Finance and Railways, and Departments of Expenditure and Revenue.

In Sweden a specialised agency, the National Agency for Government Employers (SAV), has been set up under the Ministry of the Budget as a collective bargaining agent in the central government sector.

There are countries, however, where each employing authority has the power to determine certain conditions of employment for its own staff, as in the United States. In some other countries (e.g. Mexico and New Zealand), although each employer has authority in principle to determine employment conditions, mechanisms to co-ordinate their activities have in practice achieved a high degree of centralisation.

For the past few years, there seems to have been a trend in an increasing number of countries (e.g. the Scandinavian countries and the United Kingdom) towards the decentralisation of decision-making and representation in the public service. This has stemmed from government efforts to increase flexibility in pay determination with a view to attracting skilled workers. In some countries this represents a reversal of previous trends, which in the early 1980s were rather towards centralisation, reflecting government concern to control public expenditure.

Local government

Employer representation in local government (regional, municipal and county authorities) presents somewhat different problems from those in central government. One of these concerns the complex influence of party political divisions on the distribution of authority to take decisions on labour relations matters. In central government employer representatives normally reflect a coherent set of political allegiances (although here, too, complications may arise if, for example, the Minister of Finance and the Minister of the Interior belong to different parties in a coalition government). By contrast, party political divisions between local authorities are highly probable and, where they form a negotiating team for dealing with unions, fluctuations in the political balance following local government elections can result in tension and dissension. There may also be party political differences between the central government and local authorities. This may affect the degree of control of local spending that the central government attempts to exert, mainly through the allocation of funds.

There seems today to be a trend towards closer co-ordination of bargaining activities carried out by local authorities. In a growing number of countries, including Australia, Denmark, the Federal Republic of Germany, Sweden and the United Kingdom, local authorities have grouped themselves into associations for the purpose of employer representation in negotiations with employees.

In such countries as France, Nigeria and Peru the same pay structure and other main conditions apply to both central and local government employees. Ministries or central government departments may represent local authorities in labour relations, although in France representatives of local authorities constitute the employer side in joint consultative machinery on the management of local government. In Belgium negotiations on pay and other main conditions for local government employees take place within the central negotiating machinery where employers are represented by the Minister of the Interior and other central government officials. In Italy, under the new system of collective bargaining introduced in 1983, associations of municipalities, provinces and regions are included in central government machinery for national bargaining.

On the other hand, in such countries as Canada, the United States and Japan, each local authority (state, province, municipality, etc.) has the power to determine pay and conditions for its employees. They are, however, subject to central government influence to the extent that they rely financially on allocations from central government funds.

In many developing countries labour relations at the local government level, including employer representation, still seem to lack any system, leaving each local authority individually to handle labour disputes occurring in its jurisdiction.

2. Organisations of public service employees

Collective labour relations can only work properly if PSEs have the right to organise themselves freely. Partly as a result of ILO Conventions and supervisory mechanisms this right has now been accepted in an increasing number of countries and has also led to a high degree of unionisation in the public service.

The right to organise

Most countries in the world have for a long time recognised the right of PSEs to organise. Some, such as Greece, Peru, Portugal and Spain, have done so with the country's return to democracy after a period of authoritarian rule. Governments have recognised the right either in legislation covering all workers or specifically PSEs, or by simple acceptance in practice. However, there remain countries which refuse, as a matter of principle, to recognise the right of public employees to associate in trade unions: Bolivia, Chad, Ecuador, Liberia, Nicaragua, Thailand and Yemen.

ILO standards

The ILO's position is laid down in Convention No. 87 (on freedom of association and protection of the right to organise), which has been ratified by almost 100 member States. Article 2 of this Convention provides that "workers and employers, without distinction whatsoever, shall have the right . . . to establish . . . organisations of their own choosing". The Convention covers all workers with the exception of the police and the armed forces.

A year after the introduction of Convention No. 87, the International Labour Conference adopted a second basic instrument in this field: the Right to Organise and Collective Bargaining Convention, 1949 (No. 98). This Convention does not cover "public servants engaged in the administration of the State", which has been interpreted by ILO supervisory bodies as persons who act as agents of the public authority. It contains specific provisions for the protection of individual workers against acts of anti-union discrimination and for the protection of workers' and employers' organisations against interference in each other's affairs – as well as for the promotion of voluntary collective bargaining. Like Convention No. 87, this instrument permits member States to determine the extent to which the guarantees provided for in the Convention shall apply to the police and armed forces. As at 1 June 1989, Convention No. 98 had received 115 ratifications.

Since certain categories of public servants remained unprotected by Convention No. 98, the International Labour Conference later adopted the Labour Relations (Public Service) Convention, 1978 (No. 151), and Recommendation, 1978 (No. 159). These extend to all persons employed by public authorities the protection against anti-union discrimination and interference in the affairs of public employees' organisations provided in Convention No. 98. Convention No. 151 had been ratified by 21 member States as at 1 June 1989.

The Convention also contains provisions on facilities to be afforded to representatives of public employees' organisations, procedures for determining the terms and conditions of employment of public employees, whether through collective bargaining or otherwise, and settlement of disputes. It applies to all persons employed by public authorities "... to the extent that more favourable provisions in other international labour Conventions are not applicable to them" (Article 1, para. 1). Furthermore, "public employees shall have, as other workers, the civil and political rights which are essential for the normal exercise of freedom of association, subject only to the obligations arising from their status and nature of their functions" (Article 9). Like Conventions Nos. 87 and 98, Convention No. 151 contains reservations regarding the armed forces and the police (Article 1, para. 3) as well as "high-level employees whose functions are normally considered as policy-making or managerial or . . . employees whose duties are of a highly confidential nature" (Article 1, para. 2).

Restrictions

Even though many countries have fully implemented the right to organise, some impose restrictions. For example, public employees may be permitted to form associations only for cultural or social purposes to the exclusion of activities vital to the occupational interests of their members (Kenya (central government) and Paraguay).

Moreover, it is not always possible to determine from the law in force in a country the precise extent to which public employees enjoy the right to freedom of association in practice. On the one hand, even in countries where the right to form trade union organisations is not recognised by law, associations do exist and are recognised by the government for the purpose of discussing pay and other employment conditions. On the other hand, such associations may be accorded only limited rights, and trade unions formed within a legal framework may find themselves ignored by the authorities or tightly restricted in their activities.

In examining these direct or indirect prohibitions on the right to organise of public employees, it becomes clear that restrictions are often linked to the special functions or responsibilities of the employees concerned. The police and the armed forces are obvious examples – although in some countries, where the legislation expressly excludes them from the right to form unions, the police are able to form their own associations. Some governments also exclude fire service personnel and prison staff on the grounds that they are linked to the police or form part of the armed forces.

Likewise, staff in managerial or confidential public service posts sometimes find restrictions placed on their right to organise, often in the form of a ban on joining associations of lower grade public officials or unions covering other categories of workers. Such restrictions cover senior administrative employees and some of their supporting staff, as well as staff employed in confidential positions or units (Bangladesh, Colombia, Egypt, Gabon, Mexico, Nigeria, Peru, Sri Lanka and, for a particular category, the United Kingdom). In some cases, the categories or posts excluded are clearly specified in the relevant laws and regulations. This type of ban is no doubt aimed at preventing the interference by employers in trade union activities through the participation of senior officials and at avoiding conflicts of interest.

The ILO has various mechanisms for monitoring observance of the right to organise in practice. There is a supervisory system for, and a procedure for complaints against, countries that have ratified Conventions. But there are also two special bodies which investigate allegations that States – even if they have not ratified a particular Convention – have violated the principle of freedom of association. Thus the Fact-Finding and Conciliation Commission on Freedom of Association and the Governing Body's tripartite Committee on Freedom of Association were created in 1950 and 1951 respectively. The Committee has been presented with almost 1,500 cases, of which more than 180 related specifically to alleged bans or restrictions on the right to organise of public employees (for a description of two recent cases see box 5.1). This does not include the 400 or so cases which in-

5.1 Two cases concerning the right to organise: The United Kingdom and Kenya

United Kingdom

In May 1984 the British Trades Union Congress (TUC) and other organisations presented a complaint to the ILO's Committee on Freedom of Association about an alleged infringement of trade union rights at the Government Communications Headquarters *(GCHQ)* in *Cheltenham.* In January 1984 the Government had announced that, as from 1 March 1984, GCHQ staff would no longer be permitted to be members of trade unions or have recourse to industrial tribunals. In future they would be allowed to belong only to a departmental staff association approved by their director. Staff were given a choice: they could resign their union membership, receive £1,000 compensation and continue working as before, or they could apply to be transferred elsewhere in the civil service. According to the Government, these measures were necessary to protect the confidentiality of the work of GCHQ and to ensure its uninterrupted operation, which had been disrupted by industrial action on several occasions between 1979 and 1981. It also considered that its actions were justified by Article 1 (2) of Convention No. 151, which states that the extent to which the protections embodied in that Convention apply to "employees whose duties are of a highly confidential nature" is to be "determined by national laws or regulations".

The Committee did not accept this argument. It stated that the exclusion of public servants from the fundamental right to form and join organisations of their own choosing was not compatible with Convention No. 87. It considered that Article 2 of that Convention required that *all* workers, without distinction whatsoever, should have the right to establish and to join organisations of their own choosing. The only permissible exceptions to this guarantee were in relation to members of the armed forces and the police as provided in Article 9 of the Convention.

The Committee rejected the view that Convention No. 151 in some way derogated from the rights embodied in Convention No. 87. It is true that Convention No. 98 envisages that the terms and conditions of employment of public servants engaged in the administration of the State *may* be determined otherwise than by a process of free collective bargaining, and that Convention No. 151 recognises that certain categories of public servants (including those in highly confidential positions) may be excluded from the protections set out in *that* Convention. But neither of these provisions can be interpreted as qualifying in any way the basic right to organise which is guaranteed by Article 2 of the Convention No. 87.

The GCHQ issue has also been examined by the Committee of Experts on the Application of Conventions and Recommendations on a number of occasions. Its views have been entirely consistent with those of the Committee on Freedom of Association. In their 1989 Report, for example, the Experts: (i) noted with regret that 13 employees at GCHQ had been dismissed because of their refusal to give up membership of the trade union of their choice; (ii) restated its view that Article 1 (2) of Convention No. 151 does not take precedence over the guarantees provided by Article 2 of Convention No. 87; (iii) rejected the Government's suggestion that the workers at GCHQ could be regarded as falling within the scope of the "armed forces" exemption in Article 9 of the Convention; (iv) noted with regret the fact that the Government continued to feel that no useful purpose would be served by renewed negotiations with the relevant trade unions; (v) reiterated that such negotiations offer the most appropriate means of resolving the issue in a manner which is consistent with the requirements of Convention No. 87; and (vi) urged the Government to reconsider its position on the usefulness of further negotiations.

Kenya

In November 1983 the Committee on Freedom of Association examined a number of allegations relating to the right to organise of public servants in Kenya. These allegations referred to the deregistration in 1980 of the Union of Kenya Civil Servants and the subsequent registration under the Societies Act (rather than the Trade Union Act) of the Kenya Civil Servants' Welfare Association. This Association was in turn deregistered in 1983, and its assets confiscated. In its response to the allegations submitted by the Public Services International and the Organisation of African Trade Union Unity the Government indicated that following discussions with the Deputy Director-General of the ILO "there was a favourable prospect for the re-registration of the association, subject to minor modifications of the constitution (of the association) which is currently being worked out". In its conclusions the Committee reiterated that, like all other workers, public servants should have the right to establish and join organisations of their own choosing, and asked the Government to keep it informed as to any measures taken to establish an organisation properly to represent the interests of public servants. Subsequent progress has been exceedingly slow, as is evidenced by the fact that in March 1989 the Governing Body, on the Committee's recommendation, once again urged the Government "to send a detailed report of the measures that it is going to adopt to re-establish the right to form trade unions of public servants and on the situation as regards the assets which were confiscated from the [Kenya Civil Servants' Welfare Association]".

volved allegations of a more general nature such as the total collapse of industrial relations in situations of armed conflict, martial law, and so on.

Organisational patterns

Union structures in the public service are often inherited from the private sector. Where private sector workers were unionised earlier than public servants, the latter have tended to adopt the patterns of union organisation that were already firmly embodied in the country's labour relations system. Thus in Sweden the union structure in the public service reflects the characteristics of private sector unions: a high degree of centralisation and the existence of three unions representing manual, white-collar and professional workers. In Australia the existence of a large number of small unions, mostly organised on a craft or occupational basis, is a feature common to the public and private sectors. In Canada and the United States the mixture of industrial and occupational unions found in the private sector also prevails in the public sector, although in the latter occupationally organised unions have greater weight.

The same tendency is discernible in many developing countries even though their public service union structure is more often dictated by law than in IMECs. Thus for example in Peru, where almost all private sector unions are organised at the level of the enterprise, public service unions are organised at the level of the establishment *(repartición)*. In Sri Lanka a multiplicity of trade unions with close ties to political parties is the pervasive feature of labour relations, and the public service is no exception. In the Philippines the trade union movement in the public service, emerging after legal recognition in 1987 of public servants' right to organise, appears to be developing through a multiplicity of unions as in the private sector.

In the USSR and other Eastern European countries labour relations legislation does not make any distinction between the public service and industrial sectors, the public service being defined as one branch of activity. Thus in the USSR, employees in the administrative organs of the State (at all levels) are represented by a single union, one of 32 unions organised at branch (industry) level. However, it is noteworthy that, in most of these countries, occupational groups such as teachers and nurses are represented by separate unions.

In the German Democratic Republic the national economy is divided into 16 main branches, each of which has its own trade union. The three main trade unions in the non-material sector cover employees in state institutions and the local economy, health and education. About 100 framework collective agreements are concluded each year in all the branches; these cover pay, working time, holidays and other issues, such as productivity. The management side is represented by the responsible ministries, both in the material and non-material sectors. Employment conditions of police officers, fire-fighters and army personnel are directly determined by the State.

While union structures in the public service often reflect private sector patterns, they are also affected by the peculiarities of government employment. Thus, parliamentary control over the budget means that decision-making on labour relations issues tends to be more centralised in the public service than in the private sector. This is particularly true of countries that have adopted a uniform pay system for the whole public service, but it applies to other countries too. In Italy and the United Kingdom, for instance, public service unions are relatively centralised in structure and activities.

Union representation in the public service is also frequently stratified by grade. In the United Kingdom and other countries inheriting the British system of labour relations, the tradition of craft unionism in the private sector is reflected in the mixture of grades and occupations that forms the basis of union organisation in the public service. In the British civil service (i.e. central government employment) six unions represent different grades or occupations, with the exception of the Inland Revenue Staff Federation which organises all grades in the agency. In Nigeria, since the Government restructured the trade union movement in 1978, eight unions represent different grades or occupational categories in the public service, while industrial unionism characterises the private sector. In Sri Lanka high, middle and lower grades as well as manual workers in the public service are represented by separate unions or associations, and different occupations among high level grades (staff officers) are also separately represented.

Employment status distinctions in the public service of a number of countries also affect union organisation. In Denmark the statutorily defined "public servants" are organised separately from public employees with employment contracts. In the Federal Republic of Germany industrial unionism prevails in the private sector; but in the public service the German Civil Servants' Association (DBB), which organises public servants with a statutory employment relationship *(Beamte)*, exists alongside the German Confederation of Trade Unions (DGB), whose member unions also have *Beamte* as members. Moreover, DGB affiliate unions also compete for membership of white-collar employees with a union representing the interests of salaried workers (DAG).

In a number of developing countries union structure is extensively regulated by law, and the regulations often differ between the public service and the private sector. In Malaysia a union in a statutory authority must confine its membership to the employees of that authority, and unions in local authorities must confine their membership to the local authority employees; unions in the private sector must be organised along trade, industry or occupational lines. In Mexico the Statute of Public Service Employees

(Estatuto de los Trabajadores al Servicio del Estado) lists all the unions that can be affiliated to the central organisation of the public sector unions (*la Federación de Sindicatos de Trabajadores al Servicio del Estado* (FSTSE)).

In certain countries the gradual development of public employees' unions, often before the legal recognition of their right to organise, has brought about a marked diversity of structure and function. For example, in Venezuela there are three basic forms of public employees' organisations: trade unions, allowed in the public service since 1970; associations, many of which are involved in bargaining activities; and professional colleges *(colegios profesionales)*, some of which (e.g. doctors) are also increasingly involved in bargaining activities.

In India, where, as in some other developing countries, private sector unions are largely dominated by politicians or other outsiders, public servants' organisations are led overwhelmingly by leaders who have emerged from among the rank-and-file membership. The predominance of internal leadership has been attributed to the high average level of education among public servants.

The degree of unionisation

The unionisation of public servants has been a relatively recent phenomenon in comparison with the long tradition of trade unionism in the private sector. An exception is the United Kingdom, where most of the large public sector unions have their origins at the start of the twentieth century. In a number of English-speaking developing countries the organisation of PSEs preceded the unionisation of private sector workers. However, the massive unionisation of PSEs in most IMECs and many DCs took place in the 1960s and 1970s.

While unionisation in the private sector began to stagnate or even decline in the late 1970s in many countries, it expanded steadily in the public service throughout that decade, and often well into the 1980s. Consequently, in a large majority of industrialised countries and many developing countries, the degree of unionisation in the public service is now far higher than in the private sector.

Table 5.1 shows the rate of unionisation for public and private sector workers, comparing recent years. These statistics should be used with caution: depending on the country, the statistics may refer to statutory government employees, central government employees or workers in the public service or even in the public sector as a whole; statistics on union density outside the public service may apply to the economy as a whole, non-agricultural sectors or the private sector; and the methods of collecting statistics vary widely.

It is possible to make some generalisations for the IMECs. During the 1980s unionisation in the public service decreased by more than one percentage point in most IMECs for which data are available, such as the Federal Republic of Germany, Italy, Japan and the United Kingdom, though the fall was much less than in the private sector. An important exception is Canada, where public service unionisation increased substantially.

The available statistics do not permit any generalisation about the DCs. In Sri Lanka unionisation in the public service dropped by more than 30 percentage points within three years from over 55 per cent in 1980 to 25 per cent in 1983. This was the result of a drastic change in government policy towards trade unions in the public service. Malaysia and Peru are two other DCs for which limited data are available. It is noteworthy that PSEs in DCs are only slightly less organised than their colleagues in IMECs.

Within the public service union density often varies widely from one sector to another, and there have been significant shifts in density among different sectors of the public service in the course of the past few decades. In general, unionisation is very high for education workers and relatively low for health workers – among whom, however, union density has recently been rising rapidly. For example, in the United Kingdom union density among health workers increased from 46 to 74 per cent between 1971 and 1979, while unionisation of employees in central Government was virtually unchanged (falling from 94 to 93 per cent).

The high density of union membership in the public service, at least in those countries where unions are allowed, can be explained by three main factors, usually found in combination. First, public sector management tends to be more favourably inclined towards unionisation than private employers. Changes of government in democratic societies often lead to changes in public employers, while private employers rarely change. When a political party favourable to unionism is in power, and the government aspires to be a model employer, unionism in the public services can spread rapidly. The result often survives subsequent political changes. Second, the large average size of the employing authority aids

Table 5.1. Unionisation in the public service and other sectors of the economy, 1980s comparison for two years in the 1980s (percentages)

Country	Coverage	Year 1	Percentage unionisation	Year 2	Percentage unionisation
Canada	Federal government	1983	83.4	1986	88.8
	Non-agricultural employees	1983	40.0	1986	37.7
Finland	Public service		...	1987	99.6
	Private sector		...	1987	59.8
Germany (Fed. Rep. of)	Statutory civil servants	1984	67.6	1987	66.1
	All employees	1984	41.9	1987	41.2
Italy	Public service	1980	53.0	1986	49.7
	All employees	1980	48.4	1986	39.5
Japan	Central government	1983	63.0	1986	61.4
	All employees	1983	29.7	1986	28.2
Malaysia	Public service	1983	44.3	1986	44.6
	Total employees			1986	5.8
Netherlands	Public service	1984	53.9	1987	53.0
	All employees	1983	32.0	1987	29.0
Peru	Public sector (white collar)	1985	35.9		...
	Private sector employees	1985	39.6		...
Quebec (Canada)	Public service	1983	63.2	1987	65.3
	Private sector employees	1983	24.0	1987	31.0
Sri Lanka	Central government	1980	55.5	1983	25.0
United Kingdom	Public sector	1979	85.0	1985	81.0
	All employees	1979	42.0	1985	38.0
United States	Public sector	1980	35.3	1986	36.0
	Private sector employees (non-agriculture)	1980	20.4	1986	14.0

... = Not available.
Source: ILO secretariat and government sources.

unionisation, as in the private sector where large enterprises tend to have higher union densities than small ones. A third factor is the higher job security which public servants enjoy, and the consequent low labour turnover.

3. From unilateral to joint determination of employment conditions

Since the 1960s there has been growing recognition of the right of public servants to participate in the determination of their employment conditions. This was reflected in the adoption at the 64th Session of the International Labour Conference of the Labour Relations (Public Service) Convention, 1978 (No. 151), and its subsequent ratification by an increasing number of ILO member States.

Article 7 of the Convention provides that: "Measures appropriate to national conditions shall be taken, where necessary, to encourage and promote the full development and utilisation of machinery for negotiation of terms and conditions of employment between the public authorities concerned and public employees' organisations, or of such other methods as will allow representatives of public employees to participate in the determination of these matters."

In many countries there was a gradual trend towards bilateral methods (such as collective bargaining and joint consultation) of determining employment conditions in the public service. This came about with a sharp increase in employment of teachers and welfare workers who are more likely to organise themselves than other PSEs. Moreover, the privileges of PSEs were gradually being eroded as their numbers increased, while their employment conditions deteriorated in comparison with those negotiated through collective bargaining in the private sector.

In some countries, however, the development of bilateralism was more sudden and was brought about by the transition from an authoritarian to a more democratic political system. This was the case, for example, in Spain and Portugal in the second half of the 1970s, in Argentina in the first half of the 1980s, and in the Philippines in the second half of the 1980s. Political changes were quickly followed by recognition of PSEs' right to participate in the determination of their employment conditions.

The main forms of PSE participation are joint consultation and collective bargaining, which may be informal or institutionalised. The demarcation between joint consultation and collective bargaining is often blurred because discussions within consultative machinery sometimes assume the form of negotiations. Moreover, even collective bargaining is usually subject to ultimate control by parliament, and the employer is at the same time the sovereign power.

Africa and Asia

In the great majority of developing countries pay and other conditions for public servants are determined unilaterally by the government. In many African and Asian countries PSEs are still denied the right to organise or have no means in practice of influencing their own employment conditions. And even where negotiating or consultative arrangements exist, they tend to have only limited application or have mostly remained moribund.

In a number of French-speaking African countries, for example, statutory machinery for joint consultation has been in existence for several decades, but it covers only individual questions and issues such as the organisation of services and the elaboration of statutory regulations for groups of staff. In Nigeria the National Public Service Negotiating Councils established in 1974, like their predecessors, the Whitley Councils, have not brought about any significant development of collective bargaining in the public service. (Whitley Councils are voluntarily established mechanisms, within which consultations and negotiations can take place on pay and, in principle, all other employment conditions in the public service. A distinctive characteristic of these councils, which may be organised at both the national and departmental levels, is that the staff position has to be co-ordinated between the participationg unions.) This is partly because the issues falling within the scope of the councils are in practice governed by civil service regulations, and partly because the Government prefers to determine employment conditions for its employees not by bilateral means, but through semi-political wage commissions.

The unilateral determination of employment conditions on the basis of recommendations made by wages or pay commissions is a fairly widespread practice among countries inheriting the British system of public sector labour relations. Governments have appointed such commissions mostly when pressures from public employees have reached unacceptably high levels. In India four pay commissions have so far been established (1946-47, 1957-59, 1970-73 and 1983-86) for central government employees. In Malaysia seven salary commissions have been established for the whole or part of the public service since 1967, the latest being appointed in 1977. In Sri Lanka several such commissions have been established for the whole public service since 1953, the latest in 1978; the Government also appointed a similar committee specifically for teachers in 1985. In Nigeria there have been at least three major wage reviews through ad hoc commissions since 1963 (in 1963, 1970 and 1972).

Even though governments retain the final decision-making power over PSE employment conditions, systems relying on pay commissions allow two forms of participation. First, in the course of the review proceedings, commissions receive representations from unions and associations of public servants. To this extent there are elements of consultation in the system, although it is indirect because union views have first to be reflected in the reports of the commissions and then accepted by the government. Second, in most countries relying on ad hoc commissions for pay determination in the public service, there are arrangements (modelled after the Whitley Councils) for joint consultation or negotiations on some employment conditions. This is the case, for example, of the Joint Consultative Machinery which was introduced in 1966 into the central Government of India, the five National Joint Councils established in 1973 in each of the five sectors of the Malaysian public service, as well as the National Public Service Negotiating Councils of Nigeria mentioned earlier.

In the United Republic of Tanzania pay and main employment conditions for public servants are unilaterally determined by the Government. Under a 1979 Act providing for establishment of a unitary national trade union (JUWATA), public servants are represented on several participative bodies. However, apart from a committee overseeing disciplinary actions taken against public servants, most of these bodies seem to be moribund. So far as pay determination is concerned, the Government's policy since the late 1970s has been to allow negotiations only where parties can justify wage increases by productivity packages or show that wage increases will not affect production. This has adversely affected public servants' pay, which has lagged further and further behind wage levels in private enterprises and parastatal organisations. In 1981, when the plight of teachers became a serious issue, the President established a commission to investigate and recommend means of improving teachers' employment conditions. However, as of June 1985, none of the recommendations of the commission had been implemented by the Government.

In India public servants' organisations in the central Government wield a certain clout in the determination of pay and employment conditions for their members through the Joint Consultative Machinery; consultation may sometimes lead to *de facto* bargaining, as when both sides negotiated the terms of reference for the third and fourth pay commissions. In Singapore it could be said that collective bargaining takes place to the extent that the public service is covered by the wage recommendations made by a tripartite National Wages Council, on which public sector unions are represented. In some countries in the Pacific region, such as Fiji and Papua New Guinea, that inherited the Australian tradition of labour relations, collective bargaining has been practised widely for a number of years, mainly within the framework of conciliation and arbitration machinery.

In other Asian countries there have been recent sharp changes in the labour relations scene in the public service. Sri Lanka, for example, relied on pay commissions and sporadic negotiations to determine pay and other conditions in the public service during the 1970s. But in the 1980s the Government reintroduced unilateral determination of employment conditions without negotiations. An attempt by public service unions to impose negotiations through resort to a general strike was harshly suppressed, and resulted in the dismissal of 40,000 workers.

In Malaysia, on the other hand, a strong trend towards negotiations has developed since 1985. In 1985 and 1986 the central union organisation of public employees (CUEPACS) and the staff sides of the five National Joint Councils demanded pay increases. The existing machinery of joint consultation proved inadequate to solve the dispute, which involved a nation-wide picket in October 1985 and a threat of strike action in January 1986. The Prime Minister and employee representatives subsequently agreed to set up a joint committee for negotiations on the demands.

Finally, in the Philippines public sector workers did not have the right to form unions until 1987 when the new Government recognised the right of workers in public enterprises to organise and bargain collectively and the right of public servants to form associations "for purposes not contrary to law". In consultation with the parties involved, the Government is preparing legislation to define the rights and duties of such associations.

Latin America

Labour relations in the public service in a number of Latin American countries have been highly conflictual in recent years. In Peru a strike organised in March 1985 by the Intersectoral Confederation of State Workers (CITE) lasted for 24 working days and caused a loss of 38 million work-hours, nearly five times the total recorded work-hours lost through strikes in the entire private sector in 1985. In Argentina and Brazil since 1983 and in Uruguay since 1985 there have been many strikes in the public service. The most strike-prone groups have been teachers, but strikes have also been frequent in the postal services, public hospitals and the central administration; there have been strikes even in the police and the judiciary. Thus in Argentina there were 271 public sector strikes between July 1985 and July 1986, representing 58 per cent of the total of 465 strikes during that period; a strike in the Secretariat of Industry and Commerce paralysed the administration for 46 days. In Uruguay between March 1985 and September 1986 the public sector accounted for 309 strikes out of the total of 949. In Venezuela, too, strikes in the public service have become very frequent.

The increasing incidence of strikes has led to *de facto* negotiations in the public service in a growing number of countries. In many cases, this development was prompted by the breakdown of the statutory pay fixing machinery under circumstances of rampant inflation. Such negotiations take place mostly without explicit recognition by the government of the principle of collective bargaining in the public service, and therefore without any legal framework for them.

In Peru, for example, the Constitution of 1979 provides for a unitary system of remuneration for the whole public service; under this system, public service pay is determined by the General Law of Budget *(Ley General de Presupuesto)* which Parliament approves on 15 December each year for the following year. The system became somewhat more participative in 1982 when the Government, while maintaining this basic framework, introduced a centralised mechanism of joint consultation on pay issues and a decentralised mechanism of collective bargaining on working conditions other than pay. However, the mechanism of joint consultation remained virtually inoperative (at least until the end of 1985), while public servants effectively imposed collective bargaining on pay by initiating disputes. In 1984 conflict was resolved by a government decree granting pay increases. But in 1985 another dispute resulted in the conclusion of an agreement on pay and other issues which included the establishment of joint committees to study the reform of the unitary system of remuneration, percentage adjustment of supplementary pay, the granting of tenure to personnel under contract and revision of provisions on union membership.

In Venezuela employment conditions in the public service have traditionally been determined unilaterally by the Government through legislative or administrative means. The right of public servants to form trade unions was recognised in 1970 by the Administrative Career Act, but in practice public servants had already begun to form associations with trade union functions. The first groups of government employees to embark on bargaining activities were manual workers, but office employees have also gradually become involved. Today, unilateral determination and collective bargaining coexist in a large part of the public service, the former covering such areas as recruitment, promotion and retirement systems and laying down the general framework for employment conditions, the latter dealing with additional benefits and improving the rights of public servants. Thus, for example, salaries are determined in accordance with pay scales unilaterally fixed by the President of the Republic, but they are often raised as a result of negotiations, including the general pay increase in the public service granted in 1986.

In Argentina, since the restoration of democracy in 1983, union activities have increased sharply among PSEs, as illustrated by a marked increase in the number of strikes. In 1985 the Government established a mechanism of joint consultation on pay and other employment conditions in the central administration, but this mechanism has in practice led to the development of a negotiating relationship between the parties. In a move to give this development legal sanction, the Government amended the Act on Collective Agreements in 1988 to bring the public service within its scope.

In Colombia the Labour Code allows public servants *(empleados públicos)* only the right to present petitions, but collective bargaining often takes place in practice, sometimes leading to the conclusion of written agreements. In several countries of the Caribbean region (e.g. Barbados, Guyana, Jamaica, Trinidad and Tobago) that inherited British traditions of labour relations, collective bargaining has been practised widely for a number of years, mainly within the framework of Whitley-type councils.

In some respects, public service labour relations in Latin America show similarities with those in IMECs; they tend currently to be more conflictual than labour relations in the private sector where real wages have declined less rapidly; and as a result, management in the public service is often faced with problems of recruitment and retention of staff. However, the very high rate of inflation compounds the difficulties in Latin American countries, and the gaps between the legal framework and practice are much wider than in IMECs.

Industrialised market economy countries (IMECs)

Among the IMECs the legal framework for public service labour relations varies widely. Some countries still apply the principle of unilateral determination by the government of pay and main employment conditions for public servants. Other countries, while maintaining the principle of unilateral determination, have developed systems of joint consultation.

Some IMECs have recognised the right of PSEs to bargain collectively with the government on pay and other employment conditions. There are also countries which use more than one method concurrently, such as joint consultation for pay and collective bargaining on other employment conditions (or vice versa).

However, the actual practice of labour relations in the public service is not as diverse as the different legal frameworks might suggest. Collective bargaining in the public service is everywhere subject to parliamentary control, and the ability of public employers to commit the government during collective bargaining is more limited than the ability of private sector management to commit the enterprise. As a consequence, collective agreements in the public service normally bind the government only politically and not legally. For example, in countries where parliamentary approval is required for pay increases for PSEs (and *a fortiori* in countries where the employment relationship of PSEs is defined as a statutory relationship), the results of negotiations are not considered contracts, but are usually called "memoranda of agreement" or "protocols of agreement". The absence of any legal, as opposed to political, obligation is explicit in the system of negotiations in the Belgian public service. In Sweden parliamentary control over the outcome of collective bargaining is exercised through a Parliamentary Pay Delegation which must approve agreements involving state expenditure.

The effectiveness of collective bargaining also depends heavily on the balance of power obtaining at a particular moment between the government and the public service unions. When the scale tips in favour of the government, as seems to have happened recently in a number of countries, collective bargaining in practice tends to become a process similar to joint consultation in which the government finally imposes its will.

The main events during the 1980s

As noted in Chapters 2 and 4, the impact of austerity measures on public service pay and employment was particularly dramatic during the first half of the 1980s. Thus, it is no surprise that this period witnessed a number of large-scale conflicts opposing powerful public employees' unions to the government. These head-on collisions were brought about not only by the erosion of real earnings and other employment conditions but also by government measures to suspend or modify the established labour relations machinery. Most of these measures were taken at the beginning of the 1980s when the economic situation was particularly serious.

In Belgium, in March 1981, the Government introduced a "solidarity contribution" to be deducted from public employees' pay as a price for the relative job security they enjoyed, the amount of the contribution varying between 0.9 and 2.7 per cent of salary. In the autumn of 1983 further austerity measures were taken, including the payment of salaries at the end, rather than the beginning, of each month and a 12 per cent cut in holiday allowances. This led to a major strike lasting 15 days in most parts of the public service. During the autumn of the same year the decision of the Government of the Netherlands to cut the gross pay of all public servants and all social security benefits by 3.5 per cent (later reduced to 3 per cent) provoked strikes and working-to-rule in the railways, postal services, customs and, initially, the police, from the end of October to the first week in December.

In Denmark, between 1982 and January 1987, the Government suspended the automatic cost-of-living indexation system provided for in collective agreements in both the public and private sectors. In 1985 this led to a breakdown of negotiations on new collective agreements, followed by a major industrial conflict in the private sector which led to the intervention of Parliament in the form of legislation determining pay in the two sectors. However, workers dissatisfied with the legislation resorted to unlawful strikes for a further two weeks, particularly strong support coming from public servants who felt that the legislation was especially disadvantageous for them. In the United States 12,000 federal air traffic controllers belonging to the Professional Air Traffic Controllers' Organisation (PATCO) went on strike in 1981 in their quest for higher pay and shorter working hours. Most of the controllers were subsequently dismissed – a clear illustration of the changes that took place in public sector labour relations at the beginning of the 1980s.

In Sweden a dispute between the Government and the white-collar union TCO-S in 1985 led to a strike lasting several weeks of 20,000 key employees, including civil air traffic controllers, customs clearance staff, postal supervisors and slaughterhouse meat inspectors. In the Swedish local authority sector the SACO/SR negotiating cartel took strike action in spring 1986 in a bid to restore its members' purchasing power after a long period of steady decline. Public servants in Finland went on strike over a wage dispute for about seven weeks at around the same time; at its peak the strike involved more than 40,000 workers.

The Government of the United Kingdom, while tightening its control over public sector pay by introducing a ceiling for pay increases within the framework of cash limits, unilaterally suspended civil service arbitration arrangements in 1981; it restored them in 1982 only on the understanding that it reserved the right to ask the House of Commons to set aside an award of the Civil Service Arbitration Tribunal on grounds of overriding national policy. In Japan, where pay in the national civil service is determined by the Government on the basis of annual recommendations made by the National Personnel Authority, the Government refused to implement the recommendations for 1982 and only partially implemented recommendations for the following three years. In Canada seven out of 11 jurisdictions adopted statutory public sector pay restraint programmes in 1982 and early 1983. Some of them suspended pay bargaining for a defined period during which legislation determined the level of pay increases or decreases, while others restricted the scope of pay bargaining by limiting the amount of funds available (e.g. to school boards).

During the second half of the 1980s the predominant trend seems to be a gradual return to the normal operation of labour relations machinery and the loosening of pay restraint programmes. Thus, for example, in Japan the recommendations of the National Personnel Authority for pay increases in the national civil service have been implemented in full by the Government since 1986, thus restoring the normal pre-1982 operation of the system. In Denmark collective bargaining took place in 1987 after being suspended between 1984 and 1986. In Canada the restrictive legislation on public sector pay bargaining introduced in 1982 and 1983 has mostly lapsed or been repealed. For example, by 1985 bargaining units under federal jurisdiction had ceased to be covered by the Public Service Compensation Restraint Act of 1982; in British Columbia the 1982 Compensation Stabilization Act, empowering the government to issue guide-lines for maximum permissible pay increases, was repealed in 1987.

However, in some countries labour disputes and restrictions on pay and collective bargaining have continued during the second half of the 1980s. For example, in the United Kingdom, where centralised collective bargaining within Whitley Councils has had a long tradition, the coverage of collective bargaining machinery has shrunk. Pay for over a million employees – nurses and midwives, the armed forces, doctors and dentists, professions allied to medicine, and "top salaries" (senior civil servants, judges and the senior ranks of the armed forces) – is today determined by the Government on the basis of annual recommendations made by independent "review bodies". These are all groups whose pay has proved a sensitive issue; the nurses' review body, for example, was set up after a series of disputes and strikes in the National Health Service over pay in 1982. In addition, following a pay dispute with teachers that spasmodically disrupted classrooms for two years, the Government abolished the pay bargaining machinery for teachers, called "Burnham Committees", in 1987. Under the new procedures, pay and other employment conditions of teachers are determined unilaterally by the Government on the basis of recommendations made by a special advisory committee.

Decentralisation and flexibility

During the 1980s many IMEC governments have tried to make the public service more cost-efficient. One measure adopted was to decentralise government activities, and thus also labour relations, to make them more responsive to regional and local needs. Governments also introduced greater pay flexibility to improve individual performance and make the pay structure more responsive to labour market conditions. As noted in Chapter 4, public-private pay differentials increased during the 1980s and made it increasingly difficult to attract highly qualified staff.

Finland took a step towards decentralisation with a 1988 amendment to the Civil Service Collective Agreements Act which makes it possible to conclude collective agreements at the level of government departments or institutions within the central government sector. In the Netherlands the Government's decision to set aside a significant portion of the total pay increase for 1987 for specific measures to ease recruitment bottlenecks (in spite of union demands for a fixed across-the-board percentage increase) prompted union efforts to obtain higher pay increases through decentralised negotiations.

In Sweden, too, the past few years have witnessed a gradual expansion of the scope for local negotiations within the central government sector, in particular for the allocation of individual salary grades within a given margin determined by central negotiations for each national authority. In the local government sector agreements entered into in 1988 for 400,000 public servants and academic staff belonging to SACO/SR-K and the negotiating body KTK provide for a pay rise of 11.5 per cent over a two-year period, out of which 5 per cent is earmarked for a pay "kitty". This will be distributed among the different employee groups and will also provide a basis for extending flexible individual pay rises.

In France, where a uniform pay scale has been applied to the public service for many years, there are signs of fragmentation – witness the conflicts in the autumn of 1988 involving groups such as nurses and prison staff.

The development of decentralised negotiations is discernible in local as well as central government labour relations. In countries where negotiations have been carried out by associations of local authorities at the national level, there have been moves towards greater autonomy for each local authority to conduct negotiations and determine the level of pay for its employees, as seems to have happened, for example, in Finland since 1986.

However, a notable exception to this trend towards decentralisation of negotiations exists in Australia, where negotiations in the public service take place within the highly centralised framework of the Australian Conciliation and Arbitration Commission's National Wage Case decision of 1987, applicable to both the private and public sectors (see box 5.2).

In the United Kingdom the pay restraint policies based on the annual "pay assumption" within the framework of cash limits have been phased out since 1987 and replaced by a policy of letting the market decide. This means that employees with highly marketable skills (e.g. scientists and tax staff in the civil service (central government) and computer staff, accountants and surveyors in some local authorities, including London) have been receiving much higher pay increases than other government employees. This change of tack was mainly due to the pressures exerted on public sector pay structures by competition for staff from a booming private sector. The change has also involved a growing number of restructuring exercises in the public sector, exemplified by a major job evaluation exercise carried out in 1987 for nearly a million local authority manual workers, and the regrading of nurses' jobs in 1988.

In Denmark the parties to the 1987 general pay negotiations for the public service agreed to earmark 0.2 per cent of the pay bill for flexible pay to be paid at a decentralised level for recruiting and retaining employees, remunerating special performance, and individual reclassifications.

This Danish agreement appears to be part of a more general trend towards linking public sector pay to individual performance. In Sweden, too, performance-related pay was introduced on a broad scale in the public sector in 1987. In the United Kingdom performance-related pay in the public service has so far been mostly limited to managerial grades, but there are signs of its spread among lower grades.

Public service unions have generally been wary of management's attempts to increase flexibility in pay structures, especially by way of performance-related pay, which they see as a threat to worker solidarity. However, rank-and-file employees tend to regard it as an opportunity for pay increases; and, faced with the serious recruitment and retention problems of the public service, an increasing number of union leaders appear to have come to terms with the changes.

Collective bargaining and joint consultation

Collective bargaining is today the predominant method of determining employment conditions for most PSEs in such countries as Australia, Belgium, Canada, Denmark, Finland, Italy, New Zealand, Norway and Sweden. In the United States nearly 40 states have granted the right to certain forms of collective bargaining to some or all state or local government employees. However, the white-collar employees in the federal Government have been granted collective bargaining rights only on limited non-economic matters. In the Federal Republic of Germany non-statutory employees, who make up nearly 60 per cent of all public employees, are covered by collective agreements.

In Spain an Act of 1987 provides for a system combining collective bargaining and joint consultation. Collective bargaining deals with various economic issues and such other matters as recruitment plans, job classification and promotion systems; matters involving legislation or increased budgetary provision are subject to joint consultation. The same Act establishes another joint consultation mechanism by granting staff councils and staff delegates the right

5.2 Return to central negotiations in Australia's public service

In Australia the Commonwealth (federal) public service was substantially reorganised in 1987, involving a substantial reduction of the number of Commonwealth departments with a view to achieving administrative efficiency, better policy co-ordination and improved budget processes. A change affecting public service labour relations was the abolition of the Public Service Board and the transfer of its industrial relations functions to the Department of Industrial Relations. Moreover, restructuring of public sector pay and classifications is taking place within the framework of a "two-tier wages system" introduced in March 1987 as part of the Australian Conciliation and Arbitration Commission's National Wage Case decision applicable to both the public and private sectors. While the first tier allows a general pay increase to all wage and salary earners, the second tier provides for increases of up to 4 per cent in accordance with a set of principles including work value changes, restructuring and efficiency. On 17 December 1987 the ACAC ratified an agreement between the Government and the major Australian public service clerical unions on a 4 per cent second-tier pay increase for office-based and related classifications in the Australian public service. The agreement is based on restructuring of the major office classifications to promote multi-skilling, flexibility and mobility at the workplace and improved career opportunities for staff, as well as measures aimed at promoting good industrial relations such as consultation and negotiation procedures on the introduction of new technology, a dispute settlement procedure and consultative arrangements.

to be heard on working-time arrangements, vacations and productivity bonuses.

In Scandinavian countries the scope of bargaining is wider than elsewhere, but it is still narrower than in the private sector. In Sweden, for example, it is affected by the application of the principle (generally accepted by the parties) that the right of public servants to negotiate must be exercised within the framework of political democracy. Thus collective agreements should not be concluded on matters relating to the aims, direction, scale and quality of the activities of public authorities because decision-making on these issues should be the task of the politically responsible bodies or, through delegation, of administrative authorities. In Finland annual leave and some other terms of employment, including those concerning the legal status of a public employee, have been regulated unilaterally by the Government and excluded from the scope of collective bargaining.

There are also IMECs where PSEs do not enjoy the right to bargain collectively over their pay and other main employment conditions. Most of them instead participate in some form of joint consultative machinery. This does not necessarily mean, as mentioned earlier, that they have less impact. PSEs covered by joint consultative machinery may in practice have as much influence on pay and other employment conditions as those covered by collective bargaining machinery, depending on the strength of their organisations.

One of the most far-reaching systems of joint consultation is operated in the Netherlands. It consists of a central committee in which the Government consults four federations of public service unions on matters of general interest for the whole public service (including pay), and 35 special committees dealing with matters concerning particular groups. In 1984 the system was made more effective by the establishment of an Advisory and Arbitration Committee, composed of an independent chairperson and two members each proposed by unions and by the Government, whose advice the parties may seek in the event of disagreement.

In the Federal Republic of Germany public employees with a statutory employment relationship *(Beamte)*, whose pay is determined by legislation, nevertheless participate in the process of determination through joint consultation. In Japan, where pay and conditions for national civil servants are determined by legislation on the basis of recommendations made by an independent body, the National Personnel Authority, unions are consulted over the distribution of pay increases among different groups of employees, as well as over personnel and other operational matters.

Industrialised centrally planned economy countries (IPECs)

In IPECs the rules governing the determination of pay and other employment conditions are basically identical for the public service and for industrial enterprises. Both are subject to a highly centralised system of determining pay scales, in which a governmental agency responsible for pay and working conditions plays a decisive role.

Nevertheless, differences in the nature of activities and the organisation of work between these two sectors are reflected in certain differences in the determination of pay and conditions. For example, in the USSR the management of an industrial enterprise and the union representing its employees can, through negotiations at the enterprise level, provide for various forms of incentives including performance-related bonuses and other allowances; such negotiations do not seem to take place to any significant extent in the public service.

The introduction of economic reforms in the past several years seems to have resulted in widening differences in much of Eastern Europe between the public administration and industrial sectors in methods of worker participation. Current reform efforts have led to the establishment of various bodies for workers' self-management in the enterprise in such countries as Bulgaria, Hungary and Poland, as well as the USSR and more recently Czechoslovakia. But self-management has been mostly confined to the industrial sectors. Thus for example in the USSR, two important laws have been promulgated, in 1983 and 1987, strengthening the role of workers' collectives in the management of the enterprise; however, these two laws do not apply to the public administration.

4. The settlement of labour disputes

The early 1980s saw many labour disputes between governments and their employees, particularly in IMECs and Latin America. While industrial action, such as strikes and lock-outs, may sometimes represent a necessary ultimate measure to break a stalemate, it seldom provides a real solution to a labour dispute. Strikes represent a huge loss of productive energy and it often takes a long time afterwards before mutual trust and respect are restored. There are various procedures – such as conciliation, mediation and arbitration – to solve disagreements peacefully. In conciliation and mediation a neutral third party assists the negotiating parties in their search for an agreement. In arbitration the third party settles the dispute by making a binding award.

These procedures have been widely used in solving labour disputes in the private sector, but are rarely employed in the public service. In the private sector the government is well placed to act as a neutral third party, but it is often unwilling to accept a third party in conflicts with its own employees. Many governments also consider dispute settlement procedures to be incompatible with their sovereign power. Thus, in the absence of established dispute procedures, the resort to industrial action has been regarded by public employees' unions in many countries as the only means of resolving conflicts.

Today things have changed significantly in a growing number of countries, and the obligations of the government as employer are increasingly recognised. Nevertheless, when a government finds itself in dispute with its employees' unions, there is always a risk that it will be tempted to invoke its sovereign power in order to overwhelm union opposition. The duality of the government's function clearly affects the operation of dispute procedures in the public service.

The right to strike

There are no ILO standards that expressly guarantee the right to strike. But the ILO supervisory bodies have recognised that it is one of the essential means available to workers and their organisations for promoting and protecting their economic and social interests. An increasing number of countries have recognised this right, even though they have often restricted its scope because of the special responsibilities of the public service. As a result, the legal framework for industrial action is still considerably more restrictive for PSEs than for workers in the private sector.

The ILO's supervisory bodies have held that strikes may be prohibited for PSEs who act as agents of the public authority or who work in services whose interruption would endanger the life, personal safety or health of (the whole or part of) the population. But where strikes are restricted or prohibited, appropriate guarantees must be afforded to protect the workers concerned, who are otherwise denied one of the essential means of defending their occupational interests. Such restrictions should be offset by adequate impartial and speedy conciliation and arbitration procedures, in which the parties concerned can take part at every stage and in which the awards should in all cases be binding on both parties and be rapidly and fully implemented.

There are more than 30, mainly developing, countries where the law prohibits strikes for most or all PSEs. The reasons often invoked for this prohibition include the parliamentary prerogative of establishing the national budget, including public service pay, which should not be interfered with by strikes; the absence of the restraining influence of the market for monopoly services provided by PSEs; and the need to provide essential services.

At the other end of the range, there are about 20 countries (and a number of states in the United States) where public servants' right to strike is in principle recognised in law, although its exercise may be regulated. In the United Kingdom no positive right to strike has been enacted, but it has in fact been granted by giving those taking industrial action statutory immunity from civil and criminal liability.

In between, there are various countries which in practice accept the right to strike by PSEs. In the Australian federal public service, for example, there is legislation prohibiting strikes by PSEs, but it seems never to have been applied.

In some Latin American countries, including Argentina, Peru, Uruguay and Venezuela, the Constitution recognises workers' right to strike but provides that this right must be exercised within the framework set by laws. So far, such laws have not yet been adopted in respect of most PSEs in these countries, but in practice PSEs have often gone on strike without being punished.

In yet other countries, in the absence of legislation, the courts have developed a system of case law on strike action by PSEs. The Government of the Netherlands, for example, ratified the European Social Charter in 1980, but it did not (as generally expected) enact legislation granting PSEs the right to strike. Nevertheless, the courts recognised this right in a number of judgements. Since the 1983 strikes, however, the courts have developed criteria for lawful and unlawful strikes mainly to the effect that the means of industrial action used must be proportional to the objectives sought.

There are also countries where the legality of strikes in the public service is ambiguous. In Belgium, for example, the General Statutes for Public Servants of 1937 prohibit public servants from striking. However, in practice, the Government has granted official recognition to public service unions whose internal rules explicitly refer to strikes as one of their means of action. In the view of many lawyers, this implies that the prohibitive legislation has been implicitly abrogated. In Austria the right to strike is recognised *de facto* as far as public employees under employment contracts are concerned; it is a matter for controversy for statutory employees. Other countries making this distinction between statutory public servants and public employees under employment contracts include Denmark and the Federal Republic of Germany, where statutory public servants are denied the right to strike enjoyed by employees under contract.

In the centrally planned economies of Eastern Europe the predominant political doctrine leaves no room for strikes because there is held to be no divergence in interests between management and employees. Thus, strikes are not prohibited, but the labour laws of most of these countries are silent on the subject. Poland is the only exception; the Trade Union Act of 1982 mentions strikes, mainly to lay down various conditions which make the lawful exercise of the right to strike very difficult. The Act on Rights and Obligations of Public Servants, also adopted in 1982, prohibits public servants from going on strike or taking other industrial action which may disturb the normal functioning of the service.

Regulation of industrial action

As noted earlier, many countries (mainly the more liberal IMECs) recognise in principle the right to strike in the public service, but most restrict or deny this right to certain groups of PSEs. In some countries the unions have made arrangements so as to minimise the disruptive effects of industrial action.

In Finland only those high-ranking civil servants called "employer civil servants" are prohibited from striking, while in Sweden all public servants seem to have the right to strike. In New Zealand and the United Kingdom only the armed forces and members of the police force are excluded. In France members of the police force, prison staff, judges, communication staff in the Ministry of Interior, and the armed forces, are denied the right to strike. Moreover, the Government can, subject to judicial control, designate certain officials in authority or those whose presence is deemed indispensable for public security or essential government services, and prohibit them from striking. In Italy members of the police force do not have the right to strike, and air traffic controllers may be prevented from striking in specific circumstances.

In a number of countries public service unions are required to maintain a minimum service even during a lawful strike. This applies to those employees of the Federal Government of Canada who are "designated" by the parties (or by an independent Public Service Staff Relations Board in the event of the parties' failure to agree) as performing duties essential for the safety and security of the public; for fire-fighters and air traffic controllers the proportion of "designated" employees obliged to work normally is 100 per cent. In France an Act of 1984, restoring the right to strike for employees in air transport, lists the duties that must be performed during strikes, later specified in decrees issued in 1985 and 1987. In Italy air traffic controllers may be required to provide minimum services. Moreover, a Bill recently approved by the Italian Senate contains clauses that empower a provincial governor *(prefetto)* or the Prime Minister to order public servants' unions to assure the provision of minimum levels of essential public services during strikes. Essential public services as defined by the Bill include health services, public transport, public utilities, civil protection, administration of justice, post and telecommunications, public radio and television, education, social security and customs.

The purposes for which a lawful strike can be called may also be limited. During the 1980s some countries introduced new restrictions. For example, the 1982 Employment Act of the United Kingdom narrowed the definition of "trade dispute", which diminished the scope of immunity from liability for strike action. One of the practical consequences is that "political" strikes are no longer protected from liability, as was shown by a decision of the Court of Appeal in 1984 involving industrial action by the Post Office Engineering Union as part of its campaign of opposition to privatisation. Many recent public service disputes in Britain have involved a challenge to government policies on public expenditure cuts and privatisation, and unions are having increasing difficulty in arguing that industrial action is lawful.

There are also countries that impose more stringent procedural requirements for strikes in the public service than in the private sector. For example in Mexico, for a strike to be lawful, it must be supported by at least two-thirds of the employees of the public authority concerned.

In some countries the government often intervenes in labour disputes in the public service by enacting legislation ordering strikers back to work and settling the disputes. This kind of intervention has frequently taken place in Denmark since the middle of the 1970s. Legislation either gives legally binding force to the mediation proposal made by the Court of Conciliation, or extends the duration of existing collective agreements for a few more years and sets a ceiling on pay increases allowed over this period.

Finally, in some countries unions themselves or the parties in labour relations have made arrangements for avoiding excessive disruption of essential services. In the Federal Republic of Germany, for example, the internal rules of the OTV (the largest union in the public service) and the directives of the DGB (the trade union confederation) contain strike procedures and exclude certain functions from strike activities. In Italy the three largest union confederations have agreed upon self-regulation of strikes, and in 1988 started elaborating precise rules aimed at guaranteeing minimum essential services and protecting basic public interests. Self-regulation in Italy has also received legislative support through an Act of 1983 which made union participation in public service bargaining conditional upon their adoption of the codes of conduct established by the confederations. In Sweden the Special Basic Agreement for the Public Sector contains provisions aimed at safeguarding the public interest, and specifies areas and functions, such as national security, law and order and nursing, in which the right to strike should be exercised with special care. The parties to the agreement have also set up a bipartite committee to assess whether a dispute is liable to involve undue disruption of vital services. The agreement also includes a list of posts that are excluded from industrial action.

Conciliation and mediation

Conciliation and mediation play the predominant role in settling labour disputes in the private sector, but are used in the public service to a relatively limited degree and in a limited number of countries. While arbitration usually attracts the keen interest of unions and public employers because it constitutes a direct challenge to the sovereignty of the State, conciliation and mediation do not seem to have aroused as much interest or controversy. None the less, they have come to be more widely practised today than in the past and in many instances have proved to be effective in solving disputes.

Countries where some form of institutionalised conciliation or mediation takes place in settling labour disputes in the public service include Australia, Canada, Denmark and the Federal Republic of Germany (for public employees under contract), Finland, the Netherlands, New Zealand, Norway, Spain, the United Kingdom and the United States.

Although the terms "conciliation" and "mediation" are often used interchangeably, some countries distinguish between "mediation", in which a neutral third party issues recommendations for the solution of the dispute, and "conciliation", in which the third party normally refrains from making such recommendations public. The work of the Advisory Conciliation and Arbitration Service (ACAS) in the United Kingdom highlights the distinction. ACAS normally conducts conciliation in a quiet and confidential atmosphere and attempts to facilitate talks between the parties rather than make proposals. However, where mediation is considered appropriate and the parties agree to it, ACAS may appoint independent mediators who are not its employees to make recommendations for a possible solution.

Even in countries where conciliation or mediation is not institutionalised in the public service, the government may appoint a mediator for solving a particular labour conflict. This is the case for example of Sweden, where the basic principle is that the parties themselves are responsible for settling interest disputes by agreement. Accordingly, the establishment of a permanent institution responsible for conciliation has not so far been considered desirable. If, however, collective bargaining fails and there is a risk of major industrial action being taken, the Government usually appoints a mediation commission. In France, too, the Government often appoints a mediator in order to solve a serious labour conflict in the public service, as was the case with recent conflicts involving air traffic controllers and prison guards.

Third party intervention in such countries as Canada, Denmark, the Federal Republic of Germany, France, the Netherlands, Norway, Spain and Sweden is more in the nature of mediation than conciliation because it is mainly aimed at producing proposals for a possible solution of the dispute which are often announced with a fair amount of publicity.

Conciliation and mediation are virtually absent in the public services of developing countries and the Eastern European countries with centrally planned economies. In the former, this reflects the persistent predominance of the sovereignty theory in public service labour relations, while in the latter the absence of settlement machinery stems from the assumption that there are no divergent interests between the management and employees.

Arbitration

Arbitration of interest disputes by a neutral third party has today come to be regarded as one of the key elements of public service labour relations in a growing number of countries. While private sector unions tend to dislike arbitration, public service unions in many countries have been more favourably inclined.

The attraction of arbitration for public servants is that it holds out the prospect of better settlements than those unilaterally imposed by government, without the need for industrial action which is often costly and tends to arouse public hostility. Arbitration also spares government the political and economic damage that might be caused by disturbances in the public service as a result of industrial action.

However, arbitration also means a considerable erosion of the power of governments, which are therefore often opposed to it. Lawmakers in a number of countries have also been reluctant to allow arbitrators to take decisions that are binding on the government since they are not accountable to the public or its representatives.

Some form of arbitration is today available to the bulk of public servants in a number of industrialised and developing countries, such as Australia, Fiji, India, Ireland, Malaysia, New Zealand, Nigeria, Norway, Papua New Guinea, Peru, Trinidad and Tobago and the United Kingdom. In Canada about half of the provinces provide for interest arbitration, while the federal Government gives bargaining agents a choice between arbitration without the right to strike and conciliation with that right. In the United States about 20 states have passed laws providing for interest arbitration: most of them apply to police and fire service personnel and some also to other groups of local government employees; a few apply to state employees.

Arbitration takes a variety of forms. In most systems, arbitrators can formulate awards as they feel just. However, some of the states in the United States provide for "final offer selection" arbitration, in which the arbitrator is obliged to select one of the parties' last offers for his award. The details of the arrangements for "final offer selection" arbitration vary widely.

The functions of arbitration also vary from one country to another. In such countries as Ireland and the United Kingdom, arbitration machinery has been established by agreement between the parties as an adjunct to their negotiating machinery which derives from the Whitley Councils. The availability of arbitration thus does not imply a renunciation of the right to strike. On the other hand, in Canadian provinces and American states, arbitration has been introduced as a substitute for the right to strike. However, irrespective of whether arbitration supplements or replaces the right to strike, it has generally been looked upon by public employees' unions as instrumental in their efforts to improve pay and conditions. This has been the case in particular in the 1980s as governments have pursued austerity policies, adopting very tough postures at the bargaining table.

On the other hand, governments pursuing pay restraint policies have tended to regard arbitration as an obstacle and have consequently attempted to restrict access to arbitration or its scope or subject it to government control. Thus for example, in 1981 the British Government refused "on grounds of policy" to have the issue of civil service pay and conditions referred to the Civil Service Arbitration Tribunal. Although the Government later agreed to restore arbitration for the 1982 pay settlement, it did so on the understanding that it reserved the right to ask the House of Commons to set aside the Tribunal's award on grounds of overriding national policy. More generally in the United Kingdom, and also in Ireland, as the governments have stepped up their efforts to avoid arbitration, a controversial issue has been whether public employees' unions should have the right unilaterally to refer disputes to arbitration.

In Canada measures aimed at ensuring that arbitration did not conflict with government policy were taken in 1982 and 1983 in various jurisdictions; most of them were meant to be temporary. Thus in the provinces of Ontario, Alberta and British Columbia, new legislation was introduced or existing laws amended to require arbitrators to take into account the public employers' ability to pay in the light of government fiscal policies.

In other countries arbitration has been used by the government to avoid or halt industrial action by public servants. The Norwegian Government has had recourse to compulsory arbitration on several occasions in the 1980s as a means of ending strikes, for example in 1984 when the main union organisations were involved and in 1986 when strike action was taken by the Federation of Norwegian Professional Associations and the Norwegian Union of Teachers.

In developing countries the scope of arbitration is generally considerably more limited than in the IMECs. In many developing countries pay determination is outside the scope of arbitration. In India, although the scheme for joint consultative machinery and compulsory arbitration for the central Government provides for arbitration on pay and allowances, weekly hours of work and leave, the major pay issues are in practice determined by the Government upon recommendations made by the ad hoc pay commissions referred to earlier. In Malaysia pay scales and some of the main employment conditions are determined by the Government on the basis of recommendations made by ad hoc salaries commissions; thus arbitration does not normally extend to these issues. However, complaints may be entered against alleged "anomalies" arising out of the implementation of recommendations by salaries commissions and these may lead to arbitration by the Public Service Tribunal set up in 1978. Public servants in Malaysia also have a limited possibility (subject to the consent of the authority concerned) of referring trade disputes to arbitration by the Industrial Court. In Peru the law provides for the referral of disputes over working conditions to ad hoc arbitration tribunals to be set up in each department or establishment, but pay issues are excluded.

5. Concluding remarks

Public service labour relations are today undergoing rapid transformation. The traditional view of PSEs as representatives of the sovereign power and belonging to a privileged group has been replaced by an image of workers whose pay has been deteriorating in comparison with wages in the private sector, whose job security is threatened by government policies and many of whom are frustrated and demoralised because they believe that the value of their work is not adequately recognised either by the government or by the public.

Such changes in employment conditions for public servants have naturally led to their growing militancy. They are increasingly demanding a greater say in decision-making on their employment conditions, and staging industrial action to obtain better recognition of the value of their work. In most IMECs and in some developing countries (in particular in Latin America), public servants are today engaged in bargaining activities with the government either through legally established procedures or outside any legal framework.

These developments have sparked discussion over whether the systems of labour relations in the public service and in the private sector should converge and become identical or should remain distinct. Those who hold the view that there are fundamental differences between labour relations in the two sectors argue that the State, as the representative of the popular will (or general interest), has an unassailable right to act unilaterally in matters falling within its legislative competence, a right that cannot be challenged by groups representing particular interests, such as public service unions. So far as pay determination is concerned, they argue that, because public servants are paid by the tax revenue of the community, the elected representatives of the community (such as parliament or local assemblies) should have the sovereign right to take decisions on this issue. They also argue that, because there is no alternative source of supply for public services, their monopolistic nature would distort the functioning of the private sector model of labour relations which presupposes the existence of market constraints.

On the other hand, those who think that labour relations in the two sectors should converge argue that it is possible to separate the two roles of government: that of the sovereign power and that of the employer. While as the representative of the community, the government has the sovereign power to take political decisions, its role as the employer of public servants differs very little from that of a private employer. As for the fact that the salaries of public servants are ultimately paid from tax revenue, the holders of the convergence theory argue that it is wrong to assume that public services are provided free of charge; they have their price just as the goods and services produced by private enterprises have their price. Therefore, public servants should be able to negotiate the price of their work with the public through their elected representatives and, by delegation, with public employers, just as private sector workers negotiate the price of their work with their employers.

Although many governments in the developing world still persist in invoking the sovereignty theory to reject negotiations or consultation with their employees, in a large majority of IMECs as well as a growing number of developing countries, the right of public servants to participate in the process of determining their employment conditions is today well established. In these countries the focus of the debates between the parties to labour relations is clearly shifting from the validity of the sovereignty theory towards the more practical problem: whether, in view of the crucial impact on public well-being of the work of PSEs, there should be some modifications of the private sector model of labour relations when it is applied in the public service, mainly with a view to striking an appropriate balance between the need to protect their occupational interests fairly and the need to protect the public from undue hardships caused by disruptions in the supply of essential public services.

Chapter 6

Improving public service productivity

Improving productivity and accountability in the public service requires the design and implementation of suitable measures at three levels: the individual, the agency or organisation and the system as a whole. Chapters 3 and 4 have already dealt with career patterns and wage incentives for public service employees (PSEs), that is, with incentives at the individual level. This chapter will deal mainly with productivity at the agency level, but it will also make some observations about productivity of the government system as a whole.

Productivity is difficult to measure and manage in the public service, because the goals of efficiency and equity sometimes pull in opposite directions and objectives are in any case much less clearly defined than in the private sector (section 1). The various constraints imposed by the public service environment mark another important difference with the private sector. The main productivity-enhancing measures discussed in this chapter are restructuring of government activities (section 2) and management approaches to productivity improvement (section 3).

1. Productivity measurement in the public service

Faced with often increasing demands for government services and with tight budgetary constraints, governments have devised an array of schemes to make better use of available resources aimed at "doing more with less". As a result, they have begun to show greater interest in improved management practices, cost reductions and productivity increases. A first step is to look for performance indicators of public service activities. Building on these the agencies involved, such as the Commission for the Rationalisation of Budgetary Choices in France, the Financial Management Initiatives in the United Kingdom, and the Bureau of Labor Statistics in the United States, which carries out public service productivity measurement and analysis, have tried to relate services produced to resources used, to improve services and to increase productivity.

Compared to their counterparts in the industrialised countries most public service organisations in developing countries have low productivity. In water supply and sanitation, for example, a typical European water authority might require one employee per 1,000 consumers while a typical African one would have one employee per 200 consumers. In most developing countries it is becoming increasingly evident that the inability of development projects to yield promised results is largely attributable to weaknesses in administrative services. Public services specifically designed for the poor generally remain well beyond their reach. In sub-Saharan Africa, according to one study, an inadequately staffed public administration has reduced capacity to implement policies and resulted in low standards of maintenance and operating efficiency in public facilities like rural water supply systems, roads and health services. This has led in many cases to premature destruction of expensive capital assets.

Constraints of the public service environment

In order to examine possibilities for productivity improvement in the public service, the main obstacles need to be identified. These include constraints peculiar to the public service such as the political environment within which it operates, organisational structures, the budget process and the lack of productivity measurement.

Political constraints

The behaviour of the public service is naturally influenced by the social and economic context. Managerial issues and efficiency are rarely vote-winners and have often had low priority for both politicians and career executives, including top management. Since subordinates naturally tend to follow the priorities of their superiors, they may be poorly motivated to emphasise efficiency.

A lack of stability in policies, organisational structures and staffing is another productivity barrier of a political nature. Many political objectives have a relatively short time-frame whereas productivity improvements demand continuing and consistent long-term managerial efforts which often exceed the tenure of the officials responsible. Frequent and radical policy changes can disrupt productivity through their effects on motivation and procedures for administration and service delivery. There is constant pressure to achieve quick results – to help the agency obtain more budget resources or for re-election purposes.

Organisational structures

Over the past decades both the number and size of public agencies have grown dramatically, giving rise to complex organisational structures with multiple layers of line (delivery) and staff (administrative) offices governed by numerous procedural regulations. This increases the time it takes an agency to carry out the routine and necessary steps to execute programmes. In the United States, universities and research institutions have to wait several months or more before social programme agencies such as the Departments of Health, Education and Welfare and Housing and Urban Development have reviewed and approved applications for a grant. Reams of paperwork are generated along the way.

Highly centralised decision-making can also constrain productivity by increasing the time needed to accomplish a task, irrespective of whether it originates at the top or at the bottom. This is clearly evidenced in agencies, such as police, fire departments and tax collection agencies, which use a field office structure with numerous tiers including a central or headquarters office, regional offices, field offices, and sometimes even additional intermediate offices. Many layers of line and staff positions often result in confused lines of responsibility as well as poor communications, unnecessary duplication and lack of flexibility. Centralised decision-making often hampers quick response to new situations; problems can become more intractable while the "proper" procedures are followed.

The budget process

The budget process in many countries can be another barrier to better public service productivity. Public agencies usually do not justify their budget requests or defend proposed staff increases on the basis of documented workload analyses or work measurement standards. Instead, existing productivity is accepted as satisfactory; additional staff are requested using the line of reasoning that if ten people produced 20 units last year, then 15 people are needed to produce 30 units next year. Both the level of service output and its quality tend to be determined by the amount of allocated resources, subject to overall resource availability.

As a result, many public service executives believe with reason that demonstrating productivity-related improvements results in penalties rather than rewards. Public budgeting systems tend perversely to punish managers responsible for improved use of resources by cutting their budgets while frequently giving more resources to those who manage badly. Genuine efforts to boost productivity have often been met at best with apathy or at worst with arbitrary budget cuts. It does not take long for a manager to learn how to play the "budget game": expectations of budget-cutting encourage managers to build up budget fat.

Since productivity measures are rarely used to justify budget and staff requirements, the existing budget is usually taken as a base and increments added to meet increasing service demands, even if these could be provided through higher productivity without additional resources. The size of budget and staff tends to be regarded as a status symbol and it usually determines the manager's power and salary. To cut the budget of a good manager gives the impression that he has done poorly; to increase that of a bad manager makes it appear that his influence is expanding. The incentives operate exactly counter to logic or efficient management; the system thus encourages precisely that which it can least afford.

Another negative aspect of the budget process is the line item approach to budgeting control which fails to comprehend overall departmental efforts and restricts the manager in redeploying resources in the most effective manner. Thus, managers are encouraged to spend all available funds, regardless of the workload. In addition, there is seldom significant provision for such budgeting techniques as "make or buy" analysis or "optional equipment replacement analysis". The widespread practice of the end-of-the-fiscal-year spending spree is a classic example of counter-productive practice encouraged by the politics of the budgetary process.

Lack of productivity measurement

Autonomy without measured accountability can engender corruption. Yet few public service organisations measure their own performance as they should. While most public institutions conform to regulations requiring them to prepare standard reports, these are usually prepared late, in many developing countries often several years late. The consequences are several. It is rarely possible to use techniques, such as the input-output ratio, to diagnose problems; managers and supervisory boards are seldom able to make informed decisions based on timely accurate figures; and it is difficult to set performance improvement targets and measure progress towards goals. Productivity measures, if they exist, are often unclear, unreliable and untimely.

Some authors note the tendency for analyses of public service productivity virtually to ignore quality-of-service and effectiveness measures and concentrate entirely on measures of efficiency. In other words, the public service may be more interested in the process of service delivery than in the end-result of its interventions. For example, the quality of an education system should not only be measured through exam results but also through improved employment opportunities. However, a more important barrier is that many administrators object to any attempt at measurement and evaluation on the grounds that what they do is intangible and cannot be measured. For example, some mental health professionals define output as the number of clients served and disregard quality of the service delivered. Many public service managers view productivity measurement as a "no-win" proposition. If they report a decline in productivity, their management abilities may be questioned. If gains are reflected in cash savings, their resources may be transferred elsewhere. Therefore, there has been little effort in the public service sector to develop, use and refine performance measures. Another major constraint to productivity improvement in the public service is the inadequate system of collecting data and producing information on cost and output indicators which is crucial to both planning and implementing public service programmes.

Experiences with productivity measurement

Only in a few industrialised countries is productivity in the public service measured systematically. In the United States the federal Government has been measuring productivity changes in the delivery of services since 1967. Each year 28 functions (such as auditing, medical services, personnel management, etc.), with over 2,500 output units (such as hours worked, bills collected, clients served, documents processed), are measured. These are produced by 347 organisational units, which cover 65 per cent of all federal employees – about 1.8 million out of a total workforce of 2.8 million. Data are collected annually by the Bureau of Labour Statistics, and they are analysed and published by the Office of Personnel Management.

In France the RCB (Rationalisation of Budgetary Choices) Commission, presenting its findings on the national health care system in 1984, recommended the evaluation of medical, paramedical and medico-social services in a more sophisticated way than in the past, namely in terms of cost and efficiency.

In the developing world virtually all performance information in the public service has so far consisted of qualitative judgements. Solid performance data have usually been non-existent.

Systematic reporting on productivity has considerable benefits. First of all, productivity measures help in goal-setting. They help identify the best course of action in terms of resource utilisation and cost-effectiveness. They can show what factors have most influence on results so that these can be emphasised. An analysis of past productivity trends and developments can help in decision-making for the future. Geographic variations and their causes can also be assessed, for example, in consumption of medical care. If the reason for such variations can be found, productivity may be increased through measures such as better management, different equipment and techniques. The overall effectiveness of the health care system may also be improved by shifting resources from, say, curative care to preventive care where this is indicated by the productivity data.

In addition, productivity measurement creates a climate of productivity-consciousness in public service organisations, raises questions of good or bad performance that require explanation and helps in identifying the reasons for outstanding performance from which others can learn.

The productivity measurement exercise is in itself an excellent productivity training tool and, in general, an outstanding management training method: it requires the clarification of all inputs and outputs as well as the relationship between them, and leads management to a thorough familiarisation with the objectives and procedures of the service. Productivity measures can also be useful public relation tools because they demonstrate public service performance in very specific terms.

Finally, productivity measures help in the budget process. They make it possible to calculate cost-benefit ratios and to calculate the financial implications of alternative programmes. They show where existing indicators are insufficient for management purposes, including monitoring, control and evaluation. The creation of a productivity measurement system tends to clarify the stages of a programme and assist in the evaluation of actions taken including organisational changes. Productivity indicators help in the proper allocation of central costs (accounting, personnel, etc.) to the various organisational units.

Concepts and principles

Productivity to most people means *labour productivity*: how much is produced per person per hour, day, year or some other period. However, productivity is not only a function of labour but also of many other factors whose impact needs evaluation – hence measurements such as *output per unit of capital*, *output per unit of material* and *output per unit of energy*. Since these measures relate output to one input only, they are called *partial productivity* concepts.

In order to see the combined net effect of several or all resource inputs, *multifactor* ratios and *total factor* ratios have also been developed. Multifactor measures are based on net output or *value added* by an organisation to the value of inputs bought from others such as materials or purchased components and services. This value added can be related to the combined inputs of labour and capital. Total factor productivity ratios, on the other hand, express the relationship of total *gross* output of an organisation to a combination of all input elements, including labour, capital, purchased materials, energy and other outside services. These ratios are useful to express the joint impact of all inputs on output, as well as the effect of each separately on that output.

Productivity always relates output to one or more inputs. There is no "single", "best", or "right" productivity measure. Productivity is the expression of the economic health of organisations and, just like human health, it can be diagnosed from many perspectives. Thus, several measures are required to shed light on different aspects.

Efforts to define and evaluate productivity can be grouped into three broad areas: efficiency measures, operational (or work study) measures, and effectiveness measures.

Efficiency measures compare the inputs or resources an organisation uses with the final goods or services it has produced. Specifically, efficiency refers to the ratio of the quantity of service provided (e.g. tons of refuse collected) to the cost in dollars or labour required to produce the service. In a drug abuse prevention programme, for example, this could mean high-school students counselled divided by counsellor hours expended. In an employment and training programme, it could be welders trained divided by staff hours expended. However, this approach does not determine the degree of satisfaction derived by clients or the extent to which the desired goal is achieved.

Work measurement or operational measures are mainly concerned with the activity itself rather than its results and are usually measured in terms of activity per unit of time (such as pages typed, bills processed, X-rays per hour). Work measures evaluate intermediate activity by assessing resource requirements under a given technology or set of conditions; in contrast, productivity measures relate inputs to final products.

Effectiveness measures, unlike efficiency or operational measures, examine how well a government or public service agency is meeting the public purposes it is trying to fulfil. The measures quantify a programme's impact on society or specific clients and determine whether that programme makes optimum use of inputs or resources to achieve its goals. Effectiveness refers to the degree to which services are responsive to the needs and desires of the community. Hayward (1976) defines government productivity as the "efficiency with which resources are consumed in the effective delivery of public services". The definition implies quality as well as quantity. The value of efficiency is negated if the product or service itself lacks value. For example, public transport effectiveness depends not only on how many people use it, but also on whether passengers have safe, comfortable, rapid, convenient, punctual, and reliable journeys. Thus, effectiveness relates to the outcomes (results) and impact (long-run results) of service provision. Examples of effectiveness variables for particular services include increased income, improved health, abstinence from alcohol, reduction in child abuse, and satisfaction with meal service in a day care centre for the aged.

The principal differences between efficiency and effectiveness measures lie in measuring direct output (efficiency) and the extent to which it achieves its goals (effectiveness). It is useful to contrast them as looking "inward" (efficiency) and "outward" (effectiveness). For example, an efficiency measure may indicate how many people were treated per medical staff-hour, while effectiveness measures are designed to show (if they can) what proportion of cases were treated successfully. Effectiveness measures respond to the question whether the "right thing was done" while efficiency measures show whether it was done "the right way". When, for example, a government trains unemployed people to help them find jobs, the number trained per teacher is an efficiency measure while the number finding work after training is an effectiveness measure.

However, public services should also take into consideration *equity* in service delivery, including accessibility. For example, 80 per cent of the Ethiopian population lives more than one day's walk from the nearest roads. Yet the costs associated with reaching more clients may be so prohibitive that the service itself would suffer. Productivity in terms of efficiency could fall at the same time as effectiveness based on equity could improve.

To accommodate this apparent contradiction, and giving due stress to equity, productivity in the public service may be defined as the efficiency with which resources are consumed in the effective and equitable delivery of those services. This definition comprises inputs (resources consumed), outputs, outcomes and impacts.

The complexity of productivity concepts in public services reflects their many accountability requirements: the demand for efficiency requires measuring inputs and output; the demand for effectiveness requires matching goals and achievement; the demand for service quality requires measuring an agency's responsiveness to clients' needs, convenience, and the like; and demands for equity require looking at the distribution of services. Because of the variety of demands public service productivity thus needs a variety of measures.

Measuring productivity in practice

Among the first systematic inquiries into productivity measurement techniques in public services was that of Ridley and Simon in 1938, when they suggested possible output measures for fire protection, police, public education, public libraries, personnel, municipal finance and city planning. In the case of fire protection they proposed such measures as expenditures, standards of effort (for a specific task), distribution of equipment, fire and fire loss rates, and fire and fire loss rates by type of property. However, they discussed efficiency in terms of consequences rather than direct output. The efficiency of administration was measured by the ratio of the effects actually obtained to the maximum effects possible with the available resources. Incidentally, this emphasis on consequences and evaluation was carried through into the area of Planning-Programming-Budgeting Systems (PPBS).

In 1960 Schmandt and Stephens (US) moved towards direct measurement of local government output. They developed a service level index for 19 cities and villages. The service level was defined rather crudely as the number of different activities performed for each function or subfunction. Police protection was divided, for example, into 65 different categories. In 1964 Gross suggested four possible surrogates (number of clients, the duration of the service, the intermediate or subsequent products of the service and service input factors) that could be used to estimate the quantity of intangible services, such as knowledge transfer, psychological services, media, and so on.

In 1971 the Urban Institute of the United States argued that output should be broadly defined, contending that "the volume of products or services produced" should be interpreted to include the ideas of "effectiveness and quality", not merely "efficiency and quantity". For example, to measure productivity of solid waste collection, the Institute suggested looking at output in tons of refuse collected, adjusted for changes in quality. Quality changes were assessed using two measures: an average street cleanliness rating (scale from 1 to 4), and the percentage of the population expressing satisfaction with refuse collection based on a survey. The output estimate is thus the tons of refuse collected, multiplied by the cleanliness rating and the percentage satisfied with collection. The significant aspect of this example is the quality adjustment.

Bouckaert (1988) (Belgium) suggests a three-tier approach to productivity and its measurement for public service organisations. At the first level – the agency – it is the productivity of civil servants that is measured, using the criteria of efficiency and quality of service delivery. At the second level – the service/programme level – the analysis should concern itself with the impact of the output of public services on citizens, an important element of which is equity. The third level is the political level, where politicians are the main actors. Productivity assessment at this level should determine to what extent budget reallocation, output adjustment and reorientations, investment decisions, changes and corrections in goals and objectives are the result of changing political statements and objectives. The ambiguity of such an assessment is that changing political objectives may be related to equally changing but more measurable output indicators, such as citizen satisfaction.

Epstein (1988) suggests grouping different effectiveness measures into the following four categories (see box 6.1).

- *Measures of community conditions* are important measures of effectiveness as they are the most explicit measures of community needs.
- *Measures of service accomplishments* can be more directly tied to a specific service programme than can general community conditions.
- *Measures of citizen or client satisfaction and perceptions* cover satisfaction with public services and citizens' perceptions of community conditions.
- *Measures of the unintended adverse impacts* of a service on the community examine the extent to

6.1 Measuring the effectiveness of community services: Epstein's approach

Measures of community conditions are simply measures of undesirable conditions the community will always want to reduce, or are measures of desirable conditions the community wants to increase or maintain. They include crime rates, fire incidence rates, numbers of serious traffic accidents, injuries and loss of life and property due to crimes, fires and accidents, good air and water quality, clean streets and alleys, and stable or increasing property values.

There can also be a set of equity standards for community conditions, rating each neighbourhood above or below average, or above or below certain "minimally acceptable" levels.

Measures of service accomplishments focus on programme achievements rather than community conditions. Service accomplishment measures can include both quantity and quality considerations. For example, the frequency of refuse collection is an important quality consideration. For a community with varying frequencies of collection, a useful measure of effectiveness could be the number (quantity) of households receiving two collections (as opposed to one) per week. For refuse disposal programmes, a quality measure could be the level of hazard at refuse disposal sites, and a quantity measure could be the number of communities using the service. For a street repair programme, a useful effectiveness measure could be the number (quantity) of potholes or cracks filled that do not reopen (quality) within X days after being repaired.

For programmes aimed at target groups, such as many social programmes, the number of people from the target population reached by the programme and/or the impact of the programme upon its clients can be used as measures. For example, for a job training programme aimed at the unemployed, data should include how many unemployed people completed job training courses and what were the results or impact: how many, and what percentage of, training programme graduates found jobs within three months of completing training.

Measures of response to citizen requests for services are often useful "accomplishment" measures of effectiveness. For street repairs, for example, some local governments attempt to fill every citizen-reported pothole as soon as possible, while others only repair immediately those considered imminent hazards and repair the others as part of the normal work schedule of the repair crews. Response time as a measure is important for emergency services (police, fire, ambulance, rescue operations). Some fire departments measure the extent of fire spread after the first fire-fighting vehicle arrives.

Measures of citizen or client satisfaction and perceptions provide useful measures of service effectiveness. One way to get an indication of satisfaction with government services is to keep track of the number of complaints registered by citizens. Trends in complaints can indicate problems needing special attention. However, complaints should never be used as the only measure of service effectiveness or citizen satisfaction. Complaints only reflect the views of the most vocal citizens. They do not convey whether most citizens are actually satisfied with the services they receive. Surveys of citizens or service clients provide a much more representative picture of satisfaction and perceptions. Surveys aimed specifically at the users or clients of a particular service (e.g. public transport, libraries, social services) can also be used to point up ways of improving the service.

Measures of unintended adverse impacts of services on the community have to identify the problems or needs created, or any worsening of community conditions, through the provision of a service. For example, do crews spill refuse as they collect it or disturb residents with excessive noise? Measures of adverse impacts can be collected by the use of surveys, trained observers, complaints records and other techniques.

There are many other indirect useful forms of productivity or efficiency measurement in the public service. They include *process time*, such as the time it takes to fill a purchase order or hire an employee, and *backlogs* such as the quantity of forms or letters waiting to be typed, or the number of vehicles awaiting repair. Such measures as *rates of unavailability or non-use of resources* include lost capacity, such as the percentage of vehicles or other equipment out of service, or the amount of water lost in a water supply system due to leakage, and unused capacity, such as load factors of public transport vehicles, or the percentage of personnel time spent "unproductively" (e.g., waiting for equipment or material, taking a break).

which public services create needs or problems that might not otherwise exist, or unintentionally aggravate existing problems.

A number of widely-used techniques make systematic use of performance measures to judge efficiency and effectiveness of public services. *Project management* measures track adherence to time and cost schedules stage by stage (e.g. complete facility design, receive construction bids, begin construction). Project management measures can be applied to any project with a definable end, such as the passage of a government decree, a bond issue, or development and implementation of work standards. Measures can be compiled for several projects to indicate the performance of the agencies responsible (e.g. number of projects proceeding on schedule or completed on time, number of projects within cost, total cost of projects compared to planned cost).

Programme evaluation is defined as the periodic, independent and objective review and assessment of a programme to determine, in the light of current circumstances, the adequacy of its objectives, its design and its results both intended and unintended. Evaluation will call into question the very existence of the programme. Matters such as the rationale for the programme, its impact on the public, and its cost-effectiveness compared with alternative means of programme delivery are reviewed.

The medical co-operative "Eye Microsurgery" in the USSR provides an interesting example of combining productivity evaluation of efficiency through cost-accounting and service quality (effectiveness through minimising the failure rate and keeping the operation price for the customer below the standard level) (see box 6.2).

Some public agencies use measurements designed along the lines of the *Mundel hierarchy of work units*. This approach breaks down final service outputs into well-defined quantifiable units of work, further subdivided into sub-units and operations. Various levels within the production cycle are distinguished, from resource input to the organisation's outputs or achievements. The measurement process begins with time and motion studies for each operation, moves to the measurement of intermediate and final output at the levels of work units, and ends with an attempt to measure overall service effectiveness.

Less rigorously, some periodicals have developed their own measures to evaluate effectiveness of public service activities. For example, *The Economist* (United Kingdom) has issued star-ratings and comments for each main public service programme in the United Kingdom.

2. Structural reforms and information technologies

To improve public service productivity many countries, developed and developing, market economy and socialist, are undertaking major reform programmes – often in the context of structural adjustment policies. Such programmes may include proposals for decentralisation, deregulation and privatisation, while most of them emphasise the increased use of information and other new technologies.

Decentralisation and integration

Many countries have begun a process of restructuring the public service with the purpose of decen-

6.2 Profits and productivity: Eye microsurgery in the USSR

Cost-accounting practices in the work of medical associations in the USSR has encouraged efficiency and raised the quality of work, even though resources have remained constant. This is demonstrated by various experiments now being undertaken of which the management of the technical co-operative "Eye Microsurgery" is the most well known.

Earnings of the co-operative are based on a straight capitation fee per patient treated. The fee, based on the then-existing standard average cost of an operation, has been set for a five-year period at 214 roubles per patient. The earnings finance all basic requirements including the acquisition of hospital equipment, the purchase of drugs, research, hospital food, transportation costs, heating and other administrative needs. They also cover wages and bonuses awarded to the most outstanding staff members.

Should the income of the centre exceed spending, surplus funds can be used for further development of its activities, extra payments and other incentives for employees, and social and cultural benefits for staff, including housing construction, nurseries, sports facilities, holiday centres, and so on.

According to 1987 estimates the actual cost per patient at the centre was 115 roubles, a profit of 100 roubles for each treated case.

This huge profit per patient is accounted for by the efficient work of the centre. Similar operations in other hospitals cost 260 to 280 roubles, with a ceiling price of 300 roubles, expenses which are covered by the state budget. Moreover, the failure rate is as high as 25 per cent in some of these eye clinics. In the "Eye Microsurgery" centre the failure rate has fallen and currently does not exceed 0.5 to 1 per cent.

tralising decision-making and increasing authority and accountability at lower management levels. More attention is now paid to defining clearly the division of responsibility between the central government, its agencies and local government, and laying down modalities of financial and management control. A workable compromise must be effected between two essential ingredients: autonomy – if a service is to operate efficiently; and accountability – if it is to meet the objectives of public policy.

There are plenty of examples of successful decentralisation at different levels. A number of studies in the Canadian public service, for example, concluded that as long as managers were faced with crippling administrative constraints, were afforded only limited authority, and were unsure to whom and for what they were accountable, major improvements in achieving value for money were unlikely. These studies suggested that the Government should reduce constraints on decision-making to give managers the sort of control over resources and procedures that would enable them to manage more productively. The Government should also clarify and strengthen accountability relationships, to ensure that these were clearly understood by managers, and simplify the many accountability demands at the same time as making accountability procedures more rigorous.

A 1986 government initiative enabling public managers to make changes in their budgets without going to the Treasury Board for approval was a good first step in implementing such suggestions. The main objectives of this initiative – called "Increased Ministerial Authority and Accountability" (IMAA) – were, firstly, to give ministers and senior managers the enhanced authority and flexibility they needed to deal with changing circumstances and manage effectively with limited resources, and, secondly, to increase their accountability for the achievement of results, both in programme delivery and in implementation of Treasury Board policies. One result of this initiative has been a sharp drop in the number of budget submissions from departments to the Treasury, from 5,100 in 1983-84 to 3,500 in 1986-87, or 33 per cent. Departmental contacts with the Prime Minister's Cabinet have also been significantly reduced. For example, in the area of human resources development policy, the new procedures will result in a decline of about 1,000 requests for funds annually.

Major reforms in France have entailed shifting powers and functions from Paris to the provinces, from the central Government to the local authorities at the regional, district and municipal levels, and also to the local offices of central government departments. The Civil Service Code has been extended since 1984 to cover all government levels, so that personnel at the regional, district and municipal levels now have better terms of employment. In China, a "post responsibility" system was installed to reinforce initiative and responsibility at the action officer level and to combat the ills of overconcentration of authority at the top. In Guyana decentralisation has been used to divert excess public manpower away from the capital district towards outlying areas where it could be used more productively. A system of incentives has been introduced for that purpose. In Bangladesh, major reforms are planned to strengthen the function and authority of rural subdistricts.

At the same time, along with the decentralisation process, there has been a noticeable integration (some people call it recentralisation) process – meaning an increased accountability of public organisations to government on objectives achieved and their costs. Again, this assumes a clear specification of social objectives so that the efficiency of operations can be measured. One powerful instrument, among others, is the external audit. Experience indicates that efficiency audits conducted by autonomous agencies within the government structure can play a useful role. There are a few examples where such agencies have been able not merely to monitor the performance of government departments, but also to conduct valuable in-depth studies of public organisations and, by disseminating their findings, to contribute to public understanding of the civil service. In some instances, such as Ethiopian Airlines and the New York transport department, such knowledge has helped to boost the prestige and improve the image of particular government agencies.

Deregulation and privatisation

Today more and more governments see deregulation and privatisation as important vehicles to promote efficiency. The administrative capacities of many governments are severely strained by the extent of their activities and, as noted previously, they have often also reached the limit of their financial resources. Hence, they are looking for ways to simplify regulations and to shift some of their activities to the private sector.

Deregulation

Deregulation has had and continues to have a dramatic impact on public service organisations. Recent developments in, for example, the US, the EEC, Japan, and some socialist and developing countries range from liberalisation – giving managers more flexibility in interpreting existing regulations – to full deregulation. The pace of change has varied from a steady erosion of constraints to a dramatic reduction in the regulatory framework. In the Federal Republic of Germany, for example, individual states have set up commissions for the simplification of administration. In the Ministry of Culture and Sports for Baden-Wurtemberg, the work of the local commission focuses on deregulating the administration of schools, colleges and universities. The Ministry employs 120,000 teachers and other public servants and used to manage its affairs with the help of 3,500 administrative directives. As a result of an effort at deregulation, this number has been reduced to 365. The principal aim of deregulation was to increase the autonomy of managers, encourage delegation of authority to the lowest practical level and unify formerly divided lines of accountability.

Regulations are normally introduced for a purpose – to promote equity, prevent waste and abuse, and ensure prudence and probity. But rules also have costs. There is the cost of making and administering them. There is also the cost of resulting bureaucratic actions that can be unresponsive and inflexible. However, reasonable limits need to be set on deregulation so as not to harm the social and living standards of the population. For example, over-zealous deregulation in transport and communications could impair the safety and quality of services. Labour market deregulation could bring about a dilution of acquired rights such as pension benefits, minimum wages and labour standards. Thus, the main challenge is to achieve a balance between the need for regulation and the need for an adequate level of managerial authority and flexibility.

Privatisation

As noted in Chapter 2, many governments have privatised public enterprises or are planning to do so. This section describes how some governments are also experimenting with the privatisation of government services such as education and health. The strain placed on the administrative resources of many governments by the numerous demands on them raises the question of whether social and economic development could be accelerated by moving some responsibilities to the private sector. Such an arrangement would allow hard-pressed public administrative systems to concentrate on activities that they are best equipped to provide.

The appropriate balance between publicly- and privately-provided services is something on which governments have very different views. Comparing three industrialised countries in 1986, in Sweden health accounted for 26 per cent of public sector employment, education for 18 per cent and various other welfare services for 21 per cent. In the United Kingdom, the national health service accounted for 23 per cent of general government employment, and education and social services provided by local government for, respectively, 27 and 7 per cent. In the United States health accounted in 1985 for 10 per cent of state and local government employment, which in total accounts for some 80 per cent of general government employment. This low share reflects the important role played by the private sector in the provision of health services in the United States. Education accounted for 53 per cent of US state and local government employment in the United States in 1986.

In France privatisation has affected public services ranging from television (privatisation of the national channel TF1) to the national health service. In the Federal Republic of Germany, privatisation of some locally provided public services began to be suggested in the mid-1970s, principally as a means of cutting costs. The services most frequently transferred to the private sector are: refuse collection, treatment and incineration; social services for children and the elderly; health services such as hospitals, clinics, technical services, physiotherapy, ambulances, hospital laundry; the sale of a number of local hospitals to private multinational groups; cleaning of public buildings, care of public parks and gardens, canteens, and so on.

In the education system of many developing countries the percentage of private enrolment has been declining since the 1960s, but the numbers receiving private education have increased in absolute terms. Two main reasons for this expansion have been proposed. Firstly, private schools provide a better education than public schools, and this difference in quality outweighs the cost difference. Secondly, the governments are strapped for funds and cannot meet the demand for secondary or even primary educa-

6.3 The computerisation of personnel statistics in the public service: The case of China

There are some 29 million people working in the Chinese public service (including public administration, health and medical services, teachers, scientific research staff and various other categories). Of these 5.5 million work in public administrations at central, provincial and local levels; 1.87 million in health and medical services; 7.58 million in the teaching profession; 633,000 in scientific research; and 13.4 million in other services (such as customs, police, libraries, press agencies, publishing, etc.). Almost 2 million are party cadres, who in the future will no longer be classified as in the public service.

At the moment, personnel statistics are collected manually at the provincial and district level, with delays of five to six months between the beginning and the end of the operation. Only macro-level statistics are sent to the Ministry of Personnel. To collect them, large numbers of staff have to be mobilised. In 1983, for example, a database was set up for higher professional and technical staff, limited to a number of ministries, bodies and municipalities. For this exercise, 100,000 people had to be mobilised over nine months, which proved insufficient to cover all the staff concerned. According to information received from the Ministry of Personnel, no less than 700,000 employees are engaged in the collection of public service statistics throughout the country.

In certain provinces the statistical information is registered on diskettes which are sent by mail to the Ministry of Personnel. The Ministry does not, however, have computers with the necessary power and storage capacity to make proper use of this information and to generate, for instance, checklists.

The Ministry of Personnel – established in 1988 – and its Personnel Information Computer Centre (PICC) maintain, for the time being, only the personnel files of the Ministry's own employees and of about 3,000 higher civil servants of other ministries. This number is to be increased to 9,000 or 10,000 files in the near future. With a view to improving its statistical information, the Ministry envisages setting up, as a first step, a personnel information network for higher civil servants (about 500,000) and for professional and technical personnel (about 200,000) across the country. Through this network, the Ministry expects to obtain information about the numbers of staff, their distribution and composition, their assignment and training, and so on. This information will be processed and analysed in order to provide a sound basis for policy decisions and administration.

The 13th National Congress of the Communist Party of China decided in November 1987 to establish a civil service system. Its management would be based on the law governing public servants, a draft of which is at present being discussed. In this context, the Government decided to undertake a comprehensive reform of the personnel management system and has asked the ILO for assistance. Following a preliminary assessment by the ILO of immediate needs in this area, the following priorities have been identified for improving efficiency through the introduction of a computerised personnel information system:

- The present decentralised personnel management system is working well and is suited to the country's needs. It needs, however, to be modernised and, if possible, computerised down to county and district levels, where the majority of civil service staff is employed.
- Present methods of obtaining personnel statistics are of little use for personnel policies and personnel planning purposes, since they are cumbersome and costly. By the time statistical information is ready for analysis by the Ministry of Personnel, it is already outdated. The double procedure for the day-to-day management of personnel files on the one hand and for the collecting of statistics on the other should be replaced by a single procedure, whereby statistics are a by-product of handling staff records. Furthermore, personnel administration staff need appropriate training, notably in the use of computerised methods and of personnel management procedures.
- There is a need for uniform legislation on personnel management functions such as recruitment, promotions, disciplinary sanctions, leave, mobility, and the like, and on use of the resulting statistical information.

tion, particularly in a number of African countries. The overall picture is that in developing countries in recent years lower-level general education has increasingly become the responsibility of public authorities on equity considerations, while the private sector has been more involved in specialised education such as higher-level and vocational training.

A similar trend can be observed for the health sector. On equity grounds governments provide health services free or at reduced cost. But many governments have begun to charge user-fees and concentrate their services on general and preventive health services, leaving specialised – and more expensive – care to the private sector. In fact, private health services play a leading role in all developing countries. For example, private sector expenditures in Thailand on health care were estimated in 1980 to have been four times the amount spent on health by the Government. Fifty per cent of curative health care was delivered through private pharmacies and a further 20 per cent by traditional healers. In Brazil and China, private expenditure as a percentage of total health expenditure in 1981 was more than 30 per cent, in Haiti (1980) 65 per cent, in Indonesia (1983) 62 per cent, in Jordan (1982) 41 per cent, Mali (1981) 54 per cent, and Pakistan (1982) 71 per cent.

Information technologies

The development and introduction of new technology into the public service can improve its quality, decrease costs and generate new activities. Of all new technologies, information technology (IT) is the most important and universal, and it could be applied much more extensively in public service administration and management, particularly in the developing countries. Among the major constraints on improving productivity in the public service is an inadequate system of collecting data, organising them and producing information for decision-making (see box 6.3). Even available information may be underutilised. Many United Nations advisory missions to developing countries have found frequent misuse and gross underuse of information systems, such as computers and data banks.

Applications

The most promising direction for improving public service productivity is office automation through development of IT and computerisation. For example, a pilot project in Sri Lanka for establishment of a data system at the divisional (provincial) level for village-level planning and rural development is based on the use of a micro-computer at the district level (the Kalutara district), enabling the local administrators and planners to process their data locally.

There has been a rapid development of computer data bases covering a wide range and growing number of applications, including management systems. The key developments in this field involve improving integration and access, that is, using an appropriate telecommunications network to link different systems together as well as to hook up terminals of potential business and domestic users. Many countries have already built, or are building, specific communication and telecommunication networks to allow much more data traffic. Digital telecommunications infrastructure links different IT devices and users, allowing them to communicate with each other, and so provides the potential for the growth of an enormous range of interactive information-based services which can be carried on the network. It is worth mentioning that the most important IT key components such as memory cards, terminals, videotex and teletext, word processing, micrographics, laser disks, and so on, which are likely to generate new service activities in the next 10 to 15 years, are already in existence.

Computerisation has led to the development and use in the public service of such new technologies of decision-making as Decision Support Systems (DSS), Automated Decision Conferencing (ADC), Expert Systems (ES) as well as more sophisticated and computerised Management Information Systems (MIS).

Table 6.1. Automation capabilities and how they affect productivity

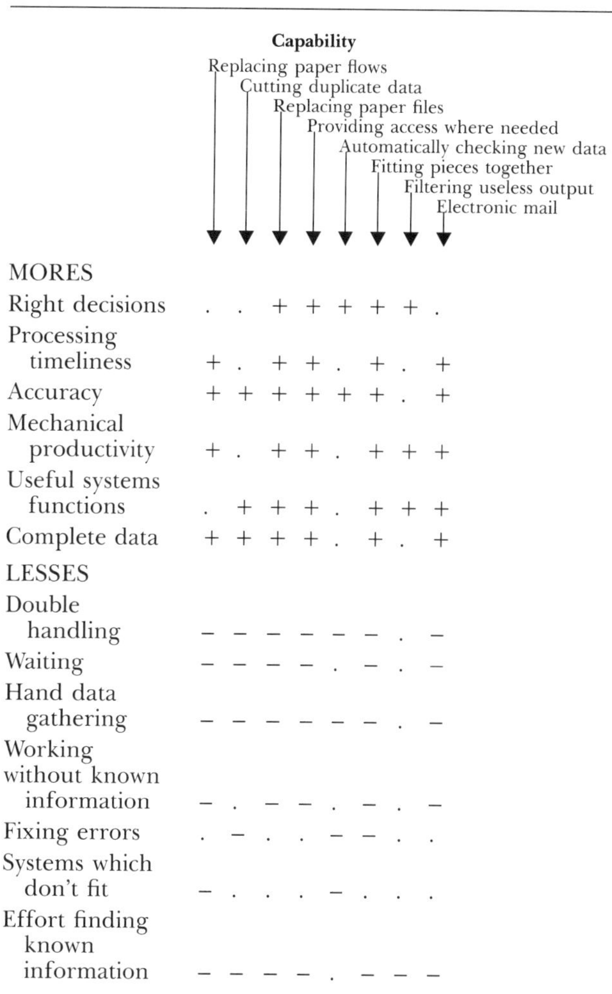

	Capability: Replacing paper flows	Cutting duplicate data	Replacing paper files	Providing access where needed	Automatically checking new data	Fitting pieces together	Filtering useless output	Electronic mail
MORES								
Right decisions	.	.	+	+	+	+	+	.
Processing timeliness	+	.	+	+	.	+	.	+
Accuracy	+	+	+	+	+	+	.	+
Mechanical productivity	+	.	+	+	.	+	+	+
Useful systems functions	.	+	+	+	.	+	+	+
Complete data	+	+	+	+	.	+	.	+
LESSES								
Double handling	–	–	–	–	–	–	.	–
Waiting	–	–	–	–	.	–	.	–
Hand data gathering	–	–	–	–	–	–	.	–
Working without known information	–	.	–	–	.	–	.	–
Fixing errors	.	–	.	.	–	–	.	.
Systems which don't fit	–	.	.	.	–	.	.	.
Effort finding known information	–	–	–	–	.	–	–	–

Source: M. K. Stankard: *Productivity by choice: The 20-to-1 principle* (New York, John Wiley and Sons, 1986), p. 238.

Thus, in the realm of public service productivity computers serve three major purposes: reducing costs, increasing resources and providing better and often new services, for example, selling access to computer facilities.

Table 6.1 summarises the relationship between office automation and productivity. It shows that the many capabilities of office automation have multiple effects on costs and productivity improvements for the consumer. Thus, introducing office automation means that productivity is improved over a whole range of activities. A 1986 survey of all 50 American states revealed that 48 state financial control officers are now using microcomputers. The Treasury Department decision to use electronic funds transfer systems for all federal benefit programmes has eliminated the need for cheques. Savings to taxpayers in the financial year 1984-85 exceeded US$7 million a month.

A Productivity Development Group Inc. (United States) survey shows that in over 200 cases studied large productivity successes were mostly attributable to automation. The Pennsylvania sales tax collection office increased collection of delinquent taxes by US$19 million in the first year of use of an on-line computerised system. In Brooklyn, New York, the fire department automated its dispatch centre, reducing response time from ten minutes to 20 seconds. Greater use of electronic deposit and transfer mechanisms in the office of the Canadian Receiver General has cut the number of departmental bank accounts from 1,000 to 22, and so reduced processing costs. To increase productivity as well as safety of hazardous chemicals inspection procedures, the hazardous chemical information file has been incorporated into the computer-aided dispatch system for the Canadian police and fire departments.

Social consequences

An important issue in considering the introduction of new technology into public services is the balance between enhancing productivity and possibly adverse social consequences. Among the negative consequences are redundancies, impaired working conditions and a reduction in the autonomy and privacy of citizens. To cope with these growing challenges many industrialised and some developing countries have introduced government-wide policies to co-ordinate new technology projects and deal with the problems that arise. In many countries, redundancies are minimised by training employees to apply and work with the new technology and by the reorganisation of jobs and work units. In Canada the Public Service Commission is notified of all vacancies, so that these can be considered for the possible placement of redundant employees before being cleared for general competition or other recruitment procedures. Most provincial governments have adopted programmes to prevent redundancies and to limit the negative impact of new technologies by retraining, counselling and reassigning employees. In Belgium an agreement concluded between the Government and the unions stipulates that the authorities must inform the unions about major computerisation plans; the unions may also raise safety and health problems posed by the use of new technologies. In the Federal Republic of Germany the Ministry of the Interior has issued recommendations on the planning and introduction of new technologies which are designed to ensure that due account is taken of the organisational and social consequences and that representatives of the staff and others concerned are involved in the process at an early stage.

In India the introduction of computers is tied to four government commitments: (1) there must be no retrenchment as a result of computerisation and any worker made redundant must be found alternative employment; (2) there must be no loss of earnings for existing staff; (3) computerisation must have no adverse effect on conditions of work and promotion prospects; and (4) adequate safeguards must be provided to protect workers' interests, including a method of sharing possible benefits. In Turkey there is also a legal provision on alternative employment for staff who become redundant as a result of technological change.

In Finland government offices are required to plan and introduce the rationalisation of office work in a way that ensures the continuity of employment of the staff. Co-operation with shop stewards is mandatory when rationalisation affects remuneration or other employment terms fixed by agreements; the staff must be duly informed at the planning stage and be given the opportunity to participate in decisions entailing changes in their tasks and working environment.

In Italy trade unions have extensive rights to information concerning planned technological innovations and processes that may alter work organisation.

In Madagascar measures to cope with technological change have been taken unilaterally by the administration and consultation of the workers affected has been discretionary. In Nigeria, however, training programmes on new technologies for civil service staff have created a favourable atmosphere for the changes to take effect. Workers are trained to use the new equipment, are alerted to any danger of exposure and are taught to wear protection (such as special glasses) if necessary. In Portugal, while there is no legal obligation to consult the unions or workers' representatives on the introduction of new technologies or structural changes, there is a dialogue between the public administration and the unions on these matters. In Côte d'Ivoire and a number of other African French-speaking countries unions are consulted when reforms are envisaged and new technologies introduced in the administration.

The introduction of new technology into the public service, and particularly into public administration, clearly can have positive and negative consequences which extend far beyond any reduction in employment.

For example, information technology could enable government departments to gain greater autonomy, a tendency that the centre may be tempted to check by tighter control which IT also permits. For public servants IT could make their jobs more interesting. Against that, it is much easier for management to monitor staff activities and compare individual work records.

In addition, in many countries, the criteria for data protection are unclear. Information is a political resource. Computerised information systems are a means of establishing control, for a time, over a problem area or a cluster of activities. Thus, new technologies strengthen the power of government over the country's citizens. The computerisation of information about the citizen inevitably leads to centralised records and information sharing between computer networks, so increasing the danger of misuse. Therefore new measures for legal protection of the citizen against privacy invasion and upholding the individual's right to privacy are necessary.

3. Management approaches to productivity improvement

Apart from structural adjustments at the macrolevel, many productivity improvement actions need to take place at the agency or organisation level. One important school of thought argues that service quality problems arise from two major sources: first, faults built in to the actual service system and, secondly, one-off problems which result from the actions of an individual employee. Of the two, built-in sources of trouble are by far the most important. Thus, service quality and client satisfaction are largely, if not completely, under management's control.

Changing managerial styles and practices

The commitment and active support of top management is a vital prerequisite of a successful productivity improvement programme. Monthly or quarterly meetings with all staff to review progress have often had beneficial influences on morale and productivity. People tend to follow the example of their superiors, so that the demonstration of top management commitment to productivity goals is helpful in itself.

In the public service sector it is also important to secure support from politicians, based on the recognition that efficient management will help them to spend public money more effectively and achieve a better return on investments. Politicians need to adopt a management philosophy which embraces approaches such as decentralisation, more freedom for managers and accountability for performance.

For management as a whole, a modern open managerial style is a requirement for higher productivity. The outmoded authoritarian style of management needs to be replaced by one which is more democratic, co-operative and delegating. Managers must learn to trust their subordinates and to allow them more independence. One of the critical issues mentioned in a recent public service sector survey in Canada was low morale among employees, stemming from lack of confidence in their leadership.

It is also important to attack such organisational matters as improving co-ordination, eliminating duplication and waste, reducing complexity and shedding excess staff. A key approach to service productivity improvement is a client-focused strategy. Unfortunately, in many countries public service organisations are too much concerned with satisfying superior authorities – ministries, government agencies and their plans and policies – rather than the users of government services.

In developing their service strategy, public service organisations should address the following five issues: knowledge of clients' needs; training and development; providing information to clients; continuous performance improvement; and measuring and reinforcing service excellence. Tackling these key areas will result in a performance-oriented organisational culture and productivity improvement. Such a strategy will also influence management practices. For example, managers should set specific and realistic productivity goals for specific programmes and types of services and follow them up to ensure that work is performed on schedule, that actions achieve results, and that productivity measurement is carried out.

There are many different management methods and techniques to improve productivity at the work unit level. Simple work reorganisation in one large service organisation reduced the time taken to type the average letter from 14.32 minutes to 12.34 minutes, without additional capital investment. At Blue Cross, an American health insurance organisation, conscious productivity improvement efforts have reduced claims-processing time per employee by 10 per cent over a two-year period. Another organisation found that its productivity could be improved by eliminating some 25 checks of the same claim, that had crept into the system over the years due to poor co-ordination.

In the Province of Ontario (Canada), in a noteworthy innovation, "The Deputy Ministers' 100 Minutes", the eight ministers on the Management Board of Cabinet set aside 100 minutes each year to discuss with each deputy minister (top-ranked civil servant) departmental achievements, problems and priorities. This has improved upward communication and top management awareness of current problems.

Developing management skills

An active, highly-skilled, well-informed and motivated civil service management, committed to the objectives of national development, is a necessary condition for the success of government policies. Achieving this state of affairs is the goal of management training and development, a goal which requires conscious effort on the part of top policymakers.

Management training and development are necessary to raise general productivity awareness and to acquire skills and knowledge in productivity improvement methods and techniques. Improving productivity awareness is important to overcome resistance to change and to secure employees' full cooperation in productivity improvement programmes. Training addresses itself to staff needs and organisational requirements that are as diverse as they are often complex and difficult to meet. It provides for the acquisition, refinement and updating of managerial knowledge and skill required to achieve high performance, as well as developing and even modifying behavioural traits and attitudes (such as putting oneself in the client's "shoes"). The scale and complexity of government services make new demands not only for aptitude in the use of up-to-date computer technologies, but also for improved interpersonal and communication skills.

Thus, appropriate education and training policies are necessary. Such training should combine familiarity with new technologies, particularly IT, with sufficient flexibility to allow for frequent changes in job specifications as technologies and service applications evolve. Individual European countries are already accumulating considerable experience in devising such policies, while the European Commission is co-ordinating the results and facilitating exchanges of information about successful initiatives. Among them are open universities, "learning resource centres", introduction of "expert systems" and social "counselling". (Expert systems are computer-software systems for knowledge processing (instead of data processing), using advanced programming techniques. Such systems make knowledge and experiences of experts more widely available for clients and customers. They can take the form of check-lists, computerised manuals or counselling (self-service) systems.)

The public service will always need managers who can harmonise political and managerial objectives, balance the mix of resources and cope with administrative constraints inherent in the public service environment. The future effective public service manager will need to develop such characteristics as: flexibility and openness to new ideas and concepts; "breadth plus depth" or multi-dimensionalism in skills and competences; leadership sensitivity to issues of ethics and morality, value systems and social codes; global orientation; decision-making capabilities under conditions of uncertainty; communication skills; good judgement; technological literacy, adaptability, and so on. For senior civil servants it will be important to play a greater role in the introduction of new technology, to provide less authoritarian leadership, to rapidly recognise and concentrate on new problem areas, and to use modern IT devices.

Management training programmes

Few public service organisations provide specialised training for productivity improvement. This requires two types of knowledge; a practical understanding of productivity concepts and techniques, for example, measurement methods; and a familiarity with operating the tools and techniques which bring increased productivity about.

Many problems in public service productivity training in developing countries arise because of the blind transfer of training programmes from Europe, North America or Japan. Very often the curricula of development administration programmes in developing countries have been based on situations prevailing a decade previously, or specific to particular countries not their own. For example, in many developing countries revenue administration is one of the most neglected fields in teaching programmes in public administration, partly because of the heritage of colonial administration which was uninterested in revenue collection.

Training programmes in most developing countries do not yet pay sufficient attention to the policy role of senior administrators, and need to concentrate much more on people-oriented skills rather than simply on analytical techniques. Public service management development also lacks a good system for training evaluation. Management development, particularly in the Third World, is measured almost exclusively in terms of participant time whereas the ultimate objective is to improve performance in client organisations. Management development professionals, who are rewarded only in terms of contract hours, have too little incentive to acquire and use the more powerful, result-oriented tools at hand such as action learning, management consulting, and so on. Finally, the clients must become partners in development training. Today fewer than 20 per cent of public agencies in developing countries have budgets for management development.

Instituting management training and development specifically for public services and particularly for public administration is of critical importance. In most countries public employees have access to a range of management training programmes and facilities. Training institutions for senior civil servants and for managerial and technical staff were recently established in Argentina (National Institute of Public Administration) and in Brazil (National School of Public Administration and Public Administration Development Centre). In the German Democratic Republic training of public employees is ensured in general training institutions and in specialised institutions, such as the Academy of State and Law Sciences. Time off from work with pay is granted for training purposes.

In Italy the High School of Public Administration organises training courses at the request of individual organisations and on the basis of collective agreements provided for in the Public Service (General Principles) Act. The emphasis is on the training of new appointees and supervisory and managerial training. In India a great diversity of training programmes exists for various levels of officials, such as cadre training programmes in the Indian administrative service, in-service training, and so on.

Paid educational leave arrangements are available to public servants in a large number of countries (Algeria, Argentina, Australia, Bahrain, Barbados, Belize, Bulgaria, Burundi, Canada, Cyprus, Czechoslovakia, Denmark, Finland, France, the Federal Republic of Germany, Guinea-Bissau, India, Honduras, Luxembourg, Netherlands, Nigeria, Portugal, Sri Lanka, Sweden, Tunisia, the United Kingdom, the USSR). In Italy educational leave is already provided for certain categories of public servants and is to be extended to all public servants. In Belgium, government and public service unions recently agreed upon the principle of paid educational leave. In other countries (Japan, Madagascar, Mali) paid educational leave does not exist.

Improving management through training and development without other organisational changes can create problems of its own. Thus, client organisations need to ensure they can use trained managers effectively. To improve actual performance, classroom training is best combined with "action learning" – on-the-job training that involves the solution of real problems – or similar "hands-on" approaches. Some of these which have been actively applied in a number of ILO projects are discussed below (see box 6.4).

Productivity improvement programmes

Success in boosting productivity requires conscious, results-oriented productivity improvement programmes at different levels – national, agency and organisation. These programmes can be aimed at raising the overall productivity of the agency or organisation, or at separate elements such as personnel policy, management styles and practices, incentive systems, new methods of work organisation and/or technology, and so on. In Malaysia in 1987 productivity improvement programmes were mainly concerned with productivity measurement and analysis in public health care (University Hospital), and productivity measurement in public services; in Pakistan, an attempt was made to improve the training services of the National Supervisory Training Centre, with ILO assistance. The Philippine Productivity Development Centre developed programmes with the objective of improving the productivity of the present administration, which involved carrying out a Survey of the Productivity Improvement Programme in the Government. In Thailand a large number of productivity promotion activities were aimed at stimulating public service organisations to continue their own productivity promotion projects.

The typical key elements of a successful productivity improvement programme are as follows:

6.4 Some management training techniques used in ILO projects

Action learning (AL). This technique, originally developed by Professor Reginald Revans of the United Kingdom, has been used in a wide variety of situations, from very large to very small enterprises, in hospitals and in rural communities. In large organisations AL may take the form of interchanging senior personnel, for periods of six months to a year, to carry out work on perceived problems in the host organisations. In smaller organisations managers usually work on their own problems. In all cases a feature of the approach is regular (e.g. monthly) meetings of the participants, at which they report their progress, discuss problems encountered, and exchange advice. These meetings are important in maintaining the motivation of the participants. Action learning has been successfully tried in many industrialised and developing countries and in different economic sectors, including the public service.

AL is based on the principle that managers learn best from doing, reflecting on the results and doing better next time. Action learning helps them appreciate this way of developing their skills. It is in effect a means of learning how to learn.

Planning for Improved Performance (PIP). This is a form of Organisation Development (OD) with a strong "do-it-yourself" flavour. The organisation itself identifies and diagnoses problem areas (which might be maintenance standards, quality control or customer relations), and develops and implements actions to remedy them. In effect, PIP results in an upgrading and "tightening-up" of overall management performance in the service organisation. PIP helps by providing a framework for carrying out the process of diagnosis (fact-finding), action plan development and implementation, and by training management consultants on how to help their clients overcome any barriers encountered in the process.

Management Development Units (MDU). MDUs are led by a "training manager" from the organisation itself and an officer of the Management Development Institute who provides "facilitator" skills – the aim being to work with enterprise management, encouraging them to solve problems through creative thinking and initiative. It is important to ensure that MDUs have no power to take decisions so they pose no threat to senior personnel. Recommendations from the MDU should take the form of proposals to be adopted and implemented by the organisation. A further technique to build confidence in the MDU's ability to solve problems, characterised as a "fail-safe" strategy, is to attract attention to itself by successfully tackling easy problems first. This approach has been tried in India and Pakistan within the framework of ILO projects.

Campaign-type programmes. Whereas action planning workshops allow managers to set targets and make plans on a variety of issues, campaigns concentrate on a single issue involving many organisations. Campaigns mobilise considerable resources to tackle a pinpointed problem. They must be designed to build momentum from early successes and to run long enough for bottom-line results to appear. In its first cycle a campaign will concentrate on breaking one important barrier, such as maintenance; then in subsequent cycles the campaign will use its tested procedures on related problems like production, quality or cost control.

(1) *Setting clear objectives and an integrated productivity plan.* Each service organisation needs to have clearly defined, practical and attainable productivity goals and objectives. Based on these goals and objectives, detailed productivity improvement plans need to be worked out annually.

(2) *Continuing productivity activity.* Effective productivity improvement is a continuing process and a long-term effort. It needs to be evaluated regularly and the results fed back to those responsible for it.

(3) *Central point of responsibility.* Public service organisations need to have a respected individual or small staff, appointed near the top of the organisation, to help implement the productivity effort. Its responsibilities should include, at minimum: stimulating, institutionalising and assisting the productivity effort; gathering and disseminating information on productivity to all staff; and providing information and data on productivity performance to top management.

(4) *Measurement of results.* Productivity measurement is needed to indicate whether progress is being made in improving productivity and how the organisation compares with other similar organisations.

(5) *Top-level interest and commitment.* Active interest shown in productivity by top managers and their visible commitment to the organisation's productivity objectives seem to be essential requirements of all successful productivity efforts.

(6) *Role and importance of management approaches.* The quality of management at all levels is a critical determinant of productivity performance. While top management needs to lead and support the productivity programme, middle management must be trained and motivated to co-operate with top management in productivity improvement programmes.

(7) *Managers' accountability for productivity improvement.* Managers will endeavour to improve productivity only if their responsibility is clearly defined and if they are held accountable for productivity performance.

(8) *Raising productivity awareness throughout the organisation.* It is a prerequisite of successful productivity programmes that all employees recognise the importance of productivity to themselves as

well as to the organisation and their co-operation must be enlisted.

(9) *Communication and training.* Successful productivity programmes require clear, consistent and frequent communications about agency tasks, objectives, productivity plans and achievements. In order to be able to contribute to productivity improvement, appropriate training facilities must be made available to all staff.

(10) *Employee involvement and incentives.* The chance for participation in decisions affecting employees is one of the most effective productivity rewards and incentives, particularly in the public service where "gainsharing" possibilities are limited.

Institutionalising productivity improvement

The shortage of people with productivity expertise is a serious obstacle to productivity enhancement. To overcome it, public service organisations have often set up specialised productivity units. The staff of these units is normally very small, ranging from one to five professionals. They usually report directly to top management although their function is to support the productivity programme of the entire organisation. The best location in the organisation is in the finance or personnel department, in order to give the productivity programme the necessary authority and credibility to motivate managers and staff.

The functions of such a productivity unit include: (1) institutionalising the productivity effort by such activities as helping to define productivity objectives, assisting managers in developing and reaching productivity goals, serving as an internal consulting group, managing the suggestion system for employees, and so on; (2) gathering practical productivity information, and disseminating it to managers and all employees; (3) developing and maintaining the organisation's productivity measurement and analysis system; (4) identifying the causes of weak productivity performance; and (5) providing top management with data on productivity performance, and information as well as recommendations on productivity improvement opportunities.

There are many successful examples of such institutional arrangements at the agency and country levels. For example, the Bureau of Management Consulting (BMC) established under the Ministry of Supply and Services of Canada is now the central management consulting agency of the Government. The BMC role is to provide a full range of general and specialised management consulting services to assist in solving public sector managers' problems and improving public administration. The BMC undertakes more than 700 consulting assignments a year on a fee-for-service basis. These services are available to all Canadian government departments and organisations and to provincial governments as well as to foreign States and international organisations.

In the United States an important role in studying public sector productivity problems is played by the National Centre for Public Productivity together with a few other productivity centres in the states, cities and some universities. Influential in municipal productivity improvement is the Labor Management Co-operation and Quality of Work Life Programme in the City of New York.

Similar sectoral, regional and national productivity centres, groups and programmes have been established in many developed and developing countries with the aim of promoting productivity improvement in the private and public sectors, including public services. An important European forum for academics and practitioners in public service productivity is the European Group of Public Administration (EGPA), established as a subgroup of the International Institute of Public Administration (IIAS).

In developing countries interest and effort in productivity improvement in the public service have been very recent developments. The first region-wide fact-finding exercise to improve productivity in the public sector was launched in 1986 by the Asian Productivity Organisation with the objective of developing measures of effectiveness, techniques of work measurement and operational analysis, and innovative approaches for improving productivity in public services. This APO survey was initiated in eight countries, covering such fields as tax audit, employee state insurance, a section of city government in charge of construction, outpatient departments in two public hospitals, a general post office, a national telecommunication commission, a post office savings bank and a public hospital.

In Latin American countries a major international role in public service productivity is played by a number of public administration institutes which emphasise education and training activities. For example, many leading government officials and technicians throughout the region, especially in the field of fiscal policy and tax administration, have attended or have graduate degrees from taxation programmes or short intensive courses provided by regional centres such as the Inter-American School for Public Administration (EIAP) of the Getulio Vargas Foundation. The Foundation, now sponsored by the Inter-American Development Bank and the Inter-American Centre of Taxation Administrators (CIAT), was supported initially by the United States Internal Revenue Service and, more recently, by the German Foundation for International Development. The Central American Institute for Public Administration (ICAP) has also provided extensive training programmes in the field of taxation.

Generally, there are now more than 30 international organisations, federations and institutions, about 20 international governmental organisations and more than 40 regional organisations and institutes dealing directly or indirectly with productivity. These organisations undertake many activities in collecting, analysing and disseminating useful information on productivity and related problems among their members. They carry out research activities, organise meetings, courses, seminars, symposia and conferences and help governments in working out national productivity improvement policies and programmes. The organisations also finance and implement many programmes.

4. Concluding remarks

Faced with often increasing demands for services and with tight budgetary constraints, governments have begun to show greater interest in improving public service productivity. A first step in this direction is to measure productivity – a concept that could be defined as the efficiency with which resources are used in the effective and equitable delivery of government services. Systematic reporting on productivity has considerable benefits; it would help in goal setting and in the budget process; and it creates a climate of productivity-consciousness. However, governments generally have been slow to introduce productivity measurement because it is often difficult to establish the link between government programmes and the achievement of broad goals, such as health, employment, economic growth, client satisfaction and so on.

Various governments have undertaken (or are undertaking) major reform programmes, which often include decentralisation, deregulation and privatisation. And most governments have made special efforts to encourage the use of information technologies, which – through the introduction of office automation and computerised administration – has led to large productivity increases in, for example, tax collection and social security administration.

Since the great majority of productivity problems in the public service stem from deficiencies built into the system, considerable improvements in productivity can be expected from changes in managerial styles and practices. This often means abandoning authoritarian styles of management and replacing them by more democratic, co-operative and delegating practices and attitudes.

There would be much to gain from more general and specialised training for public service managers. Current programmes in the developing countries are still based too much on perceptions and problems in the industrialised world and they do not pay sufficient attention to the policy role of senior administrators and to the need for more people-oriented skills. Another key problem is the lack of a system to evaluate whether management training has in fact improved performance.

Success in boosting productivity requires conscious, results-oriented productivity-improvement programmes, both at the national and agency level. Many successful public service organisations have set up special units to analyse barriers to productivity enhancement. They are usually small, yet report directly to top management because their function is to support the productivity programme of the entire organisation.

Bibliographical note

This report is based on internal papers written by various ILO departments, regional teams and regional advisers. It has drawn on a wide range of ILO work as well as a variety of outside sources, including research reports and publications of other international organisations. The principal sources used in each chapter are briefly noted below and listed alphabetically by author or organisation. Some of the specially commissioned studies or ILO working papers can be obtained from the ILO's Publications Branch.

Selected sources – By chapter

Chapter 1

The sections on industrialised countries draw on contributions by the Employment and Development, as well as the Industrial Relations and Labour Relations Department. Much of the data for section 1 on industrialised market economy countries (IMECs) are drawn from the ILO *Year book of labour statistics* and from *Employment Outlook* and *Economic Outlook* published by the OECD. Other sources and references include European Trade Union Institute (1988), United Kingdom Department of Employment (1988), Welbourne and Gomez-Meija (1988), Kassalow (1988), the Kreisky Commission (1989), Vaughan-Whitehead (1989) and Rodgers (forthcoming). Section 2 on industrialised centrally planned economy countries (IPECs) has made use of ILO (1988f), Shcherbakov (1988) and proceedings of a National Conference on Wage Reform and Economic Recovery held in Budapest, Hungary, 2-4 May 1988.

The sections on sub-Saharan Africa, Latin America and Asia draw heavily on contributions by ILO Regional Employment Teams, JASPA, PREALC and ARTEP, respectively, supplemented by information on wages from the Remuneration Section of the Labour Law and Labour Relations Branch. Information on labour relations was supplied by the ILO Regional Advisers. Special articles and studies used for section 3 on Asia and North Africa include Thamarajakshi (1987), Farooq-i-Azam (1987), ARTEP (1987) and Edgren (1988). Section 4 on Latin America is largely based on PREALC (1988). The principal reference for section 5 on sub-Saharan Africa is JASPA (1989), which benefited from Jamal (1988) and Jamal and Weeks (1988). Other sources used include Ghai (1987), Lachaud (1987) and Rodgers (1987).

Chapter 2

The statistical information in section 1 on public expenditure is taken from National Accounts publications by the United Nations and the International Monetary Fund. Background information on structural adjustment can be found in the Director-General's Report to the 1989 Session of the International Labour Conference (ILO, 1989). Much of the statistical and other information on employment used in sections 2 and 3 comes from a report to the Fourth Session of the ILO's Joint Committee on the Public Service (ILO, 1988c). The chapter also draws heavily on other ILO work and on IMF and World Bank studies on public sector employment. These include Ahmed (1988), Starr (1988), Marshall (forthcoming) and Klotz (1988). The section on public enterprises and privatisation has made use of Hemming and Mansoor (1988), van Ginneken and Sarfati (forthcoming), Edgren (1988) and ILO (1988h). That on the structure of public sector employment owes much to Heller and Tait (1983), while the discussion of temporary and non-established employment includes references to studies by Corchuelo Rozo and Urrea Giraldo (1988) and Edgren (1987). The concluding remarks on retrenchment are based on Collier (1988). Box 2.2 draws on Sheehan (forthcoming) and OECD (1988a), while box 2.3 is based on a background study from Handoussa (1988).

Chapter 3

Chapter 3 on personnel management in the public service is based largely on work by the ILO's Salaried Employees and Professional Workers Branch. The subsection on recruitment practices and procedures and much of section 2 are based on the General Report to the Joint Committee on the Public Service, Fourth Session (ILO, 1988c). The subsections on equality of opportunity and conditions of entry have drawn on the ILO's report on *Equality in employment and occupation* (ILO, 1988g). Other sources are ILO (1983a), ILO (1988b), the second survey of the United Nations Department of Technical Co-operation for Development on changes and trends in public administration and finance for development (1982), as well as the Australian Public Service Board *Annual Report 1985-86* (1986) and the *Equal employment opportunity programs* (1985).

The section on the organisation of working time in health services is an updated version of the ILO's report for the Joint Meeting on Employment and Conditions of Work in Health and Medical Services (1985). Table 3.1 is based on the most recent information available from the ILO's October Inquiry. Detailed information on irregular working times in a Parisian hospital can be found in Estryn-Behar (1988).

Box 3.1 on progress towards racial and sexual equality in the United States federal civil service is based on Lewis (1988); box 3.2 on reducing job segregation between men and women made use of Drewry and Butcher (1988) and Breidenstein (1988); box 3.3 on civil service staff in the United Kingdom is derived from an Industrial Relations Review and Report (1988); box 3.4 on decentralisation of personnel management in Indonesia draws on King (1988); box 3.5 on the transferability of pension rights was provided by the ILO's Social Security Department; and box 3.6 on the special problems of doctors in hospitals makes use of various country sources.

Chapter 4

Chapter 4, on the public service remuneration package, draws heavily on ILO and World Bank studies for information on public sector pay and on ILO research and technical assistance projects for much of the section on social security.

The main source of wage data for Africa was Derek Robinson's forthcoming study on civil service pay in Africa for the ILO. A number of World Bank papers were also consulted, notably Lindauer, Meesook and Suebsaeng (1988). Edgren (1988) was useful for some Asian countries, while much of the information for civil service pay in Latin America comes from Marshall (forthcoming). Data on industrialised countries are derived from the OECD, CMEA and national sources.

The discussion on public-private sector pay differentials uses information from Ehrenberg and Schwarz (1986), van Ginneken (1988), van der Gaag, Stelcner and Vijverberg (1988) and Jamal and Weeks (1988). Box 4.1 draws on Cartaya Febres (1988); box 4.2 on the Ugandan Ministry of Planning and Economic Development (1988); and box 4.3 on OECD (1988b).

The social security section is based to a large extent on an ILO paper for the Fourth Session in 1988 of the Joint Committee on the Public Service (ILO, 1988d). The question of the retirement age was dealt with more fully in an ILO paper to the Third Session of the Committee in 1983 (ILO, 1983b).

Generally speaking, comparative international studies on civil service pensions are few and far between. Worth mentioning are the study carried out by the "Association internationale de la fonction publique" for its Avignon Congress (1986); reports to the international conference on social security in the public sector organised by the International Social Security Association in Mexico in 1977; and the work of the MAPFRE foundation, sponsored by the big private insurance companies, on civil service pensions, for a meeting organised in Madrid in 1988. For Latin America, in particular, the work of Mesa-Lago (1978) should be added. Otherwise, the section rests heavily on national sources and, for several developing countries, on reports of ILO technical assistance teams.

Chapter 5

This chapter draws on a wide range of country studies undertaken for the ILO. Studies on IMECs are contained in a publication edited by Treu (1987), while DCs are covered in a study edited by Ozaki (1988). For information on IPECs, use has been made of a study by Timsit and Letowski (1986). Recent overviews of ILO standards on freedom of association and collective labour relations are to be found in two reports to the ILO Joint Committee on the Public Service, Fourth Session (1988a and 1988e).

The sections on the right to organise and the right to strike are based on reports by the ILO Committee of Experts and the Governing Body Committee on Freedom of Association. The discussion on union density is the result of work within the ILO secretariat, based on a great many country sources. The section on labour disputes is based on a recent article by Ozaki (1987). Further information on recent trends in public service labour relations was drawn from Incomes Data Services and *Industrial Relations Review and Report.*

Chapter 6

Chapter 6 is based on a number of original studies by the ILO Management Development Branch as well as contributions from ILO consultants, World Bank research, papers from national and international conferences and workshops, and published articles and monographs. A more elaborate version of this chapter can be found in Prokopenko (1989).

Apart from sources named in the text, section 1 on productivity measurement in the public service has, inter alia, drawn on work by Acharga (1981), Campbell (1980), Buntz (1986), Ammons (1984), Prokopenko (1987) and Mark (1986). The description of proposals for productivity measures by Ridley and Simon in 1938, Schmandt and Stephens in 1960 and Gross in 1984 is taken from Ross and Burkhead (1974). Box 6.1 draws on Epstein (1988) and box 6.2 on Antosenkov (1988).

Section 2 on restructuring of government activities makes use in particular of two Canadian reports: *Constraints to productive management in the public service* (1983), and Treasury Board of Canada (1988). Other sources include: Vandermerwe (1987), Roth (1987), Usilaner (1980), Stankard (1986) and Worthley (1986).

Section 3 on management approaches to productivity improvement draws on Deming (1975), Barras (1986) and Bernolak (1985). Box 6.4 is partly based on Boulden and Lawlor (1987).

Selected sources

Acharga, S. N. 1981. "Perspectives and problems of development in sub-Saharan Africa", in *World Development* (Oxford, Pergamon Press), Feb. 1981, pp. 109-147.

Aganbegyan, A. G. 1988. "The welfare of man – Measure of economic development", in *Social and Labour Bulletin* (Geneva, ILO), No. 4/88, pp. 411-414.

Ahmed, I. 1988. *Public sector employment: Growth and implications of structural adjustment.* Geneva, ILO; mimeographed.

Ammons, D. N. 1984. *Municipal productivity: A comparison of fourteen high-quality service cities.* New York, Praeger.

Antosenkov, E. G. 1988. *Socio-economic problems in the non-material production spheres in the USSR.* Geneva, ILO; mimeographed.

Association genevoise des médecins assistants et chefs de clinique (ASMAC). 1988. *Enquête sur les temps de présence des médecins-assistants*, cited in *La Suisse*, 30 Oct. 1988.

Association internationale de la fonction publique. 1986. *Le fonctionnaire à la retraite* (8ème Colloque d'Avignon, July 1985). Brussels, Institut International des Sciences Administratives.

Auditor General of Canada. 1983. *Constraints to productive management in the public service.* Ottawa, Office of the Auditor General of Canada.

Barras, R. 1986. "New technology and the new services: Towards an innovation strategy for Europe", in *Futures* (Guildford, Butterworth), Dec. 1986, pp. 748-772.

Bernolak, I. 1985. *Measuring and enhancing productivity in the public sector.* Reykjavik, European Association of National Productivity Centres.

Bouckaert, G. 1988. *Public productivity: Levels and instruments.* Working paper, Leuven, Belgium, EGPA Workshops; mimeographed.

Boulden, G; Lawlor, A. 1987. *The application of action learning: A practical guide.* Geneva, ILO.

Breidenstein, W. 1988. "Frauen im öffentlichen Dienst", in *Wirtschaft und Statistik* (Wiesbaden), Sep. 1988.

Buntz, C. G. 1986. "Problems and issues in human service productivity improvement", in Holzer, M. and Halachmi, A. (eds.): *Strategic issues in public sector productivity.* London and San Francisco, Jossey-Bass Inc., pp. 45-62.

Campbell, A. K. 1980. "Government and productivity", in *Dimensions of productivity research.* Houston, Texas, American Productivity Center, pp. 941-952.

Cartaya Febres, V. 1988. *Employment and labour conditions in the public sector – Venezuela.* Geneva, ILO; mimeographed.

Collier, P. 1988. *African public sector retrenchment: An analytical survey*. World Employment Programme research working paper No. 27, Geneva, ILO.

Corchuelo Rozo, A; Urrea Giraldo, F. 1988. "El empleo público en Colombia y su impacto sobre el mercado laboral urbano 1970-87", in *Boletín mensual de estadística* (Bogotá, DANE), Sep. 1988.

Deming, W. E. 1975. "On some statistical aids to economic production", in *Interfaces* (Providence, Rhode Island, Institute of Management Sciences), Aug. 1975, pp. 1-15.

Department of Employment (United Kingdom). 1984. "Women's employment in the 1980s", in *Employment Gazette* (London, HMSO), May 1984, pp. 199-209.

——. 1988. "International comparisons of industrial stoppages for 1986", in *Employment Gazette* (London, HMSO), June 1988.

Drewry, G.; Butcher, A. 1988. *The civil service today*. Oxford, Blackwell.

Economic Commission for Latin America and the Caribbean. 1988. *Balance preliminar de la economía latinoamericana*. Santiago, Chile, ECLAC.

Edgren, G. 1987. *Public services as a source of employment creation*. Paper prepared for the Second Meeting of Asian Employment Planners, 24-26 November 1987. New Delhi, ILO/ARTEP; mimeographed.

——. 1989. *Restructuring, employment and industrial relations*. New Delhi, ILO/ARTEP.

Edgren, G. (ed.). 1988. *The growing sector: Studies of public sector employment in Asia*. New Delhi, ILO/ARTEP.

Ehrenberg, R. G.; Schwarz, J. L. 1986. "Public-sector labor markets", in Ashenfelter, O. C. and Layard, R. (eds.): *Handbook of labour economics*, Vol. 2, Amsterdam, Elsevier Science Publishers BV, pp. 1219-1268.

Epstein, P. D. 1988. *Using performance measurement in local government: A guide to improving decisions, performance and accountability*. New York, National Civil League Press.

Equal Employment Opportunity Bureau (Australia). 1985. *Equal Employment Opportunity Programs*. Guidelines No. 3, Canberra.

Estryn-Behar, M. 1988. *Pathologies du personnel hospitalier féminin et conditions de travail*. Paris, INSERM; mimeographed.

European Trade Union Institute. 1988. *Collective bargaining in Western Europe in 1987 and prospects for 1988*. Brussels.

Farooq-i-Azam. 1987. *Re-integration of return migrants in Asia: A review and proposals*. Asian Regional Programme on International Labour Migration. Working paper No. 2, New Delhi, ILO/ARTEP.

van der Gaag, J.; Stelcner, M.; Vijverberg, W. 1988. *Public-private sector wage comparisons and moonlighting in developing countries: Evidence from Côte d'Ivoire and Peru*. LSMS working paper No. 52, Washington, DC, World Bank.

Ghai, D. 1987. *Economic growth, structural change and labour absorption in Africa: 1965-85*. Discussion paper No. 1, Geneva, UNRISD.

van Ginneken, W. 1988. *Public-private wage differentials: A cross-country analysis*. Geneva, ILO; mimeographed.

van Ginneken, W.; Sarfati, H. (eds.). *Employment in government services: Case studies on developing countries*. Geneva, ILO; forthcoming.

Handoussa, H. 1988. *The burden of public service employment and remuneration: A case study of Egypt*. Geneva, ILO; mimeographed.

Hayward, N. W. 1976. "The productivity challenge", in *Public Administration Review* (Washington, DC, American Society for Public Administration), Sep.-Oct. 1976, pp. 544-550.

Heller, P. S.; Tait, A. A. 1983. *Government employment and pay: Some international comparisons*. Occasional paper No. 24, Washington, DC, International Monetary Fund.

Hemming, R.; Mansoor, A. M. 1988. *Privatisation and public enterprises*. Occasional paper No. 56, Washington, DC, International Monetary Fund.

ILO. 1983a. *General report*. Report I, Joint Committee on the Public Service, Third Session, Geneva.

——. 1983b. *Recruitment, training and career development in the public service*. Report II, Joint Committee on the Public Service, Third Session, Geneva.

——. 1985. *Employment and conditions of work in health and medical services*. Geneva.

——. 1988a. *General report*, Ch. VII: "Trade union rights in the public service". Report I, Joint Committee on the Public Service, Fourth Session, Geneva, pp. 63-87.

——. 1988b. *Report of the Committee of Experts on the Application of Conventions and Recommendations*. Report III (Part 4A), International Labour Conference, 75th Session, Geneva.

—. 1988c. *General report.* Report I, Joint Committee on the Public Service, Fourth Session, Geneva.

—. 1988d. *Joint consultation, negotiating and collective bargaining rights with regard to determining pay and conditions of employment in the public service.* Report II, Joint Committee on the Public Service, Fourth Session, Geneva.

—. 1988e. *Social security, including social protection of public employees in respect of invalidity, retirement and survivors' benefits.* Report III, Joint Committee on the Public Service, Fourth Session, Geneva.

—. 1988f. "A leaner central administration", in *Social and Labour Bulletin* (Geneva), No. 1/88, pp. 45-46.

—. 1988g. *Equality in employment and occupation.* General survey of the reports on the Discrimination (Employment and Occupation) Convention (No. 111) and Recommendation (No. 111), 1958. Report III (Part 4B), International Labour Conference, 75th Session, Geneva.

—. 1988h. "Privatisation: No simple panacea?", in *Social and Labour Bulletin* (Geneva), No. 2/88, pp. 160-164.

—. 1989. *Recovery and employment.* Report of the Director-General, International Labour Conference, 76th Session, Geneva.

ILO/ARTEP. 1987. *Structural adjustment: By whom, for whom? Employment and income aspects of industrial restructuring in Asia.* New Delhi.

ILO/JASPA. 1989. *African Employment Report 1988* (Addis Ababa), Ch. I: "The challenge of employment and adjustment in Africa", pp. 1-39.

ILO/PREALC. 1988. *Evolution of the labour market during 1980-87.* Santiago, Chile.

Industrial Relations Services. 1988. "Civil Service staff appraisal – Two years on", in *Industrial Relations Review and Report* (London, Dec. 1988).

—. *Industrial Relations Review and Report* (London), various issues.

Jamal, V. (ed.). 1988. "The African crisis, food security and structural adjustment", in *International Labour Review* (Geneva, ILO), Special issue, 1988/6.

Jamal, V.; Weeks, J. 1988. "The vanishing rural-urban gap in sub-Saharan Africa", in *International Labour Review* (Geneva, ILO), 1988/3, pp. 271-292.

Kassalow, E. M. 1988. "Concession bargaining: Towards new roles for American unions and management", in *International Labour Review* (Geneva, ILO), 1988/5, pp. 573-592.

King, D. Y. 1988. "Civil service policies in Indonesia: An obstacle to decentralization?", in *Public Administration and Development* (Chichester, Wiley), July-Sep. 1988, pp. 249-260.

Klotz, V. 1988. *Trends in public service employment in industrialised market economy countries in the 1980s.* Geneva, ILO; mimeographed.

Kreisky Commission on employment issues in Europe. 1989. *A programme for full employment in the 1990s.* Oxford, Pergamon Press.

Lachaud, J. P. 1987. *Restructuration des entreprises publiques et ajustements sur le marché du travail au Sénégal: Des possibilités à la mesure des espérances.* Labour Market Programme, Discussion paper No. 4, Geneva, International Institute for Labour Studies.

Lewis, G. B. 1988. "Progress toward racial and sexual equality in the federal civil service?", in *Public Administration Review* (Washington, DC, American Society for Public Administration), May-June 1988, pp. 700-707.

Lindauer, D. L.; Meesook, O. A.; Suebsaeng, P. 1988. "Government wage policy in Africa: Summary of findings and policy issues", in *The World Bank Research Observer* (Washington, DC), Jan. 1988.

Mark, J. A. 1986. "Measuring productivity in government: Federal, state, and local", in Holzer, M. and Halachmi, A. (eds.): *Strategic issues in public sector productivity.* London and San Francisco, Jossey-Bass Inc., pp. 73-90.

Marshall, A. (ed.). *El empleo en el estado en América Latina.* Geneva, International Institute for Labour Studies, forthcoming.

Mesa-Lago, C. 1978. *Social security in Latin America: Pressure groups, stratification and inequality.* Pittsburgh, University of Pittsburgh Press.

Ministry of Planning and Economic Development (Uganda). 1988. *Census of civil servants.* Kampala.

Mundel, M. E. 1975. *Measuring and enhancing the productivity of service and government organisations.* Hong Kong, Asian Productivity Organisation.

OECD. 1988a. *Employment Outlook.* Paris.

——. 1988b. *Recent trends in performance appraisal and performance-related pay schemes in the public service.* Public management study No. 4, Paris.

Ozaki, M. 1987. "Labour relations in the public service. 2. Labour disputes and their settlement", in *International Labour Review* (Geneva, ILO), July-Aug. 1987, pp. 405-422.

Ozaki, M. et al. 1988. *Labour relations in the public service: Developing countries.* Geneva, ILO.

Prokopenko, J. 1987. *Productivity management: A practical handbook.* Geneva, ILO.

——. 1989. *Improving public service productivity: Problems and challenges.* Management Development Programme working paper No. 51, Geneva, ILO.

Public Service Board (Australia). 1986. *Annual Report 1985-86.* Canberra.

Robinson, D. *Civil service pay in Africa.* Geneva, ILO; forthcoming.

Rodgers, G. 1987. *Labour market mechanisms and urban poverty: A review of ten studies.* Discussion paper No. 7, Geneva, International Institute for Labour Studies.

——. *Non-standard and precarious forms of work in Europe.* Geneva, International Institute for Labour Studies; forthcoming.

Ross, J. P.; Burkhead, J. 1974. *Productivity in the local government sector.* Massachusetts, Lexington Books.

Roth, G. 1987. *The private provision of public services in developing countries.* Oxford, Oxford University Press.

Shcherbakov, V. I. 1988. *Results-based remuneration in the USSR.* Labour Law and Labour Relations Programme, Occasional paper No. 3, Geneva, ILO.

Sheehan, G. *Labour administration in a changing world.* Geneva, ILO; forthcoming.

Stankard, M. F. 1986. *Productivity by choice: The 20-to-1 principle.* New York, John Wiley and Sons.

Starr, M. A. 1988. *Recent wage and employment trends in sub-Saharan Africa.* Washington, DC, World Bank; mimeographed.

Thamarajakshi, R. 1987. *Youth employment in Asian countries.* Asian Employment Programme working paper, New Delhi, ILO/ARTEP.

Timsit, G.; Letowski, J. et al. 1986. *Les fonctions publiques en Europe de l'Est et de l'Ouest.* Paris, Editions du CNRS.

Treasury Board of Canada. 1988. *Increased ministerial authority and accountability: Introduction and progress report.* Ottawa.

Treu, T. et al. 1987. *Public service labour relations: Recent trends and future prospects: A comparative survey of seven industrialised market economy countries.* Geneva, ILO.

United Nations. 1982. *Changes and trends in public administration and finance for development – Second survey – 1977-1979.* New York, Department of Technical Co-operation for Development.

Urban Institute. 1982. *The challenge of productivity diversity.* Washington, DC.

Usilaner, B. L. 1980. "Can we expect productivity improvement in the federal government?", in *Dimensions of productivity research.* Houston, Texas, American Productivity Center, pp. 963-985.

Vandermerwe, S. 1987. "Deregulation in services and the marketing challenge", in *IMI Horizons,* Autumn 1987, pp. 5-7.

Vaughan-Whitehead, D. 1989. *Partage des profits et marché du travail en France.* World Employment Programme reseach working paper No. 28, Geneva, ILO.

Welbourne, T. M.; Gomez-Mejia, L. R. 1988. "Gainsharing revisited", in *Compensation and Benefits Review* (American Management Association, Saranak Lake, New York), July-Aug. 1988, pp. 19-28.

Williams, R.; Walker, J.; Fletcher, C. 1977. "International review of staff appraisal practices: Current trends and issues", in *Public Personnel Management* (Chicago, International Personnel Management Association), Jan.-Feb. 1977, pp. 5-12.

Worthley, J. A. 1986. "Computer technology and productivity improvement", in Holzer, M. and Halachmi, A. (eds.): *Strategic issues in public sector productivity.* London and San Francisco, Jossey-Bass Inc., pp. 205-213.

Statistical appendix

The fourth volume of the World Labour Report is based on a large amount of data collected by the ILO in the course of its normal activities. Most of these data have been published in ILO's *Year book of labour statistics* and its special publication on the October Inquiry (on wages, prices and working time). These data have been supplemented from other sources, such as the United Nations, UNCTAD, IMF, World Bank and OECD.

This appendix presents three extra tables derived from ILO statistical sources but not available in the ILO publications mentioned above. They provide useful background and reference information for those who wish to have a more detailed insight into recent employment and wage trends.

Table A.1 gives estimates and projections of the labour force for each year 1980-90. They are interpolated from data given at five-year intervals in the ILO's *Economically active population: Estimates 1950-1980 and Projections 1985-2025* (Geneva, 1986). All countries and territories with more than 300,000 inhabitants are shown separately, and those with a population of less than 300,000 have been included in the regional and subregional totals.

Table A.2 gives the employment shares of agriculture, industry and services for 1979, 1983 and 1987 in selected countries. Most of the data are derived from national labour force and household surveys that measure total employment. Persons not classified under any of the three main sectors were not included in the calculation of the employment shares.

Table A.3 shows real wage indices for wage earners or employees in manufacturing (1980 = 100). They are derived from the wage and price statistics published in ILO's *Year book of labour statistics*. Comparisons between countries may be difficult because the data may cover different subgroups such as employees only, skilled workers only or unskilled wage earners only.

Table A.1. Total labour force, by region, country or territory, 1980-90 ('000s)

Region, country or territory	1980	1981	1982	1983	1984	1985	1986	1987	1988	1989	1990
World	1 957 374	1 996 991	2 037 411	2 078 648	2 120 720	2 163 644	2 202 224	2 241 492	2 281 460	2 322 141	2 363 547
Developed countries [1]	541 843	546 947	552 099	557 299	562 549	567 848	571 337	574 848	578 380	581 933	585 509
Developing countries [2]	1 415 531	1 449 876	1 485 055	1 521 087	1 557 993	1 595 795	1 630 684	1 666 336	1 702 768	1 739 996	1 778 038
Africa	189 174	193 860	198 661	203 582	208 625	213 792	219 299	224 948	230 743	236 687	242 784
East Africa	66 562	68 175	69 828	71 521	73 254	75 030	76 941	78 900	80 909	82 969	85 082
Burundi	2 281	2 327	2 374	2 422	2 470	2 520	2 577	2 636	2 696	2 757	2 820
Comoros	181	185	190	194	199	204	209	214	220	225	231
Ethiopia	17 593	17 900	18 212	18 530	18 853	19 182	19 574	19 974	20 383	20 800	21 225
Kenya	7 072	7 318	7 572	7 835	8 107	8 388	8 690	9 003	9 328	9 664	10 012
Madagascar	4 097	4 176	4 257	4 340	4 424	4 510	4 605	4 701	4 800	4 901	5 004
Malawi	2 703	2 773	2 846	2 920	2 996	3 074	3 154	3 236	3 320	3 406	3 494
Mauritius	332	343	354	366	378	390	400	409	419	430	440
Mozambique	6 903	7 050	7 201	7 354	7 511	7 671	7 818	7 969	8 122	8 278	8 437
Reunion	183	188	193	198	204	209	215	220	226	232	238
Rwanda	2 670	2 744	2 821	2 899	2 980	3 063	3 149	3 238	3 330	3 423	3 520
Somalia	1 808	1 845	1 882	1 920	1 959	1 999	2 027	2 055	2 084	2 113	2 143
Tanzania, United Republic of	9 509	9 775	10 048	10 328	10 617	10 913	11 231	11 558	11 894	12 241	12 597
Uganda	6 163	6 332	6 505	6 684	6 867	7 055	7 258	7 466	7 681	7 902	8 129
Zambia	1 913	1 975	2 038	2 104	2 172	2 242	2 317	2 395	2 475	2 558	2 644
Zimbabwe	2 979	3 061	3 144	3 231	3 319	3 410	3 507	3 606	3 708	3 813	3 921
Central Africa	21 644	22 068	22 501	22 942	23 392	23 851	24 345	24 850	25 365	25 891	26 428
Angola	3 414	3 473	3 533	3 594	3 656	3 719	3 789	3 860	3 932	4 006	4 081
Cameroon	3 618	3 684	3 750	3 818	3 888	3 958	4 036	4 116	4 197	4 280	4 365
Central African Rep.	1 199	1 215	1 232	1 248	1 265	1 282	1 302	1 322	1 342	1 363	1 384
Chad	1 634	1 664	1 695	1 726	1 758	1 790	1 825	1 860	1 897	1 933	1 971
Congo	649	661	673	685	697	710	724	738	752	766	781
Equatorial Guinea	158	160	162	165	167	169	172	174	177	179	182
Gabon	502	505	508	512	515	518	522	525	529	532	536
Zaire	10 434	10 670	10 910	11 157	11 408	11 666	11 937	12 214	12 497	12 787	13 084
Northern Africa	29 823	30 706	31 616	32 553	33 517	34 510	35 547	36 615	37 715	38 848	40 015
Algeria	4 051	4 197	4 348	4 505	4 667	4 835	5 017	5 207	5 403	5 607	5 819
Egypt	11 298	11 590	11 890	12 197	12 512	12 836	13 166	13 505	13 852	14 209	14 574
Libyan Arab Jamahiriya	755	783	812	842	873	905	937	970	1 004	1 039	1 076
Morocco	5 689	5 874	6 065	6 262	6 466	6 676	6 891	7 113	7 343	7 580	7 824
Sudan	6 086	6 257	6 433	6 614	6 800	6 991	7 196	7 407	7 624	7 847	8 077
Tunisia	1 908	1 967	2 029	2 092	2 157	2 224	2 294	2 365	2 439	2 515	2 594
Southern Africa	11 103	11 404	11 714	12 031	12 358	12 693	13 041	13 399	13 766	14 144	14 532
Botswana	321	332	344	356	368	381	393	406	419	432	446
Lesotho	662	675	688	702	716	730	745	760	776	792	808
Namibia	426	436	446	456	466	477	488	500	512	524	537
South Africa	9 449	9 711	9 979	10 255	10 539	10 831	11 134	11 446	11 766	12 095	12 434
Swaziland	245	250	256	261	267	273	279	286	292	299	306
West Africa	60 041	61 502	62 998	64 530	66 100	67 708	69 423	71 180	72 983	74 831	76 726
Benin	1 775	1 811	1 848	1 886	1 925	1 964	2 008	2 053	2 100	2 147	2 195
Burkina Faso	3 420	3 486	3 554	3 623	3 693	3 765	3 842	3 921	4 001	4 083	4 167
Cape Verde	102	106	109	113	117	121	125	129	133	137	141
Côte d'Ivoire	3 547	3 643	3 741	3 842	3 946	4 053	4 157	4 263	4 372	4 484	4 599
Gambia	289	293	296	300	304	308	312	317	321	325	330
Ghana	4 353	4 469	4 587	4 709	4 835	4 963	5 100	5 241	5 386	5 534	5 687
Guinea	2 626	2 668	2 712	2 755	2 800	2 845	2 894	2 943	2 994	3 045	3 097

Region, country or territory	1980	1981	1982	1983	1984	1985	1986	1987	1988	1989	1990
Guinea-Bissau	403	408	412	417	422	427	433	439	445	452	458
Liberia	726	742	758	775	792	809	828	848	869	890	911
Mali	2 296	2 353	2 412	2 473	2 535	2 598	2 666	2 736	2 808	2 882	2 958
Mauritania	516	530	544	559	574	589	606	623	641	660	679
Niger	2 865	2 930	2 996	3 063	3 132	3 203	3 282	3 363	3 446	3 532	3 619
Nigeria	32 087	32 937	33 809	34 705	35 624	36 568	37 569	38 598	39 655	40 741	41 857
Senegal	2 641	2 690	2 740	2 791	2 843	2 896	2 953	3 011	3 070	3 130	3 192
Sierra Leone	1 279	1 293	1 308	1 322	1 337	1 352	1 369	1 385	1 402	1 420	1 437
Togo	1 114	1 139	1 164	1 190	1 217	1 244	1 273	1 303	1 334	1 365	1 397
Americas	245 260	249 990	254 812	259 727	264 736	269 842	274 457	279 152	283 926	288 783	293 722
Latin America	123 478	126 664	129 932	133 284	136 723	140 250	143 684	147 203	150 808	154 501	158 284
Caribbean	10 890	11 156	11 429	11 708	11 994	12 287	12 578	12 876	13 181	13 493	13 813
Barbados	118	120	122	123	125	127	129	131	133	135	137
Cuba	3 566	3 646	3 729	3 813	3 899	3 987	4 078	4 170	4 265	4 362	4 461
Dominican Republic	1 571	1 625	1 681	1 739	1 799	1 861	1 922	1 985	2 050	2 118	2 187
Guadeloupe	134	137	139	142	145	148	150	152	154	156	158
Haiti	2 558	2 609	2 660	2 713	2 767	2 822	2 881	2 942	3 004	3 067	3 132
Jamaica	946	974	1 003	1 033	1 063	1 095	1 124	1 153	1 183	1 214	1 246
Martinique	135	138	140	143	145	148	150	151	153	154	156
Puerto Rico	1 004	1 027	1 051	1 076	1 100	1 126	1 149	1 172	1 196	1 220	1 245
Trinidad and Tobago	397	407	417	428	439	450	460	470	480	490	501
Windward Islands	152	156	161	165	170	175	180	185	191	196	202
Other Caribbean	308										
Central America	29 185	30 123	31 091	32 090	33 122	34 186	35 278	36 405	37 568	38 768	40 006
Costa Rica	777	801	826	851	877	904	927	950	974	999	1 024
El Salvador	1 587	1 633	1 681	1 730	1 780	1 832	1 893	1 955	2 020	2 087	2 156
Guatemala	1 967	2 022	2 079	2 138	2 198	2 260	2 329	2 401	2 474	2 550	2 628
Honduras	1 078	1 119	1 163	1 207	1 254	1 302	1 353	1 405	1 460	1 517	1 576
Mexico	22 248	22 966	23 708	24 474	25 264	26 080	26 907	27 761	28 641	29 550	30 487
Nicaragua	825	856	889	923	958	994	1 033	1 073	1 115	1 159	1 204
Panama	657	676	696	717	738	760	781	803	825	848	872
Temperate South America	15 204	15 423	15 646	15 871	16 100	16 332	16 563	16 796	17 034	17 274	17 518
Argentina	10 304	10 417	10 532	10 648	10 765	10 884	11 014	11 145	11 278	11 412	11 548
Chile	3 765	3 862	3 962	4 064	4 169	4 277	4 368	4 461	4 557	4 654	4 753
Uruguay	1 134	1 141	1 148	1 155	1 163	1 170	1 179	1 189	1 198	1 207	1 217
Tropical South America	68 199	69 955	71 757	73 604	75 500	77 444	79 258	81 114	83 014	84 958	86 948
Bolivia	1 740	1 787	1 835	1 884	1 935	1 987	2 043	2 101	2 160	2 221	2 284
Brazil	44 239	45 271	46 326	47 406	48 512	49 643	50 676	51 730	52 806	53 905	55 026
Colombia	7 992	8 219	8 453	8 694	8 941	9 196	9 424	9 658	9 897	10 143	10 394
Ecuador	2 439	2 514	2 592	2 672	2 755	2 840	2 924	3 011	3 100	3 192	3 287
Guyana	291	300	309	318	328	338	347	355	364	374	383
Paraguay	1 048	1 081	1 115	1 150	1 186	1 223	1 258	1 295	1 333	1 371	1 411
Peru	5 374	5 530	5 691	5 857	6 028	6 203	6 380	6 561	6 748	6 940	7 138
Suriname	104	106	109	112	114	117	120	124	127	131	135
Venezuela	4 947	5 119	5 298	5 482	5 673	5 871	6 057	6 248	6 446	6 650	6 860
Northern America	121 783	123 306	124 849	126 411	127 992	129 593	130 741	131 900	133 068	134 247	135 437
Canada	11 848	12 018	12 191	12 366	12 543	12 723	12 848	12 974	13 101	13 230	13 360
United States	109 873	111 225	112 593	113 979	115 381	116 801	117 824	118 855	119 896	120 945	122 004
Asia [3]	1 157 836	1 184 810	1 212 412	1 240 658	1 269 561	1 299 138	1 325 521	1 352 440	1 379 906	1 407 929	1 436 522

Region, country or territory	1980	1981	1982	1983	1984	1985	1986	1987	1988	1989	1990
East Asia	630 161	644 917	660 019	675 475	691 292	707 480	720 606	733 975	747 593	761 463	775 590
China	547 061	560 548	574 368	588 529	603 039	617 906	629 835	641 995	654 389	667 023	679 900
Japan	57 097	57 622	58 152	58 687	59 227	59 772	60 250	60 732	61 218	61 708	62 202
Other East Asia	26 004	26 723	27 462	28 221	29 001	29 803	30 506	31 226	31 962	32 716	33 488
Hong Kong	2 531	2 595	2 660	2 727	2 796	2 866	2 914	2 963	3 013	3 064	3 115
Korea	22 567	23 193	23 835	24 496	25 175	25 873	26 494	27 131	27 782	28 450	29 133
Korea, Democratic People's Rep. of	7 838	8 073	8 314	8 563	8 820	9 084	9 346	9 615	9 891	10 176	10 469
Korea, Republic of	14 729	15 120	15 521	15 933	16 355	16 789	17 148	17 515	17 890	18 273	18 664
Mongolia	773	796	819	843	868	893	919	945	972	1 000	1 029
South Asia	527 676	539 893	552 393	565 183	578 268	591 657	604 905	618 450	632 298	646 457	660 932
East South Asia	149 345	153 040	156 827	160 708	164 684	168 759	172 680	176 692	180 798	184 999	189 297
Burma	15 170	15 464	15 764	16 070	16 381	16 699	17 012	17 331	17 655	17 986	18 323
Indonesia	56 253	57 620	59 021	60 455	61 925	63 430	64 934	66 473	68 049	69 662	71 314
Kampuchea	3 300	3 358	3 418	3 478	3 539	3 602	3 633	3 664	3 695	3 726	3 758
Lao People's Democratic Republic	1 839	1 873	1 907	1 942	1 978	2 014	2 057	2 101	2 146	2 192	2 239
Malaysia	5 338	5 495	5 657	5 823	5 995	6 171	6 341	6 516	6 696	6 881	7 071
Philippines	17 533	17 978	18 434	18 902	19 382	19 874	20 369	20 876	21 395	21 928	22 474
Singapore	1 117	1 138	1 159	1 181	1 203	1 225	1 239	1 254	1 268	1 283	1 298
Thailand	23 581	24 166	24 766	25 381	26 010	26 656	27 208	27 772	28 347	28 935	29 534
Viet Nam	24 930	25 652	26 395	27 159	27 946	28 755	29 543	30 352	31 184	32 038	32 916
Central South Asia	343 964	351 498	359 197	367 065	375 106	383 322	391 572	400 000	408 610	417 404	426 388
Afghanistan	4 797	4 831	4 866	4 901	4 936	4 971	5 200	5 440	5 691	5 953	6 228
Bangladesh	25 133	25 835	26 557	27 299	28 061	28 845	29 703	30 587	31 496	32 433	33 398
Bhutan	575	586	597	609	620	632	644	657	670	683	696
India	265 320	270 674	276 136	281 709	287 393	293 193	298 915	304 750	310 698	316 762	322 944
Iran, Islamic Rep. of	11 072	11 437	11 815	12 204	12 607	13 023	13 441	13 873	14 319	14 778	15 253
Nepal	6 139	6 279	6 422	6 568	6 717	6 870	7 033	7 200	7 371	7 546	7 725
Pakistan	25 415	26 237	27 086	27 963	28 868	29 802	30 543	31 303	32 082	32 880	33 698
Sri Lanka	5 457	5 546	5 637	5 730	5 824	5 919	6 006	6 094	6 184	6 275	6 367
West South Asia	34 366	35 350	36 362	37 403	38 474	39 576	40 650	41 753	42 887	44 050	45 246
Cyprus	292	296	299	303	307	311	314	317	320	323	326
Democratic Yemen	485	499	513	528	543	559	576	593	611	629	648
Iraq	3 551	3 682	3 819	3 960	4 107	4 259	4 418	4 584	4 755	4 933	5 118
Israel	1 446	1 477	1 509	1 542	1 576	1 610	1 647	1 686	1 725	1 765	1 806
Jordan	645	673	703	733	766	799	834	871	910	950	992
Kuwait	501	532	565	600	637	677	706	736	768	801	835
Lebanon	742	748	753	759	764	770	797	825	854	884	915
Oman	280	295	310	326	343	361	369	378	387	396	405
Qatar	107	114	121	128	136	145	152	160	168	177	186
Saudi Arabia	2 752	2 872	2 996	3 126	3 262	3 404	3 530	3 661	3 796	3 936	4 082
Syrian Arab Republic	2 188	2 264	2 343	2 424	2 509	2 596	2 690	2 788	2 889	2 993	3 102
Turkey	19 090	19 528	19 977	20 436	20 905	21 385	21 829	22 281	22 744	23 215	23 697
United Arab Emirates	530	558	587	617	649	683	702	722	742	763	784
Yemen	1 472	1 511	1 550	1 591	1 633	1 676	1 728	1 782	1 838	1 895	1 954
Europe [3]	217 952	219 611	221 282	222 966	224 663	226 373	227 429	228 490	229 556	230 626	231 702
Eastern Europe	56 400	56 723	57 049	57 376	57 705	58 036	58 294	58 553	58 813	59 074	59 336
Bulgaria	4 480	4 481	4 481	4 482	4 482	4 483	4 481	4 480	4 478	4 477	4 475
Czechoslovakia	8 025	8 056	8 087	8 118	8 150	8 181	8 222	8 263	8 304	8 345	8 387
German Democratic Rep.	9 116	9 195	9 275	9 355	9 436	9 518	9 548	9 579	9 609	9 639	9 670
Hungary	5 220	5 219	5 218	5 217	5 216	5 215	5 227	5 239	5 252	5 264	5 276

Region, country or territory	1980	1981	1982	1983	1984	1985	1986	1987	1988	1989	1990
Poland	18 519	18 657	18 797	18 937	19 079	19 221	19 317	19 413	19 509	19 606	19 704
Romania	11 038	11 113	11 188	11 264	11 341	11 418	11 498	11 579	11 660	11 742	11 825
Northern Europe	39 469	39 692	39 916	40 141	40 368	40 596	40 748	40 901	41 054	41 208	41 363
Denmark	2 705	2 721	2 736	2 752	2 768	2 784	2 797	2 811	2 825	2 838	2 852
Finland	2 381	2 402	2 423	2 445	2 466	2 488	2 501	2 514	2 527	2 540	2 553
Iceland	117	119	121	123	126	128	130	131	133	134	136
Ireland	1 259	1 280	1 301	1 322	1 344	1 366	1 388	1 411	1 434	1 457	1 481
Norway	1 962	1 977	1 992	2 008	2 023	2 039	2 057	2 075	2 093	2 111	2 129
Sweden	4 163	4 178	4 192	4 207	4 222	4 237	4 253	4 270	4 286	4 302	4 319
United Kingdom	26 765	26 897	27 030	27 163	27 297	27 432	27 498	27 565	27 631	27 698	27 765
Southern Europe	54 180	54 711	55 247	55 789	56 336	56 888	57 308	57 731	58 157	58 587	59 019
Albania	1 211	1 246	1 283	1 321	1 359	1 399	1 435	1 473	1 511	1 551	1 591
Greece	3 669	3 691	3 713	3 735	3 758	3 780	3 794	3 809	3 823	3 837	3 852
Italy	21 936	22 099	22 263	22 429	22 595	22 763	22 877	22 992	23 107	23 223	23 339
Malta	132	133	135	136	138	139	140	142	143	145	146
Portugal	4 346	4 389	4 432	4 476	4 520	4 564	4 599	4 634	4 669	4 704	4 740
Spain	12 896	13 058	13 221	13 387	13 555	13 725	13 868	14 013	14 159	14 307	14 456
Yugoslavia	9 958	10 061	10 165	10 270	10 377	10 484	10 558	10 632	10 707	10 782	10 858
Western Europe	67 905	68 484	69 069	69 658	70 253	70 852	71 077	71 303	71 529	71 756	71 984
Austria	3 364	3 392	3 419	3 447	3 476	3 504	3 517	3 530	3 543	3 557	3 570
Belgium	3 947	3 976	4 004	4 033	4 063	4 092	4 104	4 116	4 128	4 140	4 152
France	23 559	23 771	23 985	24 201	24 419	24 639	24 790	24 942	25 095	25 249	25 404
Germany, Fed. Rep. of	28 336	28 546	28 758	28 971	29 186	29 403	29 385	29 366	29 348	29 329	29 311
Luxembourg	152	153	153	154	154	155	155	155	155	155	155
Netherlands	5 461	5 539	5 618	5 698	5 779	5 861	5 918	5 976	6 034	6 093	6 153
Switzerland	3 062	3 084	3 106	3 128	3 150	3 173	3 181	3 189	3 196	3 204	3 212
Oceania	10 219	10 410	10 605	10 803	11 005	11 211	11 399	11 589	11 783	11 981	12 181
Australia-New Zealand	8 077	8 221	8 368	8 517	8 668	8 823	8 961	9 100	9 242	9 387	9 533
Australia	6 744	6 864	6 985	7 109	7 236	7 364	7 480	7 598	7 718	7 839	7 963
New Zealand	1 334	1 358	1 382	1 407	1 432	1 458	1 480	1 502	1 524	1 547	1 570
Melanesia	1 875	1 917	1 961	2 005	2 051	2 097	2 141	2 187	2 233	2 281	2 329
Fiji	206	211	216	221	226	231	235	240	244	248	253
Papua New Guinea	1 514	1 547	1 580	1 614	1 649	1 685	1 720	1 755	1 791	1 828	1 865
Other Melanesia	155	160	165	170	175	181	187	192	198	205	211
Micronesia-Polynesia	266	271	276	281	287	292	297	303	308	314	320
Micronesia	115	117	120	123	125	128	131	133	136	138	141
Polynesia	148	151	154	157	161	164	167	170	173	176	179
USSR	136 934	138 182	139 441	140 712	141 994	143 288	143 951	144 617	145 286	145 959	146 634

... = not available.

Notes: The regional figures also include data for countries with small population generally those with less than 300,000 inhabitants in 1980 which are not shown separately.

[1] Developed countries: Australia, Canada, Europe, Japan, New Zealand, USSR and the United States. [2] Developing countries: Africa, Asia, excluding Japan, Latin America, Melanesia, Micronesia and Polynesia. [3] Excluding USSR.

Source: ILO: *Labour force projections*.

Table A.2. Share of three main sectors in total employment, 1979, 1983 and 1987

	Agriculture			Industry			Services			Total		
	1979	1983	1987	1979	1983	1987	1979	1983	1987	1979	1983	1987
North Africa and West Asia												
Egypt	42.5	39.7 [1]	...	22.0	22.2 [1]	...	35.5	38.1 [1]	...	100.0	100.0 [1]	...
Tunisia	35.5	32.9 [1]	...	34.3	35.9 [1]	...	30.2	31.2 [1]	...	100.0	100.0 [1]	...
Cyprus	20.1	17.5	15.6	33.5	31.8	30.3	46.4	50.7	54.1	100.0	100.0	100.0
Israel	5.9	5.5	5.2	31.9	30.3	29.4	62.2	64.2	65.5	100.0	100.0	100.0
Syrian Arab Republic	32.8	30.6	...	31.2	29.2	...	35.9	40.1	...	100.0	100.0	...
Bahrain	3.1	2.7 [1]	...	40.0	34.8 [1]	...	56.9	62.5 [1]	...	100.0	100.0 [1]	...
Latin America and Caribbean												
Barbados	...	8.0	8.0	...	23.4	22.4	...	68.5	69.7	...	100.0	100.0
Bolivia	46.9	47.4	47.4	20.7	17.4	12.8	32.4	35.2	39.8	100.0	100.0	100.0
Brazil	31.9	27.1	25.9	24.0	25.4	24.2	44.1	47.6	50.0	100.0	100.0	100.0
Costa Rica	28.6	28.3	27.2 [2]	24.0	21.8	23.1 [2]	47.3	49.9	49.7 [2]	100.0	100.0	100.0 [2]
Chile	16.8	15.8	...	24.2	18.1	...	59.0	66.0	...	100.0	100.0	...
Guatemala	...	50.9 [1]	51.9	...	19.4 [1]	16.7	...	29.7 [1]	31.4	...	100.0 [1]	100.0
Jamaica	34.5	33.3	32.7 [2]	16.6	18.0	19.2 [2]	48.9	48.7	48.1 [2]	100.0	100.0	100.0 [2]
Panama	30.4	29.3	27.3	17.9	17.9	17.7	51.7	52.8	55.0	100.0	100.0	100.0
Paraguay	47.1	44.8 [1]	...	20.6	22.1 [1]	...	32.4	33.2 [1]	...	100.0	100.0	...
Puerto Rico	5.0	5.4	3.7	27.0	25.1	25.1	68.1	69.5	71.2	100.0	100.0	100.0
Trinidad and Tobago	10.8	8.6	11.7	38.6	37.8	29.1	50.6	53.6	59.3	100.0	100.0	100.0
Venezuela	15.4	14.8	14.3	27.9	25.7	27.6	56.7	59.4	58.1	100.0	100.0	100.0
South and South-East Asia												
Hong Kong	1.2	1.2	1.5	50.6	45.0	42.9	48.2	53.8	55.5	100.0	100.0	100.0
Korea, Republic of	35.8	29.8	21.9	30.1	29.1	34.0	34.1	41.1	44.1	100.0	100.0	100.0
Malaysia	37.2 [3]	30.6	31.8	24.1 [3]	25.9	23.2	38.7 [3]	43.5	45.0	100.0 [3]	100.0	100.0
Pakistan	55.0	52.9	50.9 [4]	18.5	19.5	20.3 [4]	26.5	27.6	28.9 [4]	100.0	100.0	100.0 [4]
Philippines	51.9 [3]	52.0	47.8	15.4 [3]	13.8	14.6	32.8 [3]	34.2	37.6	100.0 [3]	100.0	100.0
Singapore	1.5	1.0	0.9	35.3	36.0	35.1	63.2	63.0	64.0	100.0	100.0	100.0
Thailand	64.9	63.1	63.8	13.5	13.0	12.5	21.6	23.8	23.7	100.0	100.0	100.0
Industrialised market economies												
Australia	6.6	6.6	5.7	31.2	28.0	26.2	62.2	65.4	68.0	100.0	100.0	100.0
Austria	...	9.9	8.7	...	38.8	37.8	...	51.3	53.5	...	100.0	100.0
Belgium	3.1	2.9	2.7	34.4	30.4	28.0	62.5	66.6	69.3	100.0	100.0	100.0
Canada	5.7	5.5	4.9	28.9	25.5	25.3	65.4	69.0	69.8	100.0	100.0	100.0
Denmark	7.3	7.5	5.8 [2]	32.8	28.5	28.1 [2]	59.9	64.0	66.1 [2]	100.0	100.0	100.0 [2]
Finland	13.6	12.5	10.2	34.2	32.7	30.7	52.3	54.8	59.0	100.0	100.0	100.0
France	8.8	7.8	7.0	35.7	33.3	30.4	55.4	58.9	62.6	100.0	100.0	100.0
Germany, Fed. Rep. of	5.8	5.6	5.2	44.2	41.8	40.5	50.0	52.6	54.2	100.0	100.0	100.0
Greece	...	30.0	27.0	...	28.6	28.0	...	41.4	45.0	...	100.0	100.0
Ireland	19.7	16.9	15.1	32.7	29.5	27.6	47.7	53.6	57.2	100.0	100.0	100.0
Italy	14.6	12.2	10.3	37.2	35.5	32.0	48.2	52.3	57.7	100.0	100.0	100.0
Japan	11.2	9.3	8.3	35.0	34.9	33.9	53.8	55.9	57.8	100.0	100.0	100.0
Netherlands	5.8	5.4	5.0	33.6	28.5	26.5	60.6	66.0	68.5	100.0	100.0	100.0

	Agriculture			Industry			Services			Total		
	1979	1983	1987	1979	1983	1987	1979	1983	1987	1979	1983	1987
Norway	8.4 [3]	7.6	6.6	29.3 [3]	26.9	26.6	62.4 [3]	65.4	66.8	100.0 [3]	100.0	100.0
Portugal	...	23.5	22.2	...	35.4	...	...	41.0	43.3	...	100.0	100.0
Spain	19.8	18.6	15.1	36.6	33.5	32.3	43.6	47.9	52.5	100.0	100.0	100.0
Switzerland	7.2	6.7	6.5 [2]	39.6	37.8	37.7 [2]	53.2	55.4	55.8 [2]	100.0	100.0	100.0 [2]
United Kingdom	2.7	2.7	2.4	38.6	33.4	30.2	58.7	64.0	67.4	100.0	100.0	100.0
United States	3.6	3.5	3.0	31.5	28.2	27.3	64.9	68.2	69.6	100.0	100.0	100.0
Industrialised planned economies												
Czechoslovakia	13.4	12.8	12.3	48.0	47.5	47.3	38.6	39.7	40.4	100.0	100.0	100.0
Hungary	21.9	23.3	20.7	41.8	38.9	38.1	36.3	37.8	41.2	100.0	100.0	100.0
Poland	30.2	31.3	29.2	38.7	36.7	36.7	31.1	32.0	34.2	100.0	100.0	100.0
Romania	31.4	29.7	29.3 [4]	44.4	44.9	45.2 [4]	24.2	25.4	25.5 [4]	100.0	100.0	100.0

... = not available.
[1] 1982. [2] 1986. [3] 1980. [4] 1985.
Source: ILO: *Year book of labour statistics*.

Table A.3. Index of real earnings in manufacturing (1980 = 100), 1980-88

Country	Time unit	Coverage	1980	1981	1982	1983	1984	1985	1986	1987	1988
Sub-Saharan Africa											
Burundi [1]	mo	em	100.0	144.7	124.4	105.1	127.2	124.1	122.6	115.0	...
Ghana	mo	em	100.0	57.6	53.8	40.3	75.7	100.8	127.9	...	...
Kenya	mo	em	100.0	97.7	86.1	80.9	81.6	77.1	77.1	78.6	...
Malawi	mo	em	100.0	100.2	133.0	94.0	71.3	62.1	61.7	...	...
Mauritius	da	we	100.0	100.6	92.9	98.5	98.9	98.9	103.7	120.9	...
Sierra Leone	wk	we	100.0	81.5	78.7	47.5	38.0	30.9	29.7	10.7	...
Tanzania, United Republic of	mo	em	100.0	90.6	...	...	...	...	...	...	...
Zambia	mo	em	100.0	82.8	77.9	71.0	59.2	...	...	...	...
Zimbabwe	mo	pe	100.0	109.4	114.1	105.3	98.3	103.2	...	...	...
Latin America											
Bolivia	mo	em	100.0	89.7	65.2	87.5	50.3	...	...	...	...
Colombia	hr	we	100.0	100.4	105.7	110.2	117.5	114.5	120.0	122.1	...
Costa Rica	mo	ip	100.0	90.7	76.4	85.9	80.0	91.3	104.1	101.6	...
Dominican Republic	mo	em	100.0	99.7	103.2	99.0	86.8	...	...	...	...
Ecuador	hr	we	100.0	99.5	92.4	80.0	79.3	...	...	...	...
El Salvador	hr	we [2]	100.0	92.1	83.9	86.3	78.2	69.0	...	...	...
Guatemala	hr	we	100.0	100.8	105.6	108.9	79.5	68.6	...	...	...
Honduras	wk	em	100.0	109.1	...	...	101.0	109.4	...	...	...
Mexico	mo	we	100.0	102.4	101.0	74.2	71.3	71.7	64.3	64.4	...
Panama	hr	we	...	100.0	97.9	105.9	111.6	111.1	...	...	...
Peru [3]	da	we	100.0	95.4	96.6	78.9	66.4	53.7	79.7	87.6	...
Puerto Rico	wk	we	100.0	100.0	100.0	106.7	108.9	111.5	115.8	114.7	...
Uruguay [4]	mo	em [5]	100.0	106.7	103.5	82.1	80.2	97.6	...	...	...
Venezuela	mo	we	100.0	100.2	...	...	...	...	64.4	73.6	...
Asia and Northern Africa											
China	mo	es	100.0	98.0	97.8	97.9	115.0	115.5	124.1	126.6	...
Hong Kong [6]	da	we	...	...	100.0	100.0	104.8	110.9	116.5	124.0	...
Israel	mo	ip	100.0	111.6	113.7	118.0	122.5	109.8	121.1	132.1	137.6
Jordan	da	em	100.0	110.7	114.7	115.5	112.5	118.3	123.7	...	...
Korea, Republic of	mo	em	100.0	99.0	105.9	115.0	121.5	130.4	139.2	150.6	...
Malaysia	mo	we	...	100.0	89.0	...	...	...	...	...	...
Pakistan	mo	we	100.0	94.8	...	...	...	...	...	...	...
Singapore	hr	we	100.0	108.4	114.0	124.2	133.5	138.5	...	...	...
Sri Lanka	da	we	100.0	87.0	77.2	78.1	77.8	88.3	86.7	88.7	...
Thailand	mo	em	100.0	105.1	112.3	109.3	...	...	...	...	...
Turkey	da	ip	100.0	90.5	52.5	54.7	49.7	...	...	...	...
Industrialised market economies											
Australia	hr	we	100.0	102.0	108.3	103.9	104.8	104.3	100.8	...	...
Austria	mo	em	100.0	100.9	102.3	104.2	103.6	106.5	109.7	112.3	114.5
Canada	wk	em	100.0	99.7	99.5	97.7	98.9	99.7	98.9	97.7	98.4
Denmark	hr	we	100.0	97.7	97.9	97.7	95.9	95.9	96.1	101.9	...
Finland	hr	we [7]	100.0	100.8	101.6	102.8	105.9	108.0	110.5	114.3	...
France	hr	we	100.0	101.5	103.3	106.3	105.2	105.2	106.6	107.8	...
Germany, Federal Republic of	wk	we	100.0	98.2	96.7	97.1	98.0	99.2	102.6	106.1	...
Greece	hr	we	100.0	102.1	112.7	112.0	119.4	119.9	109.9	103.5	...

Country	Time unit	Coverage	1980	1981	1982	1983	1984	1985	1986	1987	1988
Ireland	wk	we	100.0	100.2	95.3	96.7	99.2	101.5	105.4	106.0	...
Italy	hr	we	100.0	104.1	104.1	104.7	104.6	106.0	...	...	...
Japan	mo	em	100.0	101.3	102.3	104.0	106.4	106.9	108.4	111.0	112.0
Netherlands	wk	em	100.0	99.1	100.6	100.1	97.4	96.9	98.1	...	...
New Zealand	hr	em	100.0	103.6	101.8	96.7	98.4	92.6	95.3	...	...
Norway	hr	we	100.0	97.1	96.3	96.4	98.5	100.5	103.2	110.2	...
Portugal	hr	we	100.0	101.1	98.4	91.6	84.6	86.8	92.7	...	...
Spain	hr	em	100.0	106.0	106.8	109.0	110.2	111.2	112.3	116.7	...
Switzerland	hr	we	100.0	99.3	100.1	100.6	...	...	...	...	...
Sweden	hr	we	100.0	97.2	94.7	92.2	95.1	96.1	98.6	101.3	...
United States	wk	we	100.0	99.9	97.7	101.5	102.8	102.5	103.2	102.1	...
Yugoslavia	mo	es	100.0	95.7	92.4	79.5	79.4	80.9	87.7	82.1	...
Industrialised centrally planned economies											
Bulgaria	mo	es [7]	100.0	104.4	107.0	108.1	110.6	113.8	116.2	120.8	...
Czechoslovakia	mo	es	100.0	100.9	98.2	99.6	101.1	100.9	102.1	104.0	...
Hungary	mo	es	100.0	102.4	101.6	99.0	103.9	106.1	107.3	107.3	...
Poland	mo	es	100.0	103.7	77.9	83.0	85.5	88.4	90.9	85.9	...
Romania	mo	es [8]	100.0	99.5	...	...	...	...	...	...	...
USSR	mo	es	100.0	101.0	100.8	102.1	106.2	108.5	109.0	110.5	...

... = not available.

[1] Bujumbura. [2] Males. [3] Lima area. [4] Montevideo. [5] Private sector. [6] Wage rates. [7] Including mining, quarrying and electricity. [8] Including mining and public utilities.

Note: mo – monthly; wk – weekly; da – daily; hr – hourly; em – employees; we – wage earners; pe – persons engaged; ip – insured persons; es – employees in the socialised sector.

Source: ILO: *Year book of labour statistics.*